The Feminist, the Housewife, and the Soap Opera

Charlotte Brunsdon

Clarendon Press · Oxford

OXFORD

UNIVERSITY PRESS

Great Clarendon Street, Oxford OX2 6DP

Oxford University Press is a department of the University of Oxford.
It furthers the University's objective of excellence in research, scholarship,
and education by publishing worldwide in

Oxford New York

Athens Auckland Bangkok Bogotá Buenos Aires Calcutta
Cape Town Chennai Dar es Salaam Delhi Florence Hong Kong Istanbul
Karachi Kuala Lumpur Madrid Melbourne Mexico City Mumbai
Nairobi Paris São Paulo Singapore Taipei Tokyo Toronto Warsaw

and associated companies in Berlin Ibadan

Published in the United States
by Oxford University Press Inc., New York

First published 2000

British Library Cataloguing in Publication Data

Data available

Library of Congress Cataloging in Publication Data

Data available

ISBN 0–19–815980–3
ISBN 0–19–815981–1 (Pbk.)

1 3 5 7 9 10 8 6 4 2

Typeset by Graphicraft Limited, Hong Kong
Printed in Great Britain
on acid-free paper by
Biddles Ltd,
Guildford and King's Lynn

Oxford Television Studies

General Editors
Charlotte Brunsdon and **John Caughie**

OXFORD TELEVISION STUDIES offers international authors—both established and emerging—an opportunity to reflect on particular problems of history, theory, and criticism which are specific to television and which are central to its critical understanding. The perspective of the series will be international, while respecting the peculiarities of the national; it will be historical, without proposing simple histories; and it will be grounded in the analysis of programmes and genres. The series is intended to be foundational without being introductory or routine, facilitating clearly focused critical reflection and engaging a range of debates, topics, and approaches which will offer a basis for the development of television studies.

For Jan and Bob

Acknowledgements

EVERY effort has been made to trace copyright holders. The author apologizes in advance for any unintentional omission or neglect. I am grateful to Margaret Duerden, Reference Librarian of Central Television Birmingham for her assistance in attempting to trace the copyright holders of the *Crossroads* material, and to Siân Parry of BFI Stills. Acknowledgement is hereby made to ATV Licensing, *The Birmingham Evening Mail*, *The TV Times*, and the former *See Red Women's Workshop*.

This book has been a long time in the making, and I have incurred too many debts to list them all here. However I must thank my interviewees, Ien Ang, Christine Geraghty, Dorothy Hobson, Terry Lovell, and Ellen Seiter, who gave their time frankly and with good will, and have been consistently supportive of the project. I must also acknowledge the British Academy for funding a trip to Western Australia in 1996 to present a paper on 'Personal Narratives' and the University of Warwick which has enabled this project to come to completion through the provision of sabbatical leave. Andrew Lockett, then of Oxford University Press, deserves a particular mention for persistency, as does Richard Johnson, then of Birmingham University, for perseverance beyond the call of duty, and Erica Carter for editorial advice. Many students, in a range of institutions, have been essential to the development of these arguments.

I have had help with transcriptions and typing from Jason Jacobs, Anna Janmaat, Anne Lakey, and Rachel Moseley.

With the usual disclaimers, I must also thank Lucy Bland, Erica Carter, John Caughie, Pam Cook, Gill Frith, Ann Gray, Annette Kuhn, Maureen McNeil, and Angela McRobbie who have all offered important support and argument at particular times. David Morley has lived with the project for a long time and learned not to say a word about it.

Elements of the Introduction, Chapters 1 and 3 have been published as:

'Pedagogies of the Feminine', *Screen* 32/4 (1991), 364–81.

'Identity in Feminist Television Criticism', *Media, Culture and Society*, 15 (1993), 309–20.

'The Role of Soap Opera in the Development of Feminist Television Scholarship', in R. C. Allen (ed.) *To Be Continued . . .* (London: Routledge, 1995), 49–65.

A note on the text. This book contains interview material and references to my original transcripts. These references have been retained in the text to enable the reader to gauge the sequence in which comments were originally made.

Contents

List of Figures

The motives that impelled me at that time to make this choice are not totally clear to me. I am diffident about those that come to mind today because I would not like to project into the past intentions that have been maturing in the course of these many years. Gradually, I came to realize that many events and connections of which I was totally unaware contributed to influencing the decisions I thought I had made independently: a banal fact in itself, but always surprising because it contradicts our narcissistic fantasies.

Carlo Ginsburg, 'Microhistory: Two or Three Things I Know about It' (1993: 23)

Introduction

THIS book traces the development of British and US feminist television criticism through particular attention to the study of one genre, the soap opera, in the years from 1975 to 1986. It is the study of the development of a certain kind of academic television criticism, rather than television production, and is thus less concerned with soap opera on television than with soap opera in the seminar room. My starting point was the astonishing elevation of this genre from its despised cultural status up to the mid-1970s to its present central position on many syllabuses of media and communication studies in primary, secondary, and tertiary education. How did this happen?

Although soap opera was well established by the mid-1970s as a staple of many broadcasting economies, and British serials such as *Coronation Street* had been running since 1960, there was little discussion of soap opera as such, and broadcast programmes were generally regarded as of low prestige. Thus the 1970s annual handbooks of the Independent Broadcasting Authority, the publication in which independent television and radio is presented to audiences and advertisers, normally grouped 'serial drama' inconspicuously in the larger 'Drama' section which highlighted more prestigious productions. For example, the 1978 handbook devotes one page of fifteen drama pages to a section headed 'To Be Continued', while the 1977 handbook makes no special mention in fourteen pages of drama coverage (IBA 1978*b*: 44–59; 1977*b*: 14–29). The IBA Annual Report and Accounts, without the constraint of the address to the public, tended to be rather more explicit, as we see, for example, in this extract from the 1977–8 Report:

> Many viewers particularly enjoy serial stories. *Coronation Street*
> and *Crossroads* continue to draw very considerable audiences
> although not every member of their audiences is equally
> appreciative. (IBA 1978*a*: 13)

In Britain, it is the single play, the classic serial, and the literary adaptation, rather than the economically significant but culturally humble domestic serial, which have been most significant in the presentation of television drama promoted by the institutions of

broadcasting. Similarly, in the academy, the early concerns of culturalist students of television were with either the general place of
television in working-class life, or the political, the real, and the
public (Hoggart 1958; Caughie 1980; Laing 1986).

Raymond Williams had, however, in 1974, explicitly addressed the
relative valuation of literary adaptation and domestic/naturalist
serials, arguing for the significance of the 'essentially new form' which
engaged with 'the run of ordinary experiences' (1974: 55–6).[1] Williams
was, however, the exception. Thus Fiske and Hartley's 1978 *Reading
Television* (now in its third edition) has no discussion of soap opera as
such, although there is mention of *Coronation Street* in a discussion
of class and television (Fiske and Hartley 1978: 106). Similarly, Len
Masterman's influential *Teaching about Television* (1980), while it too
discusses crime drama, also has no discussion of soaps. Work by the
Media Group of the Centre for Contemporary Cultural Studies in the
1970s displays the same patterns of concern and value (for example,
Hall, Connell, and Curti 1976). Morag Shiach, surveying this work in
her *Discourse on Popular Culture* (1989), observes:

> They impose a very clear hierarchy of programmes worthy of
> serious critical attention, and have little to say about other,
> more trivial, forms of television. There is, of course, a gender
> dimension to this emphasis. Public affairs are seen as serious and
> political, while forms such as soap opera or quiz shows, which
> are widely consumed by women viewers, are seen as trivial and
> irrelevant to the business of political analysis. (1989: 194)

Although Shiach is right about the seventies, she is not right in terms
of the subsequent curricula of media and television studies in
schools, colleges, and universities. Since 1980 books (in English) on
soap opera have been published by Allen (1985), Ang (1985), Brown
(1994), Buckingham (1987), Buckman (1984), Cantor and Pingree
(1983), Cassata and Skill (1983), Dyer et al. (1981), Geraghty (1991),
Gripsrud (1995), Hobson (1982), Intintoli (1984), Kilborn (1992),
Kingsley (1988), Matelski (1988), Mumford (1995), Nariman
(1993), and Nochimson (1993). There has also been substantial
discussion of soap opera in works edited or authored by Allen (1995),
Brown (1990*b*), Fiske (1987), Kaplan (1983*a*), Modleski (1982),
Taylor (1989), Tulloch and Moran (1986), Seiter et al. (1989), and
Silj (1988).

---

1 Raymond Williams's interest in naturalist television drama was partly a continuation of
his interest in drama as a contemporary social force, an interest which had led him to
add the discussion of a film, Bergman's *Wild Strawberries*, to his 1968 revised edition
of *Drama in Performance*. See also his collected television criticism, once again witness
to the unusual seriousness with which he took the new medium (O'Connor 1989).

The British broadcast schedules have been dominated by serial drama, from imported prime-time shows like *Dallas* and *Dynasty* in the late 1970s to mid-1980s, to the new generation of British realist drama initiated in 1982 by Channel Four with its Liverpool soap, *Brookside*. Following this, the massive investment by the BBC in *EastEnders* transformed the profile of broadcast serial drama. The success of commercial television's police soap, *The Bill*, which was moved from two to three evenings a week in 1992, marks the culmination of a transformation of the genre apparent throughout the period. By 1994, all three major British soaps, *Coronation Street*, *Brookside*, and *EastEnders*, had moved to three evenings a week, while *Eldorado*, the attempt at an upbeat *EastEnders* on the Costa del Sol had come and gone. Since then, broadcast of the core British soaps has further increased. While the look and concerns of British serial drama have been transformed—in ways which, following Geraghty (1991), we can generally characterize as a masculinization of the genre (although this process is characterized too simply if we ignore the other major serial success of the period, the Australian import *Neighbours*)—so too has its academic and critical profile, and it is with this process that I am here concerned.

The critical writing about soap opera which partly constitutes its new place in the syllabus has been mainly by feminist critics, and so teaching and learning about soap opera also involves thinking about ideas of femininity, feminine pleasure, and feminism. Indeed, just as it is possible to trace the growing respectability of soap opera as an academic area of study in the period from the mid-1970s on, it is also possible to show that it is in precisely this period that feminist critique moves from the streets to the academy. Or, less controversially, that feminism begins to have an academic existence, to be known as feminism, rather than 'Women's Liberation', as the second wave first named itself.[2] Both soap opera and feminism have moved together from outside to inside the academy in the period since 1975, and it is this move that is our topic.

As I reread those early articles by women such as Carol Lopate (1977), Michèle Mattelart (1982), Dorothy Hobson (1980), and Tania Modleski (1979), which tried to engage seriously with popular women's television, I became more and more aware of the reciprocity of the processes involved. While the feminist critics were consciously addressing and thinking about soap opera as a genre for women, this work was also one site in which the labour of 'writing as a feminist' was being elaborated. The constitution of television soap opera as a legitimate object of study for both feminists and, ultimately, other

---

2 Discussions of the history and significance of this shift in name are offered—with different inflections—by Catherine Hall (1992) and Denise Riley (1992).

academics was also a process in which the subject of this studying was constituted. The feminist, and, more specifically, the feminist intellectual, produces herself in this engagement with this popular television genre, just as she produces a text for media studies.

So my study of the early feminist engagement and revaluation of soap opera inexorably led me to an interest in the historical construction of the feminist critic. To investigate this figure, I interviewed some of the feminist critics who conducted the early work on soap opera, asking them what they remembered of this early endeavour, and how they now thought about it. These interviews, and the close textual analysis of the early articles that I had made, convinced me that my first model, which had two terms—soap opera and feminism—was inadequate. I saw a shadowy third term—most neutrally, 'the television viewer', sometimes, in the early articles, 'the housewife' or 'the ordinary woman'—who was understood to motivate, and in some cases, through her tastes and desires, to be the focus of, the enquiry. The feminist engagement with soap opera, historically, has an ambivalent relation with this figure. She both is and isn't the feminist herself. Hence my title.

This is not an investigation of soap opera, nor is it a history of feminism. But it is a history of the encounter of soap opera and feminism, traced across a variety of sites—articles, books, images, and interviews. In these various texts, I want to examine the fluctuating and differentiated constitution of what I would argue are the central personae of feminist television criticism: the feminist television critic and the character in some ways produced as her other—the ordinary woman, or housewife. I would, however, also see the field of 'soap opera studies' as an exemplary site in which to explore the critical dilemmas of cultural and television studies at the end of the twentieth century as we move into a period which is best characterized as post-public service broadcasting. That is, in relation to a genre which has been characterized as primarily talk, I want to look at the patterns of talk—the discursive construction of soap opera in the late 1970s and 1980s.

Particularly potent in this history is the figure of 'the housewife' or 'ordinary woman' who is figured in a complex set of ways in feminist research. It is because of, on behalf of, this 'ordinary woman' that much research has been conducted. It is also, as I will hope to show, on to this figure that recalcitrant feminine desires are projected. However, at the same time, it is with this figure that unity is desired, assumed, and felt. Thus while the ostensible focus of enquiry is feminist research into soap opera, and the key figure of the feminine viewer therein, this requires investigation of the contradictory position of feminist intellectuals in the late 1970s and 1980s, whose academic training permits entry to the predominantly masculine academy, but whose origins, gender-formation, and the discrimination they meet, return them endlessly to that which has been forbidden, disavowed, or abandoned—the pleasures, concerns, and accoutrements of femininity. One way in which the painful contradictions aroused here can be handled is through a classic splitting, in which the femininist academic investigates her abandoned or fictional other—the female consumer of popular culture.

The history told here, then, juxtaposes the detailed analysis of published material with the detailed analysis of interviews with scholars about their early research on soap opera. The interviews reveal how different women started doing research on soap opera in the 1970s—it seems only fair to offer my own account.

Personal Stories This book has been a long time in the making. In the late 1970s, I was trying, along with the other women interviewed here—and the many others discussed herein—to *write* feminist television criticism. In the 1990s, mainly because of my experiences as a teacher in the changed context already outlined, I found myself able, and strongly motivated, to *write about* feminist television criticism. Trying to write as a feminist about a popular generic television form like soap opera was one thing in the late 1970s—it is quite another in the 1990s. The contexts, the programmes, the audiences, the motivations of and for such writing have all changed.

I want to start by discussing this lengthy making in quite personal terms. I want to do this partly because I have given a central place in this project to a series of interviews with scholars whom I know through conducting research on television soap opera in this period. These are explicitly personal interviews, even though they are mainly about intellectual work. They could perhaps be better described as long conversations, in each case between two clearly identified people, the interviewee and myself. In this context, it would seem both disingenuous and counter to the 'ethnography of ourselves' spirit of the original project to withhold information about myself. However, there is also the issue of indicating to the reader something of the origins of the text she is reading. What I say about myself is thus offered not because I think it interesting in itself, but because I consider it in some ways necessary to enable the reader to orient herself, to understand something of how this project came about, whose voice speaks, and the types of criteria which are likely to be used in the making of judgements.

This autobiographical turn is not currently unusual in critical intellectual work, assailed as its practitioners are by anxieties about inappropriately speaking for others and a reluctance to appear to endorse the grand narratives which might permit an impersonal voice. There is also a long and specific history of the use of personal voice in feminist writing. Nor is the self-reflexivity of the project at present uncommon, particularly in the way in which it can be seen to contribute to a more general stocktaking of the role of feminism within the academy, as we can see from the spate of retrospective collections currently available. These range from works for which a large number of retrospective essays on the same topic were commissioned—such as Greene and Kahn's *Changing Subjects: The Making of Feminist Literary Criticism* (1993), Butler and Scott's *Feminists Theorize the Political* (1992), or the special issue of *Camera Obscura* on *The Spectatrix* (1989)—which thus have a survey-like status, to individuals' collections of their essays which span the period of the development of feminist academic work and frequently have retrospective prefaces and essays—such as books by Sally Alexander (1994), Catherine Hall (1992), Laura Mulvey (1989), Angela McRobbie (1991), Michele Wallace (1990), and Pam Cook (1999). They also include anthologies from significant journals of the period such as *Screen* (Screen Editorial Group 1992), *m/f* (Adams and Cowie 1990), and *Feminist Review* (Feminist Review Collective 1986; 1987). What is particular to my project is the tightness of its focus on inaugural feminist research in one genre, in combination with what it seems most appropriate to call its 'soap operaticness'. By this I mean its group cast: Ien Ang, Charlotte Brunsdon, Christine Geraghty, Dorothy Hobson, Terry Lovell, and Ellen Seiter; its reliance on episodic and anecdotal narrative; and its elevation of the personal— indeed, its determination that the public and historical can and must be understood as it shapes, and is also shaped by, the concerns of personal life.

Because the formative context in which I had to think about feminism in the academy was the Centre for Contemporary Cultural Studies (CCCS), this work can also be considered to contribute to the group of reflections on the 'Birmingham years' which have been emerging since the late 1980s, although I am not suggesting that CCCS originated research on soap opera. I am thinking here of articles by, for example, John Clarke (1991), Stuart Hall (1992), Richard Johnson (1991), and Lawrence Grossberg (1997) which offer accounts of what is now characterized as the Birmingham project. Although there have been two feminist collections published under the aegis of Birmingham cultural studies, *Women Take Issue* (Women's Studies Group 1978) and *Off-Centre* (Franklin, Lury, and Stacey 1991a), which offer accounts of doing feminism and cultural studies, and some individuals have offered some reflection on feminism and the Centre, the girls' story is relatively unrecorded

(McRobbie 1991).[3] In some senses, what follows in this introduction is a contribution to that too.

I first registered at the CCCS at Birmingham University in 1975 with an idea that I wanted to do something on romance and romantic love, although my enrolment, after term had started, was specifically motivated by a desire to leave London because of a difficult turn in my personal life, rather than a strong desire to study in that institution then. In fact, I didn't know very much about CCCS, although I had enjoyed my admission interview, and had known enough to try and read Raymond Williams—*The Long Revolution*, I think—on the train journey to Birmingham. I was also very attracted by the idea of working in groups with other graduate students on the 'contemporary'—more so after my first week of trying to do a Ph.D. on 'Interruptions in Transparency in Fictional Narratives' at University College London. It was the first year of the new MA course, and so I joined CCCS with about twelve others, which must have been a considerable disruption to an institution which had mainly recruited Ph.D. students up till then.

I followed the MA course, and joined the Media and Women's Studies Groups. I tried most sub-groups in that first term, partly spoilt for choice, partly trying to find out what this strange place I had come to was about, and partly searching for a context in which I could pursue my interest in love and romance. I tried 'Sub-Cultures', but this was just after the publication of *Resistance through Rituals* (Clarke et al. 1975), and the group had dissipated. I knew that I didn't mean 'Love' in the way that hippies had, and 'hippies' were a possible new topic in that sub-group. I was also very shocked by the idea of observing people—like hippies—and then writing about them. As will be evident, I was not familiar with sociology as a discipline. This seemed to be a betrayal of the people observed, and a potential reporting of them to authorities. I couldn't really understand why this should be a form of radical intellectual work, but as I didn't really understand what that was if it wasn't directly agitational, I just lumped the incomprehensions together and left the group.

The Media sub-group, which seemed a likely place to pursue what I would retrospectively call my 'Images of Women' interest in Romance, had just completed a period of work on the BBC 'flagship' current affairs programme *Panorama* (Hall, Connell, and Curti 1976). Several members of the group, including Ian Connell, Stuart Hall, and Dave Morley, were trying to win SSRC (Social Science Research Council) funding for a project on the audience 'decoding' of

---

3 *Feminism for Girls* (McRobbie and McCabe 1981) could be seen as the third feminist collection to emerge from CCCS. As I discuss elsewhere, this collection certainly marks the end of a first phase of publication of CCCS feminist work (Brunsdon 1995).

television programmes, hoping to interrogate the theoretical model of Hall's recently published 'Encoding and Decoding in the Television Discourse' (Hall 1973). The engagement of the Centre as a whole with Marxism was in a fiercely Althusserian moment, with passionate argument about the determinacy—or otherwise—of 'the last instance' and a correlative commitment to the study of theories of the State.

Much of the media group's first year after the *Panorama* project was spent introducing new Centre members to the already established paradigms of the 'Centre' approach to the media. There was a fierce debate in the group when it came to the choosing of a case study. Should the group stay with the overtly political hard current affairs and news—the traditional areas of leftist media research (the first of the Glasgow 'Bad News' books had just been published (Glasgow University Media Group 1976))—or could we venture into the domain of the everyday and commonplace? Roz Brody and I (a *de facto* gendered group) argued that soap opera in general, but *Crossroads* in particular, would be the most appropriate topic of study. Roz was a regular *Crossroads* viewer, but I didn't watch the programme. However, I didn't like watching any 'heavy' television, so the prospect of studying *World in Action* or *Newsnight* was grim. At least soap opera promised stories, and seemed closer to love and romance than I was going to get anywhere else. The Women's Studies Group, my other hope, was doing a long collective reading of Juliet Mitchell's *Psychoanalysis and Feminism* (1974).

The soap opera proposal was regarded as a rather ludicrous suggestion—an object of study that just wasn't serious enough for the media group. When some of the men obviously couldn't believe that we thought *Crossroads* might be worth investigating, and clearly had no intention of doing so themselves, I began to realize that gender was imbricated in all this in quite a complicated way. It wasn't just to do with the concerns of the programme, it was something to do with the more general cultural meaning and value of this type of programme. We stuck our ground though, partly buoyed up by Dorothy Hobson's emerging research findings that many women specifically avoided the news, and helped by the fact that the group had just 'done' the key current affairs programme on British television (Hobson 1978*a*). I think our main motive, though, was just not being able to bear the prospect of endless hours of current affairs. A curious compromise was reached—our case study would be *Nationwide*, broadcast in the Midlands at the same time as *Crossroads*. Clearly not soap opera—but not hard news either. Retrospectively, I think Antonio Gramsci— who was rapidly replacing Althusser as top CCCS theory man—with his stress on the significance of common sense in the securing of hegemony, must have been a stronger ally than I thought at the time. His theorization of the significance of everyday life offered an accept-

able justification for spending time on this evidently trivial programme (Hoare and Nowell-Smith 1971).

The *Nationwide* project took off. It was before the days of domestic
video recorders, and we used to watch the programme together every
night in each other's houses. It was very exciting and involving, and I
forgot about romantic love and soap opera. I also forgot—or didn't
see how—to ask the type of questions of our material that would now
seem obvious. So although we knew that the *Nationwide* construction
of the family was critical to our analysis, and realized that the home
was a different place for men and women, we didn't record obvious
data like the gender of interviewers unless the items were obviously
sexist. I thought of myself as a feminist, I was also attending the
Women's Studies Group, and had been very active in the establishing
of a CCCS women-only group, 'Women's Forum'. But if not actually
working on 'women and . . .', it seemed terribly difficult to articulate
feminist questions and concerns. I think this was partly because of
the strength and resonance of the *Nationwide* world-view, which did
rather take us over so that we spent a lot of time making not very
funny *Nationwide* jokes with each other. But I think it was also to
do with the relative unfamiliarity of feminist questions within the
university (I use the term generically) in England in 1976. There were
so few feminist academic books published that we just read everything—anthropology, history, literary criticism—whatever its topic.[4]
Feminist questions weren't always very sophisticated questions—
they were generally of the 'What about women?' type. Going with the
flow of stimulating, enjoyable, collective, intellectual work was more
compelling than constantly interrupting to say 'What about women?'

I abandoned romance and started to think about a Ph.D. topic
on common sense and everyday life. Later, Dorothy Hobson and I
recorded some *Crossroads* episodes, but never really did much with
them together. Ph.D.s were rarely completed at CCCS in those days—
the priority was collective work and publishing—and I threw myself
into writing up the *Nationwide* work and planning *Women Take Issue*
(Brunsdon and Morley 1978; Women's Studies Group 1978).

So my first attempt to think about soap opera was a complete failure. But I think two aspects of that failed project were significant. The
strength of the reaction against the suggestion of working on soap
seemed in itself interesting, and the gendering of this disdain seemed
very clear. What I grasped less clearly were the class dimensions of
soap opera's reputation, which, ironically, given what we ended up
saying about the substitution of region for class in *Nationwide*, I think
I misrecognized as region. I was still maintaining close links with

---

4 Contemporary collections such as Mitchell and Oakley's *The Rights and Wrongs of
  Women* (1976) give a very clear sense of the cross- and inter-disciplinary character of
  the feminist project at this stage.

London (where I had grown up) and was very struck by how rude Londoners were about Birmingham if I said I was living there—'Poor you!' If I mentioned soap opera as well, the rudeness about Birmingham was combined with incredulity. I began to feel very defensive about Birmingham and *Crossroads* (which was made there), as I learnt for the first time in my life how Southerners appeared from North of Watford. So, in a complicated way, the *Crossroads*/soap opera project was always a defensive one for me, even before it really started. A defence of the idea that these programmes might be worth studying, a defence of watching them rather than serious programmes, a defence of Birmingham—and I think a defence of my own decision to leave London, avant-garde film culture, my family of origin, and the study of high culture in a literature department.

My main subsequent engagement with soap opera was as a teacher, and it has been thinking through the way in which students have dealt with it that I have had to reformulate some of my own ideas. Most significant, but perhaps also most difficult to write about usefully, is the very changed context of the encounter with soap opera in the academy. My first encounter was as a postgraduate when I was deeply involved in arguments about the canon which were significant throughout the academy on a very broad scale. The political historical context was of the 1970s Labour governments in which, although unemployment was rising, the rhetoric of Thatcherism was not yet present. The disjunction between these conditions of the address to soap opera as an object of study—and, specifically, the horizons of expectations of those making this address—and the expectations of those students to whom it later fell to study this material was significant. In the early stages of thinking about teaching soap opera, I felt or experienced it as a kind of gap, a something that didn't fit about the relationships between 'feminism' and 'soap opera' and female students. I thought I often taught the topic rather badly, and also noticed what I read as a kind of disappointment in the students, as if they had expected the topic area was going to give them something it seemed not to.

When introducing soap opera into the undergraduate syllabus in the early 1980s, as part of a course dealing primarily with aesthetics, to gender-mixed third-year groups, I always taught it alongside television crime series. There were strong intellectual reasons for doing this. Students were introduced to the two dominant forms of popular fiction on British television, both of which have rarely been granted elevation to the category of 'the aesthetic'. The comparison between the two kinds of generic fiction was instructive formally, institutionally, narratively, and in terms of audience address, production values, and critical reputation. There was much that could be taught and learned through the comparison of these two genres. However, I think I was also, almost instinctively, operating a 'crowd control' tactic. I could keep the male students quiet during the study of soap opera, if they had the promise of a boy's genre to follow. Or, tacitly, I could accept a certain kind of gendered self-selection for class attendance in those weeks, which could be perceived as 'fair' because most students did have, or wished to appear to have, stereotypically gendered genre tastes. I am not writing here of teaching in that metaphor of the disrupted classroom, an inner city comprehensive, but in a highly selective course in a well-regarded Midlands university. However, exactly the same note of ridicule that I remembered from the first time we had proposed studying soap opera at CCCS reappeared in this equally privileged context. Soap opera was perceived by all students to be so evidently gendered that any collective screening seemed occasionally to demand the dissenting staging of masculine identities. Female students complained privately to me that they weren't allowed to watch quietly—and indeed that their view of the screen would be deliberately if intermittently obscured. The same stories emerged from screenings of 'weepies' in other film courses. I also experienced similar disruptions and noisy viewings while teaching in the USA, where the perpetrators were mainly lesbian and feminist students (unsympathetic male students having self-selected themselves out of the classes). These dissenting women were I think quite clearly responding to the same provocation of conventional femininity: soap opera as a genre of a weaker gender, of femininity as she should not be inhabited.

Other patterns also emerged in the teaching of soap opera. I regularly used an exercise on television autobiography in which each person in turn recounted the viewing history in their family of origin. Here, in a context where students knew we would be studying soap opera, year after year, mainly working-class students recounted the way in which the theme tune of *Coronation Street* (which we had just watched) would trigger memories of home and, quite often, feelings of homesickness. Quite often, this programme in particular, but other soaps as well, seemed very directly to make students think of their mothers—it was 'their' programme, and the theme tune made university fade and schooldays return. So in the classroom, the gendered and class status of soap opera was repeatedly affirmed, but in violently contrasting ways: anticipation, frustration, repudiation, and nostalgia.

Working as an external examiner in the 1980s, I read countless scripts which represented—as candidates were required to do—what Allen, Ang, Geraghty, Hobson, Modleski, and Seiter had said about soaps. John Fiske's influential *Television Culture* was published in 1987, the first general book on television to explicitly take on a feminist agenda. Day schools were arranged for teachers who worked on soaps as part of Media Studies and Communications Studies courses in schools. In all of this material there appeared audiences called 'women' who had certain characteristics as viewers, one of which was watching soaps. The students I taught who were most enthusiastic about soaps were female, but I noticed that they seemed to have a very awkward relationship to this category 'women'. They wrote about soaps being a 'women's genre', and all the accompanying orthodoxy, in a quite detached way. The 'women' produced in early feminist writing seemed, in the main, to have no real connection to their lives or sense of themselves. Or if they did make a connection, it was usually one of denial, 'Well, I don't feel like that'. 'Women' were someone else. There was a gap, a something that didn't fit, between the mode of address of the now canonical texts and the people who were now having to study them.

The gap lay partly between different understandings of 'women'. There were the women—or girls, as they usually thought of themselves—that they, the students were, which was in some ways the same category as that addressed by the programmes, as was shown by the upset over disrupted screenings. On the other hand, these programmes, for both boys and girls, were more to do with mothers. There were feminists, who were women, but who weren't the same as other women. I might be an example of this. And there were the women in the material they were reading, the 'housewives' and 'ordinary women', who didn't seem to be any of these.

These different 'gaps' are complexly produced in the interplay of the different histories with which I am partly here concerned. For example, the increased sophistication of feminist critical work, the changing place of this work within the academy, the incorporation of some feminist ideas into the common sense of girls' and women's magazines, and the changing expectations of growing up female all effect hesitations and shifts in the encounters with a pedagogic feminism. Perhaps most germanely, these 'gaps' could partly be explained through what has sometimes been called the generation gap in feminism. In this model, feminism, particularly in its academic and institutional forms (who is senior, who gets published, who is the token woman) is dominated by the generation of white, now (and often in origin) middle-class professional women radicalized in the late 1960s and early 1970s—the women of 'Women's Liberation'. Andrea Stuart gives an evocative account of what is at stake here when she discusses why *Elle* is the magazine of choice for young women of her generation:

After the dour censoriousness of the past generation of feminists, *everything* about *Elle* was voluptuous. True to its implicit post-

> modern philosophy there was not hierarchy—the pictures of
> food were just as sexy as pictures of celebrities or pictures of
> Guatemala. *Elle* tapped into a new generation's attitudes and
> expectations with which the feminist establishment simply
> hasn't caught up. (1990: 31–2)

Made in 1990, this is an argument that had surfaced before, although
not always in terms of generation. Stuart herself is very keen to stress
differences between women: '[Elle] recognised that feminist assumptions about automatic connections between women are pretty hard
to swallow' (1990: 31). Ien Ang, in the conclusion to her book on
Dallas, had argued against the over-politicization of pleasure which
seemed to inform so much feminist cultural analysis in the 1970s and
1980s (1985: 130–6). Janice Winship, in a 1985 discussion of the then
new young women's magazine *Just Seventeen*, had pointed to the way
in which young women had taken on some feminist attitudes about
femininity and autonomy, but had ignored the tone of 1970s feminism. She argued that it was imperative that 'old feminists' learn from
these changes, which brings her argument back to Stuart. Angela
McRobbie, writing about the same magazine in 1994, and partly
reflecting on her own research with young women in the late 1970s,
also points to the way in which femininity and feminism have become
articulated in a quite different way in young women's lives in the later
1980s and 1990s (1994: 165).

This is one way of thinking of the gaps that I had noticed.
Feminism, to the young women in the seminar room, seemed to
mean moralism, miserabilism, and the posing of false unities between women—and their reading of founding feminist texts rather
confirmed this. These attitudes coexisted with assumptions that they
would work for a living, that they might not necessarily get married,
and that their sexuality was their own business. That is, as both Lynn
Spigel and Angela McRobbie have recently observed of young women
(in Spigel's case they were also her students), their ideas of themselves
and their futures were evidently strongly shaped by feminism, but
this was not a connection or acknowledgement that they often, or
willingly, made (McRobbie 1994; Spigel 1995).

Work using the generation gap model has two tendencies. Either,
as with Stuart, Winship, and McRobbie, the call is for 'old' feminism
to get modern. Or, as with Spigel, the call is for young women to 'only
connect'. There are grounds for both approaches. However, what I
want to do here is to step aside and use this lack of connection as a way
of periodizing feminism. To suggest that this 'gap' is not just a failure
to connect by one or other generation, but can be read symptomatically. It shows that one period is over—at least for all those who
didn't live through it, and perhaps for most of those who did. But

also, these gaps can be thought of as empirical proof of the arguments that feminist theorists such as Denise Riley have been concerned with about the historicity of the category 'woman', and the way in which what it means to be a woman has varied (1988). It becomes possible to argue that 1970s feminism has had a shaping influence on late twentieth-century discourses of femininity, that it has thrown some of the previously dominant discourses—such as notions of 'a woman's place'—into relief and thus denaturalized them. However, contrary to the ambition of 1970s feminism, which was, at least in part, an ambition to *abolish* conventional femininities—to end housewifery and sex objecthood for ever—this has been achieved in complex, contradictory, and to some extent unpredictable negotiations with traditional femininities. Who would have predicted Mrs Thatcher—or 'power-dressing'? So that from the 1990s, 1970s feminism itself, instead of being a final femininity, is much more apparently a particular political movement with some fairly clear sociological political roots which had a particular impact in its attempt to compete in the discursive field of the feminine. One of the sites where these competing definitions of femininity were harnessed together was in the not very significant debates about the academic study of soap opera. A minor site, but perhaps a rather illuminating one, since it brings together so many key players—the feminist, the housewife, and the television viewer. How had these characters come together in the late 1970s and early 1980s? How was it for them?

Structure   The book is in three parts. The first surveys the attention paid to soap opera in 1970s feminism, tracing the way in which this genre, like romance fiction and Hollywood melodramas, becomes a particularly attractive, if contradictory, object of study for feminist scholars. The second, in three chapters, suggests that much attention to soap opera can be characterized as 'worrying responsibly'—of course, also, a key characteristic of the narrative drive of much soap opera. This part of the book offers a more detailed historical reading of the discourses through which the object of study, soap opera, is constituted and introduces the three protagonists of my title. Chapter 2 returns to the classic research on radio soap opera in the USA in the late 1930s/early 1940s and examines how the genre, its heroines, and its listeners are figured in the literature. Chapter 3 analyses the language and concerns of three pioneering 1970s feminist commentators on soap opera, suggesting that the continuities between the work of the 1940s and the 1970s are greater than is usually supposed. Thus the return to the 1940s permits a greater understanding of what is new in feminist approaches to soap opera, while also revealing the familiarity of much that was thought to be new. In the discussion of the 1970s writing, the emerging figure of the feminist intellectual, and her contradictory response to conventional femininity, is focused on. Chapter 4 offers an engagement with the television soap opera as such, and studies in detail one of the most significant women of 1970s British soap opera, Meg Mortimer of *Crossroads*. It is suggested, which is in accord with the hypotheses of the 1940s scholars about similar figures, that her appeal lies partly in the way in which she represented the fantasy embodiment of a housewife, even though the *mise en scène* of the programme, *Crossroads*, was downmarket television naturalism.

Part III is composed of the presentation of interviews with five women who conducted research on soap opera in the period of the study: Christine Geraghty, Dorothy Hobson, Terry Lovell, Ien Ang, and Ellen Seiter. Here, the resources of oral history are mobilized to investigate how the stories traced so far were experienced by individuals. Each interview is dealt with separately, with a presentation of some biographical details and discussion of published work preceding the interview. The analytic procedures are discussed in Chapter 5, the introduction to the interviews. The interviews are followed by a long chapter, Chapter 11, which pursues the issues of connection and difference across the interview data, beginning to address some of the issues raised in this micro-history.

The project of the book is thus one of a limited and specific cultural history, aimed at producing understanding of the way in which soap opera was produced as an object of study through the agency of feminist critics. The method, centrally, involves the juxtaposition of accounts and analyses of different types of writing and speech. If Parts I and II trace different histories which together might provide a 'thick description' of the constitution of soap opera as an object of study within the academy, Part III explores the memories and reflections of living that history by key participants. The structure of the book thus echoes its argument. My original object of investigation was the transformed status of soap opera and its move into the academy. What I discovered though, was that one could not understand this without also paying attention to the similar move of feminism and feminist intellectuals in the same period.

1

Mapping the Fields

1

Women's Genres and Female Agency

THIS book traces the historical engagement between feminism and soap opera in the 1970s and 1980s, suggesting that this engagement can be read as representative or typical of the Western second-wave feminist engagement with the media and popular culture generally. The category of 'women's genres' has been increasingly used since the mid-1980s to refer to a cross-media, interdisciplinary area of textual production and study. This can be understood to include romance fiction, women's and girls' magazines, television soap opera, film melodrama, and 'weepies'. A radical definition would also include fashion, make-up, knitting, dressmaking, and other aspects of traditional women's and girls' culture and media. 'Women's genres' are the media, skills, and practices of conventional femininities. There was a large increase in academic publishing on these topics in the 1980s and this has become an increasingly popular area for the attention of feminist academics (see, for example, Modleski 1982; Coward 1984; Parker 1984; Radway 1984; Ang 1985; Wilson 1985; Winship 1987; Doane 1987; Mann and Spigel 1988; H. Taylor 1989; Gaines and Herzog 1990; McRobbie 1991; Bobo and Seiter 1991; Basinger 1993; Radner 1995; Sparke 1995). This book suggests that there has been a particularly privileged relationship between this burgeoning scholarship on women's genres in the 1980s and the coming-into-being of a new figure within the academy: the feminist intellectual.

When Annette Kuhn surveyed the literature on 'Women's Genres' in 1984, she was concerned with research on film and television, and particularly with the different conceptualizations of gender and spectatorship therein. Kuhn pointed to the increased feminist interest in 'gynocentric' genres such as film melodrama and soap opera which have mass appeal for female audiences. Within the literature she reviews, recurrent interest is expressed in the representation of and identification with central female protagonists, female desire, narratives modes and rhythms specific to femininity, and the modes of female spectatorship (Kuhn 1984). Although I too want to concentrate on audio-visual women's genres in tracing a certain overdetermination in the production of soap opera as a privileged object of study for feminist scholars, I want briefly to place the work on film and television women's genres within a broader perspective. This has two parameters: the feminist 'return to the feminine' which begins in the later 1970s, and the search, within much feminist research across disciplines, for instances and evidence of female agency. I would argue that the critical writing on film melodrama and soap opera that Kuhn surveys cannot be understood without reference to a much more general feminist reconsideration of mass cultural forms addressed to female consumers such as women's magazines and romance fiction.[1] This focus on 'mass' forms for female consumers coincides with a more general 'turn to the audience' and validation of the audience for/consumers of commodity culture as active meaning makers rather than passive consumers. If the active meaning maker in the cultural studies of the 1970s was the subcultural youth (Clarke et al. 1975), celebrated for his ability to wrestle creatively with mass media cultures, in the 1980s it was the television viewer, perhaps most iconically as celebrated by John Fiske (1987*a*), a potential guerrilla of the living room sofa.

(i) Women's Genres: The Feminist Engagement

In the potent imagery which has come to symbolize the origins of second-wave feminism, it is the hostile engagement with the images of conventional femininity in the late 1960s and early 1970s which has proved most enduring. The mythical bra-burning, the protests at the Miss America pageant in 1968, the flour bombs at the British staging of the Miss World contest in 1970, the image of the bra-less woman

---

1 While I do not intend to deal with film melodrama at any length—Christine Gledhill offers a very authoritative mapping of the field in her 1987 *Home is Where the Heart Is*, while Marcia Landy's collection (1991) reprints nearly every relevant article published in the 1970–90 period—it is important to note that the feminist 'return to the feminine', which directs critical attention to the film melodrama, occurs simultaneously with a new attention to this genre within film studies. This was inaugurated not through feminist concerns, although the representation of the family was an unavoidable topic and Freud not long absent, but through an attention to the work of directors Douglas Sirk and Vincente Minnelli (Willemen 1971; Elsaesser 1972). Film studies, while institutionally marginal, was one of the most overtly politicized and theoretically engaged disciplines in Britain in the 1970s, symbolized through the reach and reputation of the journal *Screen*. And it was in this journal, *Framework*, and the *Brighton Film Review* that the first radical rereadings of film melodrama appeared. The argument, far from initially offering a revaluation of melodrama in feminist terms, actually valorized directors such as Douglas Sirk for their 'Brechtian' handling of pulp feminine fiction and their transcendence of this generic material (Willemen 1971). Although work by Elsaesser (1972), Nowell-Smith (1977), Pollock (1977), and Mulvey (1977) also posed the issue of the representation of the family, and film form as marked with the contradictions of patriarchal capitalism—all concerns informed by feminism or amenable to feminist transformation—it is important to remember that there was a separately developing interest in melodrama in film studies in the 1970s which plays into, and is reworked by, specifically feminist concerns with genres aimed at women.

with unshaven legs—these events and images have dominated the popular media representations of feminism and the feminist. The feminist is primarily perceived as against the feminine. The story I want to tell is a different one, which does indeed start with this repudiation, but is then mainly occupied with a reinvestigation and re-engagement with the feminine, most commonly sought in 'women's genres'. My proposal is that we can use a repudiation–reinvestigation –revaluation schema as one way of characterizing the relationship between second-wave feminism and mass cultural feminine forms. This type of periodization has been used by other feminists offering retrospectives on the development of feminist scholarship in a particular disciplinary area: for example, Catherine Hall in the development of feminist history (Hall 1992), or Ann Rosalind Jones on the development of US feminist literary criticism (1993: 72). This three-part schema covers the period discussed in this essay, although I here concentrate on the latter phases. Periodizations and autobiographical accounts that echo these phases can be discerned in the interviews below. It is another way of thinking the transformation from a movement for women's liberation to a feminism which has a primary existence within the academy, and, as Jennifer Wicke (1994) has argued, in the celebrity zone, where it has been spoken by women as different as Princess Diana and Oprah Winfrey. It also offers us, at perhaps a more colloquial level, a way of thinking about the way in which women who identify as feminists look and dress and how this has changed since the early 1970s. I should stress that it is offered only as a schema—something to think with—and although I do think there is a traceable historical sequence through these phases, I am not suggesting that the divisions between phases are clear, or that all feminists proceeded in orderly fashion from 'repudiation' to 'revaluation'.

So in this schema the most 'movement' moment of second-wave Western feminism in the late 1960s/early 1970s is a moment partly formed in and through a repudiation of conventional and traditional femininities and their appropriate genres. For example, to quote from a founding text for the British Women's Liberation movement, Germaine Greer's *The Female Eunuch*:

> If *Sweethearts* and the other publications of the same kind with their hallucinated love imagery are American, it is unfortunately true that they find a wide distribution in England. There are also trash weeklies called *Mirabelle*, *Valentine*, *Romeo* and, biggest of all, *Jackie* selling upwards of a million copies a week to girls between ten and sixteen years of age, which set forth the British ideals of romance. (1971: 172)

The early feminist response to what were called 'the mass media' was suspicion and contestation. Against those images and fictions was

Fig. 1.1. *See Red Collective* poster, 'What do you mean it hurts? Don't you want to look pretty?', *c.*1977 (London). This is a companion poster to 'Sisters, examine every aspects of our lives' which was stylistically similar, but with attention to housework and sexual harassment as well as beauty and fashion. 'Sisters' proved impossible to reproduce as it was silver and white.

posed the demand for 'real women'. Media such as women's magazines or teenage girls' comics were seen as primary sites for the reproduction of patriarchal definitions of femininity. Traditional sites of feminine skill and interest, such as fashion, cooking, and various kinds of home-making were also regarded with great suspicion. As a popular poster from the London *See Red Collective* put it in 1978, 'Sisters, examine every aspects of our lives' (see Fig. 1.1). Of course, my summarizing argument makes things sound very clear—this distancing from conventional femininity was contradictory, partial, and painful, as well as vehement and disciplining. It was also a process understood and experienced rather differently for women of different origins who found themselves differently placed in relation to hegemonic femininity. These contradictions are attended to in many of the retrospective accounts of second-wave feminism which are now available, such as Greene and Kahn's *Changing Subjects: The Making of Feminist Literary Criticism* (1993) and Micheline Wandor's book of interviews with British feminists, *Once a Feminist* (1990). For example, Janet Rée recalls holding the meetings of an early women's group at her home:

One woman stormed out because she said I was always trying to
make people feel at ease and wished I would stop. I was always
smiling at people. It was awful. She said she was fed up with
people just sitting around, middle-class women not getting out
and actually doing things. I felt she was completely right. I was
a hostess—can you imagine, I always made cakes. And tea
and coffee. I've always loved making a kind of home. All the
peripheral things like cooking and sewing, having a nice warm
room, all that. It was really important. But I was very mortified
and recognised the justness of that description of myself. I might
as well have been hosting the Women's Institute. That was the
subtext. (1990: 100)

The complexity of the feelings expressed here, the contradictory
identification with different modes of femininity, across time, 'can
you imagine, I always made cakes', reveals what a complicated process 'coming to consciousness' as a feminist was. This anecdote also
points to the way in which class, as Catherine Hall has argued, was
a significant, if difficult, consideration in British feminism from the
early days (C. Hall 1992: 10), and can be contrasted with Valerie
Walkerdine's defence of the significance of glamour and fantasy for
working-class girls and women, in the course of which she has
recently observed:

The period of feminism which made me most unhappy with
myself was the one in which I wore dungarees and no make-up,
at least partly because it replaced the to-be-looked-at-ness
with the trappings of working-class masculinity, dungarees,
for example! To me the issues have always been far more
complicated than the simple abandonment of the trappings of
working-class femininity for those of working-class masculinity.
(Walkerdine 1997: 168)

As several other accounts, both in Wandor's collection and other histories, suggest, motherhood was a particularly problematic site for
the new feminism—but that is another story (C. Hall 1990; Snitow
1992; Kaplan 1992). So what I've called a 'repudiation' of traditionally
feminine skills and media—for example, the things that Janet Rée
says she 'always loved', or the glamour that Valerie Walkerdine 'always
liked . . . very much indeed' (1997: 168)—has, in a quite complicated
way, also to be understood, certainly in some cases, as a 'renunciation',
a giving up of the morally and politically wrong.

In ways explored in more detail in the analyses of the interviews
below, this feminist repudiation of women's genres in the 1970s and
1980s is strongly articulated through (Eurocentric) class-inflected
aesthetic hierarchy and the relative legitimacy of different cultural

practices.[2] That is, although the language of repudiation is a discourse of gender, there is a symmetry between feminist and conventional high cultural dismissals of 'mass culture'. This symmetry can perhaps most usefully be understood to indicate the contradictory imbrication of class and gender heritages and expectations. So on the one hand, we have, as already quoted, Janet Rée being criticized, and criticizing herself, for her middle-class niceness, but on the other, it is impossible to ignore the convergence of traditional aesthetic judgement and feminist critique in their assessment of soap opera and romances. In both systems of judgement, soap opera and romance are trash. These mass-produced genres of femininity were perhaps most threatening, in the context of the apparent class mobility of the post-war expansion of the British education system, to young, generally white, educated women who aspired, like their male counterparts, to be citizens. One way we can perhaps understand this vehement feminist repudiation of women's genres, which points to the enormous contradictoriness of political consciousness, is as a refusal to *be*, in Fay Weldon's resonant 1971 phrase, 'Down among the Women'. First-world feminism founds itself partly through repudiating first-world femininity.

So it is with this history, and in this context, that the first cautious investigations of women's genres are made. As Janice Winship put it in the preface to her 1987 book, the culmination of over fifteen years' research on women's magazines:

'Admitting within feminist circles that I was doing research on— of all things—women's magazines used to make me feel just as comfortable as when I hastily muttered an explanation of my 'study' to politely inquiring friends of my parents . . . Whether feminist friends voiced it or not I felt they were thinking that if I really had to do research (intellectual work has always been somewhat ambiguously tolerated in the women's movement) I should do it on something more important politically: 'Surely we all know women's magazines demean women and solely benefit capitalist profits. What more is there to say?' I experienced myself as a misfitting renegade who rarely dared to speak up for magazines, however weakly. (1987: p. xiiii)

The conditions of, and reasons for, the re-engagement with feminine genres are complex. They range from the textually and politically investigative—what is being said here about women, and by whom?

2 I am using Bourdieu's notion of 'legitimacy' in cultural taste here. He explores French taste codes in terms of class, and while he does address gender, it is usually in a metaphorical sense (Bourdieu 1984). More difficult to integrate is the complex colonial history of the construction of ethnic specificity and difference in 'European' aesthetics.

—to the recruitist—we have to discover/investigate what women like, so we can change these desires—to the defiantly celebratory—well, it may not be feminist, but I still like it. What I would argue is that the most productive position, the one from which the most nuanced and sophisticated analysis proceeds, combines some of these elements, but is articulated through a much greater degree of self-consciousness and a recognition of subjectivities both formed in, and ambivalent towards, conventional femininity.

In the 1980s came the first publication of the research by feminists in a range of disciplines of culturally devalued forms such as romance fiction (McRobbie and McCabe 1981; Modleski 1982; Radford 1986; Radway 1984; H. Taylor 1989), melodrama (Cook 1983; Gledhill 1987; Harper 1983; Kaplan 1983*b*; Mulvey 1986), girls' comics and school stories (Frith 1989; McRobbie 1991), women's magazines (Winship 1987; Hermes 1993), and fashion (Wilson 1985; Evans and Thornton 1989; Gaines and Herzog 1990). Thus the feminist research into soap opera is part of a much more general re-engagement with the mass cultural forms and fictions of femininity undertaken by feminists, usually, but not always, in the academy.

This move was generally motivated by what Ien Ang has called 'feminist desire' (Ang 1988). Ang used this formulation in a review of Janice Radway's pioneering book *Reading the Romance* where she was criticizing what she characterized as the pedagogic motivation of Radway's research: 'its aim is directed at raising the consciousness of romance reading women' (Ang 1988: 184). So for Ang, in this context, 'feminist desire' is what Angela McRobbie designated 'recruitist' in an early sensitive essay about the relationship between feminist researchers and the women or girls 'on' whom they might be working (McRobbie 1982*b*: 52). Although this kind of recruitist feminist desire is clearly present to some extent in very many feminist critics working on these genres, I think we can, at this point, usefully extend the notion of 'feminist desire' to include a less activist and more self-reflexive moment, which is constituted through the desire to understand femininity. A feminist desire to understand the complexities, desires, and contradictions of femininity which is conceptualized variously and plurally as a position, an identity, and a psychic formation (Brownmiller 1984; Coward 1984; Rose 1983). Traditional first-world femininity is made strange by feminism—it is denaturalized, and therefore the multiplicity of textual sites on which it is elaborated become areas for possible investigation.

Different writers stress different aspects of this feminist investigation of femininity, using different theoretical approaches to different ends. A most significant division is that formed in attitudes towards psychoanalysis, and it is an embrace of psychoanalytic theory which distinguishes the work, for example, of Jacqueline Rose (1986),

Elizabeth Cowie (1984), and Laura Mulvey (1989) in the approach to femininity, and which has underpinned one of the key divisions in feminist scholarship. This is commonly represented as a division of feminist work into an 'empirical' or pragmatic US tradition and a theoretical (psychoanalytic) French school (Moi 1985 offers an early version of this history). The interviewees discuss their own negotiations of this historical division in Part III. For our purposes here, as significant—indeed symptomatic—is the extent to which the writer sees herself as included within the category 'feminine' to be investigated, for this often indicates the extent to which conscious identity is understood as amenable to rational improvement.

Rosalind Coward, for example, in the preface of her 1984 book *Female Desire*, a best-selling text of 're-engagement', says:

> In *Female Desire* I'm not approaching 'feminine' pleasures as an outsider; nor as a stranger to guilt. The pleasures I describe are often my pleasures. Food, cooking, clothes, novels, soap operas, houses, nature programmes—these are all my enjoyments.
> I don't approach these things as a distant critic but as someone examining myself, examining my own life under a microscope.
> But nor will I treat these pleasures as sacrosanct. Good girls enjoy what they're given but what they're given may not always be good for them. (1984: 14)

Although there is a clear tension here between the agenda set up in the last sentence, when criteria for the distinction between different pleasures are implied, and the earlier identity claimed with other enjoyers of 'feminine' pleasures, Coward is at pains to stress how much she has invested in this project. Cora Kaplan too, writing about 'Fiction, Fantasy and Femininity', is careful to introduce her essay with a discussion not only of her passionate involvement in reading books like *Gone with the Wind* and *The Thornbirds*, but also of her commitment to the self-presentational modes of femininity:

> Both my parents found my slavish addiction to fifties femininity, its fashions that harnessed thrust and spiked us and its macho-femme versions of sexual difference, regressive and worrying. For me however, my political and sexual desires, utopian and transgressive, were bound together, which made my passionate response to *Gone with the Wind* even more contradictory . . .

> It was over twenty-five years before a novel triggered the uncontrolled level of fantasy response that I had experienced with *Gone with the Wind* and, not surprisingly, I encountered it first as a television serial. Colleen McCullough's *The Thorn Birds* seduced me away from a more respectable piece of viewing—*The Raj*

Quartet—and so profoundly affected was I by the first episode I saw (not the first in the series) that I rushed out to buy the paperback. (1986: 118–20)

Inscribed within Kaplan's account is a profound sense of contradiction. She both distances herself from her parents' view of her 'slavish addiction to fifties femininity' and, through this phrase and the vocabulary of torture used subsequently ('harnessed', 'thrust', 'spiked'), endorses and enhances their judgement. She presents 1950s femininity as perverse—but does this through her presentation of her own involvement in it, not through disavowal. Similarly, when she describes the impact of *The Thornbirds*, she very precisely includes a sense of aesthetic hierarchy ('more respectable'), but once more describes a passionate attachment.

These examples reveal a different kind of feminist engagement with texts of femininity. It is not just a recruitist project—an investigation of the pleasures of others. There is a self—a feminist self—to be investigated too.

(ii) Female Agency and the Female Viewer

The second important general motivation for the re-engagement with feminine genres is the search for feminine agency. This has equivalencies with feminist interventions in other disciplines, but is complicated by the particularly strong contrast between the (actual) gender of the makers of most film and television and the (image of) the gendered spectator or consumer of these media. Most other feminist explorations of women as agents have sought to establish the contribution of women as makers, rather than consumers, of culture. Thus for example, in relation to art history, one of the earliest feminist books was entitled *Old Mistresses* (Parker and Pollock 1981). In literary studies, Gilbert and Gubar's *The Madwoman in the Attic* (1979), using an image from *Jane Eyre*, poses a structural metaphor for the position of women writers in relation to the institution literature. Elaine Showalter, with *A Literature of Their Own* (1977), insists on the existence of women writers. Early feminist history was similarly dominated by the desire to reveal the presence of women, as titles like Sheila Rowbotham's *Hidden from History* (1973b) indicate. In all of these areas a key object of the feminist endeavour was the discovery and location of women as agents—agents who made history, wrote books, and painted pictures.

This search for female agency in relation to television has focused on three main areas: women as producers, women as image, and women as audience, and my argument will be that it is in consideration of women as audience and image that the research on soap opera has been most significant. Although there have been women film directors, and significant early feminist work was addressed to the rediscovery of figures such as Dorothy Arzner, Germaine Dulac, and Ida Lupino, these women have been much less visible than women stars and fans (Cook and Johnston 1975; Flitterman Lewis 1990; Kuhn 1995b). Similarly, key females in the production of television serial drama, such as Irna Phillips and Hazel Adair, fade in contrast to the overwhelming femininity of the image of the housewife viewer (Seiter 1989). It is not that there aren't the possibilities for the patient historical investigation of women's roles in the production of film and television—as we see, for example, in the work of Lauren Rabinovitz (1991) and Sue Harper (1983)—but, as with the reading of novels and popular fiction, and against, for example, the viewing of oil painting, spectatorship in these genres is overwhelmingly feminized, both connotationally and empirically. Although feminism may have directed attention to these genres, it was not feminism that gendered 'weepies', soaps, and women's magazines. What were women doing in this consuming of fiction, following of recipes, watching of soap opera?

In consideration of women as producers there have been two types of investigation: first what we might call the 'hidden from history' approach, when the careers and contributions of key female pioneers, such as Dorothy Arzner or Irna Phillips are documented; secondly, and this was particularly a feature of the 1970s, the exploration and recording of patterns of female employment in the film and television industries. Research in this area, particularly the early collation of documentation about the employment of women in the media industries, has usually been developed outside the academy and has often been funded by interested parties such as trade unions.[3] Liesbet van Zoonen (1994) in her survey of feminist media studies, has concentrated particularly on research into women as producers, addressing the complex issue of whether any research in this area establishes convincingly that producer gender in fact makes a difference. For our purposes what is most significant is that, perhaps because of the extreme gender stratification visible in television internationally, this has proved a much less fertile ground for feminist research. The very structure of the field has concentrated emphasis on women as viewers, rather than programme makers.

The study of women as image has employed a range of methodologies, from content analysis to textual and narrative analysis, and ranges across 1970s agitprop polemic, to large-scale quantitative surveys funded by advertisers and broadcasters, to cultural or media

---

3 Thus e.g. Margaret Gallagher has produced a number of reports since her 1981 UNESCO survey *Unequal Opportunities* (e.g. Gallagher 1984) while the ACTT was also active in collecting statistics about the employment of women within the film industry (ACTT 1975). In the USA, the US Commission on Civil Rights produced an influential report in the 1970s, *Window-Dressing on the Set: Women and Minorities in Television*.

studies analyses of femininity on screen. What is significant is the importance of soap opera, both actually and connotationally, to the analysis of the images of women and television. One reason for this is given in Gaye Tuchman's much-quoted 1978 formulation of 'the symbolic annihilation of women', which provided a vivid hypothesis about the absence of women on television, as well as specifying their generic presence: 'with the exception of soap opera, where men make up a "mere majority" of the fictional population, television has shown, and continues to show, two men for every woman' (p. 10). Gaye Tuchman's discussion of soap opera in this article, stands, along with Mildred Downing's 1974 piece on 'The Heroine of the Daytime Serial', as an early US attempt to think of women on television soap opera in the context of second-wave feminism. There have since been a series of studies within, particularly, US mass communications which have focused on soap opera and have included an investigation of the type of roles available for women, and the type of women likely to fill them (see, for example, Cantor and Pingree 1983).

Within the expansive field of quantitative content analysis, we find that soap opera is a favoured research site. There has been substantial—and continuing—interest in mapping the contours of life on television through the content analysis of soap opera, while there is rather less attention to other genres (Frentz 1992). Within cultural and media studies—as with quantitative content analysis—soap opera was mainly attractive to feminists as an object of analysis because it was perceived to be both for and about women. But within the cultural studies context, there has been a tendency towards rather broader cultural analysis. Here, there is a recurring concern with the meaning and status of soap opera as mass feminine culture. Soap opera is a significant instance of the historical connotative femininity of mass culture pointed out by scholars such as Patrice Petro (1986) and Andreas Huyssen (1986), and particularly of the privileged place of television within this historical aesthetic gendering. Soap opera, within this connotational set, metonymically signifies the worst of television, and thus the genre is interesting to some scholars for what it means as much as what it is. It was to this gendering of aesthetic judgement that feminist critics were partly addressing themselves, as we see in this comment from 1981 by Terry Lovell writing about *Coronation Street*:

> *Yet within this almost universal denigration*, soap opera does provide the pleasures of validation, and of self-assertion, which must surely go some way to accounting for its lasting popularity with women (1981: 51; my emphasis)

Ien Ang, writing about a quite different programme, *Dallas*, a little later, offers precisely this recognition of a pleasure that is off the critical map in the wording of her original advertisement to attract viewer/respondents: 'I like watching the TV serial *Dallas* but I often get odd reactions to it' (1985: 10). Much later, when these ideas about the place of soap opera within class, gender, and aesthetic hierarchies have become an accepted element of approaches to the programmes —rather than just governing these approaches unconsciously—we find this structure of feeling incorporated into an article title by Pertti Alasuutari, 'I'm Ashamed to Admit It But I Have Watched *Dallas*: The Moral Hierarchy of Television Programmes' (1992). It is also historically significant that 1978 saw the launch and subsequent international success of *Dallas*. So the interest in television programmes directed at women/housewives displayed by feminist critics coincides with popular serial melodrama as a worldwide phenomenon. Feminist work on soap opera develops alongside studies of the international reception of *Dallas* (Katz and Liebes 1985), as well as the reconsideration of film melodrama already alluded to.

(iii) Women as Audience

Early feminist research on soap opera was often conducted in the context of enquiry into 'the housewife's day'. It was the housewife and her housework which was the starting point, rather than any organization of the television text. Carol Lopate (1976) discusses US daytime game shows and soaps in a more general discussion of the rhythms and preoccupations of daytime television, itself motivated by the issue of what was available for the housewife, while Dorothy Hobson's work on *Crossroads* (1982) emerged from earlier research on the daily culture of young working-class women at home (Hobson 1978a). Concerns with domestic time, rhythm, and the engaged role of the viewer recur in the work of Modleski (1979), Seiter (1981b), and Mattelart (1982). This initial focus, on ways and rhythms of viewing, rather than detailed textual analysis, could be seen to characterize feminist approaches to television domestic serial drama. So although there is detailed work on *Coronation Street*, *Dallas*, *Dynasty*, *General Hospital*, and *Brookside*, the overarching concerns do seem to have been more with the involvement and pleasures of female viewers in the patterns of domestic viewing (Dyer et al. 1981; Swanson 1981; Feuer 1992; Geraghty 1992). That is, unlike the exquisitely detailed film analyses that we find in the work of feminist critics like Elizabeth Cowie (1984) or Mary Ann Doane (1987), the emphasis in television research has been on 'the real world of women watching'—or indeed, not watching, to incorporate a common research finding.

Early discussion of women television viewers was thus not genre-specific. Subsequent ethnographic work has tended either to be so, or, as with the work of Gray (1992a), Morley and Silverstone (1991), and

Moores (1993), to locate television viewing within the whole complex of media usages within the household. Genre-specific work is almost always, internationally, research on soap opera, in its many national guises, and is a particularly attractive genre of choice for ethnographic researchers for a range of reasons. For feminists, as we have seen, the connotational gendering of the genre is significant, and offers a sufficient rationale. However, it is also the case that many of the features of the genre can be seen as epitomizing much of what is specific to television: seriality, intimacy, domesticity, repetition, and the mundane. So soap opera, and the study of soap opera, can function as a *mise en abyme* for television watching generally. There are also pragmatic reasons. The longevity of series like *Dallas*, *Coronation Street*, or *Neighbours* and the way in which, as texts, they exceed any specific viewing occasion, make them ideal focuses for research projects which necessarily take place in time. Although the researcher may not be watching the same episode with each subject, they can be confident that they are in some ways watching the same show. Similarly, because of the way in which soaps partly have their existence in day-to-day conversations away from the television set, talking about soap can seem to be a much more natural, unstaged research situation than setting up special viewings of a particular programme or play.[4]

As is clear, the feminist interest in television programmes was from the beginning usually formulated through ideas about the audience. Several early analyses of soap opera make hypotheses about how women respond to the genre, and many later studies attempt to test these ideas (see Moores 1993: 39–49). Thus the Tuebingen/ Volkswagen study explicitly tests some of Modleski's formulation (Seiter et al. 1989*a*), while Andrea Press asks questions drawn from a variety of cultural studies work (1991*a*). Ien Ang (1985) offers both an extensive reading of *Dallas* and an audience study. This work must, however, be seen in the broader context. Thus while feminist researchers were particularly concerned with the way women 'read' or enjoyed television programmes, there was a new attention to audience 'decoding' in general, as any review account of media research in the 1980s indicates (for example Corner 1991 or Moores 1993).

Feminist reception studies thus have to be understood both within and as influential on a more general 'turn to the audience' characteristic of popular media study in the late 1970s and 1980s. This turn to the audience, noted, with different inflections and in the process of different arguments, by Ang (1989*b*), Curran (1991), Morley (1989), Schröder (1987), and Corner (1999), emerged from two quite distinct

---

4 For example, in both David Buckingham's work (1987) and Dorothy Hobson's later work (1990), the research topic is partly, precisely, talking about soap opera.

traditions, those of the 'Uses and Gratifications' paradigm within mass communications/communication studies and the rather more heterogeneous body of work known as cultural studies. With different histories, aims, methodologies, and research agendas, a series of projects—most notably the international Liebes and Katz *Dallas* project (Katz and Liebes 1985; Liebes and Katz 1990), the Morley *Nationwide* (1980) and *Family Television* (1986) surveys, and Radway's 1984 romance-reader research—were conducted. Indeed, one of the key ways in which we can understand the impact of feminist work on the academy is through the gendering of the audience which is accomplished through this scholarship. While the focus on a female audience is not historically unusual (Allen 1987), the new feminist work, as we shall see in more detail later, engaged sympathetically with the figure of the female viewer and has had significant impact on the academic understanding of who the audience is and how it should be conceptualized. It has also opened up discussion of domestic space and the social relations of viewing, as we see particularly in the work of Lynn Spigel and Ann Gray (Spigel 1992; Gray 1992*a*; Morley 1992). However, as the empirical work with female audiences has accumulated, the analytic significance of the categories of 'women' and 'gender' have become more problematic. As in so many other areas of scholarship, the primarily political objective of putting women 'in' generates a complex set of philosophical, epistemological, and methodological issues.[5] Two nodal points of argument can be isolated.

First, and posed most challengingly by Ien Ang and Joke Hermes in what was commissioned as a review essay on gender media and reception study, there is the question of whether categories of gender can be used to interpret audience behaviour without making essentialist assumptions about the characteristics of gender (1991). In a discussion which focuses on seemingly incompatible findings about the articulation of class and gender in the work of Press (1990) and the Tuebingen study (Seiter et al. 1989*a*), Ang and Hermes make a radical critique of the use of socio-demographic variables such as class and gender in the interpretation of audience data, arguing that the concentration on female audiences in particular has tended to produce gender as an *a priori* category. While wishing to retain notions of a social world structured in significant difference, they argue for a radical contextualism and particularism in the analysis of data, and the absolute historical contingency of the articulation of all variables such as gender.

---

5 This issue is clearly not one limited to television audience studies. For discussion in other fields, see e.g. Scott (1988) on history, Miller (1993) on literature, and Pollock on art history (1993).

While many scholars stop short of Ang and Hermes's absolute contingency—possibly, partly, out of pragmatic panic at how and when
to introduce a category such as gender in an analysis if it can only be
allowed to emerge *post facto* in any particular specified historical context—their argument is both a strong version and symptomatic of
a more general contemporary anxiety about how to 'do' gender in
media analysis. For example, Cathy Schwitchenberg argues that gender and genre have to be disarticulated in feminist audience studies
otherwise it is impossible to understand, for instance, women who
like sports, or lesbian women who defy feminine norms of beauty
(Schwitchenberg 1994).

The second recurrent problem in feminist reception study, again,
not a problem specific to this scholarly field, is that of the historical
and categorical exclusions hidden in second-wave feminism's category 'women'. Here, as elsewhere, it has been those speaking, or
forced to speak, in the name of 'difference' who have highlighted the
homogeneity of 'women' as Trinh T. Minh-ha elegantly argues in her
'Difference: "A Special Third World Women Issue"' (Trinh 1989).
Jacqueline Bobo and Evelyn Reid have produced accounts of black
women viewers' responses in the US and UK (Bobo 1988; Reid 1989),
while Bobo and Seiter have written an extended analysis of the reproduction of racist patterning in, for example, the selection of samples
for ethnographic research (1991). Class has proved somewhat more
comfortable, at least superficially, to the mainly white researchers
working in this field, although I will discuss this further in relation
to another key issue, that of the relationship between researcher and
researched, which is taken up at the end of the chapter. Studies of
audiences have generally been studies of the domestic, and, as Bobo
and Seiter have argued, of an ethnically specific domestic (1991). This
picture is slightly altered by the burgeoning work on audiences as
fans and fan identity as such, which would include Constance Penley's
research on *Star Trek* fans and that of Lisa Lewis on fandom in general
(Penley 1992; Lewis 1992). The public sphere is also addressed in the
emerging US research on the reception of women rappers by young
African-American women (Rose 1990; Roberts 1991) which perhaps
adds substance to an argument that white feminist work in television has mainly stayed within the sphere of personal life and the
domestic—of which, of course, soap opera is an exemplary instance.

There is thus a body of feminist ethnographic work on television
that we can place in at least two contexts. First we can see this research
as contributing to, and to some extent determining of, an increased
concern with the audience in television and cultural studies. Secondly we can relate this work to feminist ethnographies of the feminine and the rendering visible of female experience. This latter field
includes not only the directly relevant ethnographies of consumption,

but also, for example, Ann Oakley's extensive sociologies of house-work and maternity (Oakley 1974; 1981a), Valerie Walkerdine and Helen Lucey's research on the socialization of young girls (1989), Ann Phoenix's investigation of the lives of young mothers (1991), Ruth Frankenburg's analysis of the experience of being a white woman (1993), and Beverley Skeggs's ethnographies of young white working-class women in the North of England (1997).[6] While these ethnographies of femininity, as we can see from their topics, encompass a wide range of female experience, it is clear that a unifying thread of concern in all this work is the relationship between researcher and researched. That is, feminist research has been particularly attentive to the power relations of the ethnographic research encounter, although this attention, as the work of Ann Phoenix (1994) and Beverley Skeggs (1997) suggests, has historically been rather differently inflected through understandings of the differing significance of gender, class, and ethnicity in the research process. Mainly because of the founding political aspiration of the unity of women ('sisterhood', in the currently deeply unfashionable terms of second-wave feminism), the relation-ship between researcher and researched has been a necessary and recurrent issue for feminist research, as indeed titles of articles which have made significant contributions to this debate indicate. For example, Ann Oakley offered a major challenge to the sociologic-al conventions of interviewing research subject with her polemic 'Interviewing Women: A Contradiction in Terms' (1981b). Angela McRobbie asked further questions about the role of the researcher in her piece 'The Politics of Feminist Research: Between Talk, Text and Action' (1982b). Janet Finch also poses questions about the responsi-bilities of the researcher: ' "It's Great to Have Someone to Talk To": The Ethics and Politics of Interviewing Women' (1984). Ann Phoenix, writing ten years later, offers a slightly different focus: 'Practising Feminist Research: The Intersection of Gender and "Race" in the Research Process' (1994).

So the commitment to the investigation of female experience and agency with which this chapter has been concerned has its own epistemological consequences. The researcher in this feminist work is implicated in the field of study much more directly than the visiting anthropologist or participant observer. Or, to put the epistemo-logical issue plainly, the feminist researcher—as woman—recognized her implication in the research scenario much more explicitly than has sometimes been the case in both sociological and anthropological

---

6 There is a fascinating body of work published in the 1960s which anticipates the later concerns with ethnographies of feminine experience but which does not use explicitly feminist frameworks, e.g. Hannah Gavron's 1966 *The Captive Wife*, Nell Dunn's 1965 *Talking to Women*, and Sue Kaufman's 1968—although this is perhaps too late to be included here—*Diary of a Mad Housewife*.

endeavour.[7] As Ann Gray says quite unequivocally, after introducing autobiographical material about her own life, and particularly her class/gender origins:

I consider this shared position as quite crucial to the quality of the conversations that I had with the women and that the talk that ensued was, in most instances, enriched by that shared knowledge. To put it quite directly, I am a woman in my study. (1992a: 34)

This self-inscription within research destabilizes ideas of objective investigation and findings in a way which is comparable to, and often simultaneous with, the challenge other types of feminist research offered to established disciplines, the challenge Susan Bordo formulates as the argument that there is no such thing as a view from nowhere (Bordo 1990: 137). Clearly these ideas of the locatedness of all knowledge and the interrogation of existing paradigms offer interconnections between currents in, and influences of, feminist thought and more general contemporary challenges to existing regimes of knowledge.[8] As writers such as Meaghan Morris (1988) and Michele Barrett and Anne Phillips (1992) have shown, the relationships between feminist and postmodern thought are complex and contradictory. However, in relation to the specific field of feminist ethnography it is worth noting that a particularly marked element of feminist writing in this area is the explicit inclusion of emotional response in the account of fieldwork. This ranges from the expressions of warmth, sympathy, and identification—of being women together —apparent in the work of the 1980s, to the more conflicted exploration of difference found in later work.

In tracing the feminist investigation of soap opera alongside the feminist revaluation of other women's genres, I have suggested that the profound ambivalence of second-wave feminism towards conventional cultures of femininity has not been sufficiently explored. This will be one of the tasks of this book. By implication, this argument fragments the rather unitary representation that this feminism currently attracts, but in contradictory ways. First, one could hypothesize that the faultline of class mobility through education for postwar girls might be particularly salient in understanding the virulence of the rejection of—and the compulsiveness of the return to—the

---

7 In fact, of course, both sociology and anthropology have long histories of self-conscious research, as we see from debates in ethnomethodology, e.g. Clifford Geertz's responses to the critiques offered by contributors to Clifford and Marcus's (1986) *Writing Culture* (Geertz 1988).

8 The contradictory relationships between feminism and postmodernism are challengingly posed by Meaghan Morris (1988). Nicholson (1990) and Barrett and Phillips (1992) offer substantial engagement in the issues.

mass cultures of the feminine. Perhaps also relevant here would be the significant presence, within British feminism, of white women with public school/Oxbridge educations. That is to say, the different class and ethnic experiences and cultures of femininity have been a recurrent, if sometimes unconscious, concern of second-wave British feminism. Secondly, when examining the ethnographies of female experience produced by these feminist researchers in the 1970s and 1980s one finds not only the commonalities of gendered experience, and what sometimes amounts to an assertion of the sameness of women, but in fact also a documentation of difference, the revelation that gender is lived out in specific circumstances. In the scrupulous discussion of methodology we find in, for example, the work of Hobson (1978*a*), McRobbie (1982*b*), and Gray (1992*a*), there is not just an epistemological challenge to the accepted ideas of what knowledge is and how it is produced. There is, simultaneously inscribed across texts which are concerned with the understanding of experience as gendered, a recognition of issues of power difference which can be understood as a metonymic inscription of class. As Ann Gray puts it, she is 'a woman in her study', and that shared experience is what contributes to the quality of her interviews, but of course, she also isn't, and that difference, at the moment of interview, is best understood through a sense of the 'gendering' of individual identity as never accomplished in isolation. Persons are never 'just' gendered. Gray *is* a woman *in* her study—but through education she has become the woman who conducts her study. Gray's retrospective description of undertaking research offers us a complex individual history of the interplay of class, gender, and ethnicity in a particular instance (Gray 1995). And it is this complex interplay which marks the interviews in Part III as the speakers recall what they thought they were doing when they turned to soap opera as an object of study.

2

Early Work on Soap Opera: 'Worrying Responsibly'

Introduction to Part II

My own book, *Reading the Romance*, was only one
intervention in this complex and ongoing struggle
to redefine feminine subjectivity and sexuality. My
objective was to place the romance with respect not
only to the discourses of patriarchy but also to those of
feminism. Although I tried very hard not to dismiss the
activities of the Smithton women and made an effort
to understand the act of romance reading as a positive
response to the conditions of everyday life, my account
unwittingly repeated the sexist assumption that has
warranted a large portion of the commentary on
the romance. It was still motivated, that is, by the
assumption that someone ought to worry responsibly
about the effect of fantasy on women readers.

(Janice Radway 1994: 214)

THIS section offers detailed textual analyses of three different
modes of engagement with the soap opera and the housewife.
One is clearly scholarly, the second ambivalently so, while the
third takes as its primary material a television soap opera and associated publicity material. In contrast with the opening chapter which
traced a history across a range of writing and imagery, these three
chapters are organized as closely read case studies of different kinds of
material, distinguished historically, and through country of origin,
genre, and medium. I suggest that analyses of these different kinds of
text allow us to identify recurrent figures and tropes in both soap
opera and the analysis of the genre. In addition to the housewife, who
is represented both *in* and as a viewer *of* radio and television serials,
the most significant of these is the person—herself—that Janice
Radway describes in the epigraph to this introduction, the 'someone'
who 'ought to worry responsibly about the effect of fantasy on
women readers'. By juxtaposing detailed analyses of this very different
material, I show both how soap opera—as text and scholarship—is
dominated by this someone who worries responsibly and how this
figure is differently constituted at different historical moments.

The first chapter of this part, Chapter 2, examines the research into
the audiences for radio soap opera from the early 1940s conducted in

the USA under the aegis of the Bureau of Applied Social Research.[1] This work, by Rudolf Arnheim, Helen Kaufman, and Herta Herzog, is one of the earliest sustained enquiries into the soap opera and the soap opera audience (Lazarsfeld and Stanton 1944). Herzog's contribution, in particular, is also significant in the development of what has come to be called the 'Uses and Gratifications' approach to media usage. This approach, as described by James Halloran in a much-cited comment, shifts the research question from what the media do to people to what people do with the media (Halloran 1970: 34). Although Herzog's research is sometimes cited in later 'culturalist' studies of soap opera, there is little engagement with it outside the work of Robert Allen (1985), and there is a way in which the more prescient elements of her presentation are not always recognized.[2] It is partly to reinscribe Herzog's research into the history of approaches to soap opera that I discuss it here, where I recontextualize it into the group of research reports with which it first appeared. All of these research reports are dominated by the figure of the housewife, both as representation and interviewee, and this is, to a large extent, what is explored below. However, Herzog and Arnheim, in particular, as authors, inscribe themselves as people who 'worry responsibly'.

The second set of texts, discussed in Chapter 3, are three early articles which mark the first second-wave feminist engagement with soap opera. The authors are Carol Lopate, Michèle Mattelart, and Tania Modleski. The piece by Carol Lopate is generally recognized as the first feminist article on soap, while the other two writers are the most significant of the early feminist writers on soap not interviewed later in the book.[3] As her object of study is the Latin American *tele-novela*, Michèle Mattelart's work can be located as inaugural within the now extensive field of scholarship on Latin American *telenovelas* which is not here my primary concern.[4] However, Mattelart's feminism

1 Paul Lazarsfeld, originally from Vienna and associated with the Frankfurt School, was director of the Bureau for Applied Social Research in this period. Allen (1985: 216) offers a fascinating account of the Bureau's work which draws partly on Lazarsfeld's own memoir (1969).

2 For example, Modleski (1982) lists Herzog in her bibliography but makes no mention of her work in the chapter on soap opera. Although Herzog was a member of the primary grant recipients for the Tuebingen project in 1986–9, and a member of the week-long symposium on 'Re-Conceptualizing the Media Audience' in 1987, her paper was removed from the final collection, published as *Remote Control* (Seiter et al. 1989), on the advice of US readers for the publishers, and against the wishes of the editors (private communication with editors).

3 For further discussion of the criteria of selection of the interviewees, see Ch. 5, below. The selection of the interviewees to some extent determined the choice of articles discussed in this chapter. See also Ch. 3 n. 1.

4 See here the work of Jesus Martín-Barbero (Martín-Barbero and Muñez 1992; Martín-Barbero 1995). Lopez (1995) provides the key references for other Latin American work, while work such as that of Thomas Tufte (1995) provides new empirical analysis of the role of *telenovelas* in articulating the hybridity of Brazilian national identity.

distinguishes her work from much other Latin American work in this area, and it seemed particularly important to offer some consideration of the theoretical paradigms she deploys which can very clearly be related internationally to other feminist work of the late 1970s and early 1980s (see also Lopez 1995). Tania Modleski's work is well known within literary, film, television, and cultural studies since her study of soap opera was conducted alongside the study of other popular cultural forms. Of the three pioneering authors here discussed, it is Modleski who is the most widely known and frequently cited in relation to the study of soap opera. My particular interest in discussing her work here—apart from the way in which its historical significance demands attention—is twofold. First, through juxtaposition with other early work—notably Lopate's, but also that of interviewees Seiter and Hobson—I want to recontextualize Modleski's contribution and suggest that ideas which she formulated with such effect were very much 'in the air' in late 1970s feminist criticism. This is particularly true of the juxtaposition of the formal qualities of the soap opera with the rhythms of the domestic day. Secondly, in the context of my particular enquiry, it is significant that Modleski, despite her own pioneering work on popular feminine genres, has polemically opposed empirical studies of the audiences for popular mass culture, most notably in the preface to her edited collection *Studies in Entertainment* (1986). This she has done on the grounds that the critic who engages in this work can become complicit with the culture industry (1986: p. xii), and also through a particular idea of the feminist critic and her relation to other women:

> Located, until recently, on the margins of the academy, the feminist critic has contributed to the forging of a woman's culture based on this insight [the personal is political] and has felt herself to be part of a broader movement of women on whose behalf she could sometimes speak because through consciousness-raising, she in fact *did* speak *to* them—as one of them. Her work is, then, ideally plurivocal, not denying the differences of other women but learning about them through dialogic exchange rather than through ethnographies that posit an unbridgeable gap between the critic's subjectivity and the subjectivity of 'the others'.
> (1991: 44)

This argument, with its elevation of a political connection between the feminist critic and 'other women', rather than an ethnographic one, clearly engages with the terrain of this history. My interviewees, three of whom have conducted audience research, could be described as generally pro-ethnography of the type which Modleski here attacks, and proceed, in Chapters 6 to 10, to inflect the terms Modleski here invokes slightly differently. However, it is also instructive to see how Modleski herself first formulates these relations between the feminist critic and 'women', and this is the concern of Chapter 3.

The juxtaposition of these two bodies of work, one from the 1940s, the other from the 1970s, and the close textual analysis which is the main method used to examine them, suggests that there may be more continuities between the paradigms employed than is usually acknowledged. Herta Herzog, an Austrian Jewish refugee writing in the USA in the 1940s, Carol Lopate writing in the USA in the 1970s, and Michèle Mattelart writing in France and Chile in the 1970s and 1980s all express concern about the interrelation between soap opera, women, and civic life. Each writer, differently, but with more shared concerns than one might expect, worries responsibly about the effect of fantasy on women viewers. However, the mode and expression of this worry is different, as we shall see.

Chapter 4 shifts the terrain from critical approaches to women and soap opera to a brief examination of the potential for fantasy offered by one of the ur-housewives of 1970s television soap opera, Meg Mortimer (Noele Gordon) of *Crossroads*. In the retrospect on her own work from which my epigraph comes, Janice Radway links her own *Reading the Romance* (1984) with Tania Modleski's *Loving with a Vengeance* (1982). She suggests that both books are 'transitional events in the struggle over the genre' (1994: 216), but also reflects that 'Policing, it seems to me, was the real work enacted by conservative, leftist and early feminist critiques of romances and their readers' (1994: 215). In light of this argument, and the changes which she goes on to trace in the romance genre itself, Radway insists on the significance of a concept of fantasy in future approaches to romance, approvingly citing the work of Cora Kaplan (1986) and Alison Light (1984). Soap opera is not romance, and the critical history, while comparable, as we see in a collection such as Pearce and Stacey's 1995 volume *Romance Revisited*, *is* different. However, the person who worries responsibly figures largely in the critical literature on both genres, and indeed, as we see in Chapter 3, it is in this guise that the feminist first engages with the genre. One of the differences between the feminist engagement with the two genres is the deployment of fantasy as a concept. Indeed, soap opera can be placed against both romance and women's pictures as the genre which is primarily addressed through notions of the real. In Chapter 4 I address the way in which fantasy is not much used in discussion of soap opera—unlike romance—and also suggest that it is a concept which may have particular resonances in the imagination of ordinary femininity successfully achieved.

2
The Housewife in 1940s Mass Communication Research: Arnheim, Kaufman, and Herzog

IN *Speaking of Soap Operas* (1985), Robert Allen argues that it is impossible for any contemporary critic—or viewer—to approach soap operas without also engaging with the connotational encrustation that both the genre and its viewers have attracted. He supports this argument with a survey of the mass communication research done on radio soap operas in the 1930s and 1940s in the USA, arguing that more recent research has inherited key paradigms, the most significant of which is the 'difference' of the viewer. He puts this argument as follows:

> The Warner and Henry study is but one further example of the penchant of investigators to collapse the entire soap opera audience into a single social and psychosocial category whose members could be regarded as 'different' from everyone else and whose interest in soap operas is seen as deriving not from a genuinely aesthetic impulse but from a psychopathological . . . need for role reinforcement. (1985: 28)

Allen's argument—which clearly draws on and benefits from the feminist work I discuss in Chapter 3—is illuminating and well supported. It is particularly convincing in that he addresses both the construction of the soap opera text and the profile of the viewer in research. Writing within the US context at a time when the study of soap opera took place within mass communications departments very much more frequently than in contexts where 'Television Studies' was taught, part of Allen's agenda was clearly a challenge to mass communications as a discipline. This project, while explicitly addressed at various points in the main body of the text, emerges with a vengeance in the footnotes, which offer lengthy critical analyses of the US tradition in empirical audience studies.[1] I want to return to some of the pioneers of research that Allen discusses, for, without his agenda, I think this work can be read slightly differently. In some ways, my interest is very close to Allen's, and there are clear homologies in our projects in that I am explicitly investigating the way in which the figure of the housewife is constructed in research about soap opera. However, I want both to pursue the argument further than he does, to investigate the feminist work which is a significant context for Allen's work, and to go less far, to dally a little longer in what Lazarsfeld himself understood as 'administrative research', to read some of the work from the 1940s sympathetically and symptomatically. Unlike Allen, though, I am not offering any kind of survey of the paradigms of US mass communications work in this field. This work, and the arguments against it that can be mounted by students of reception theory and cultural studies, has already been most efficiently achieved in *Speaking of Soap Operas* (Allen 1985). Here, instead, I want to examine the personae we find in the 1940s US research on radio soap opera which was conducted for the most part by scholars trained in the German intellectual tradition who were refugees from Nazism in Europe.

(i) Arnheim and Kaufman

For many years, Herta Herzog's 1942 article 'What Do We Really Know about Daytime Serial Listeners?', which was published with other articles on daytime serials by Rudolf Arnheim and Helen Kaufman in *Radio Research*, 42–3, remained the single most significant study of the (radio) soap opera audience (Herzog 1944; Allen 1985: 23). Herzog addresses the question she poses in her title through the analysis of the findings of four surveys conducted in the USA in 1940–2, and concentrates exclusively on women viewers. Before discussing Herzog's research in detail, I would like to offer a brief account of the research with which it was published, Arnheim's 'The World of the Daytime Serial' and Helen Kaufman's 'The Appeal of Specific Daytime Serials' since together this work, although concerned with radio soap opera, lays out many of the areas of concern that are rediscovered by the feminist critics of the 1970s and 1980s in relation to television soap opera. This is not to argue for a simple convergence in the 1980s between the traditions of 'uses and gratifications' research and the more cultural studies work, which is where most feminist research can be most usefully located (Ang 1989*b*; Schröder 1987), but to suggest that there are homologies, not

---

1 Allen (1985: Ch. 2, pp. 216–18 n. 3, pp. 218–21 n. 8).

only in the serial world of the 1940s and 1970s, but also in the figure of the housewife that this research constructs and investigates. At this point it is also important to note Robert C. Allen's argument that despite repeated research findings from the late 1930s onwards that soap opera listeners were not very different to non-listeners, that indeed the majority of American women listened to soap opera, research projects were consistently designed to investigate 'the difference' of the soap opera audience (Allen 1985: 25). This difference, as Allen, following earlier feminist work, points out, is constituted by the genre's 'almost exclusively female audience' (1985: 25).

Kaufman provides one of the early examples of the investigation of this audience, a detailed report on two of the surveys that Herzog includes in her synthesizing account. Kaufman is investigating the extent to which 'the specific content of a serial' accounts for its appeal to specific groups of listeners. These groups she initially designates as young and old, rich and poor, but in the surveys attention is paid to educational level and rural/urban habitation as well as age and income. Kaufman finds some differentiation in appeal through a very simple notion of audience identification with a central figure —young heroine likely to be preferred by younger audience, etc.— except in the case of the serial (*Against the Storm*) which she considers more likely to appeal to more sophisticated listeners, where she uses aesthetic criteria such as 'skilfully handled' (Kaufman 1944: 94), 'well written' (1944: 95). Although the surveys offer some correlation between appeal and audiences, these are not very marked when considered against factors such as the broadcast schedule. More interestingly, Kaufman observes that many listeners 'read' each serial they listen to in terms of their own concerns, so not only are different listeners' accounts of the same serial noticeably contrasted, but indeed the same listener seems to manage to recreate the same concerns across distinct texts. Kaufman does not, however, as this account might imply, dispense with the text altogether, and insists on the significance of 'similar psychological satisfactions' in determining a listener's choice to stay with a scheduled sequence of series. She remains confident that there are correlations that can be made, and argues for the necessary development of 'finer indices to describe the listeners' and also for the development of 'finer categories to describe the content of the serials to which they listen' (1944: 106). Here we can note that one direction US research has taken has been the development of quite elaborate, but static, 'finer categories' for the analysis of the *content* of serial drama, which has produced a noticeable expansion of published research (Katzman 1972; Greenberg 1980; Frentz 1992). The question of whether this increasingly elaborate apparatus of manifest content analysis has fulfilled Kaufman's ambitions is not pursued here.[2] The significant innovation of the feminist work in the 1970s and 1980s though, was not in the study of the content of the serials, but in the shift in attention to their form. It has been the attention to the ritualistic, interrupted, everyday consumption of soap opera that has transformed the approaches to the genre. In this, the study of the ways in which the genre is watched, soap opera scholarship has been a leading site in the changed critical approaches to television which characterize the cultural studies' scholarship of the 1980s.

Rudolf Arnheim's essay is interesting both for the detailed delineation of soapland which it offers, much of which, like James Thurber's early article 'The Listening Women', is still relevant today, and for its speculations on the position of American women (Thurber 1948). Arnheim sees the serials as a stereotypical product, thus justifying 'a statistical approach', in which the producers and sponsors are concerned to meet the demands and desires of the listeners. He thus expects a content analysis to yield 'not only something about the programs, but also something about the listeners. These stories are likely to offer a picture of the world such as a particular social group would wish it to be' (Arnheim 1944: 35). This leads him, after a detailed description of the serial world, elements of which I summarize below, and within which specific attention is paid to the differential roles of women and men, to try and produce 'a psychological formula of soap opera'.

This Arnheim founds on the notion of identification. He argues that there is a 'surprisingly uniform' positive object of identification, a figure of moral perfection, a 'leader by personal quality' who is almost always a woman. Against this good character, there are ranged bad and weak individuals. The listener is actually like the weak characters, but her attention is drawn towards the good one, who suffers at the hands of the evil ones. He continues:

> she is encouraged to view failures as happening only to other people, and is confirmed in her belief that her suffering is caused not by herself, but by the imperfection and villainy of others. There is little effort to make the listener aware of her prejudices and resentments; rather, she is carefully flattered. Men are shown to be inferior to women, the working class is ignored, learning is depreciated. The egocentric and individualistic concept of a world in which the community appears mainly as a threat from outside is supported—hyenas howling round the campfire, with the law of the jungle as the only resort. Only private problems exist. (1944: 77–8)

---

2 Olivier Burgelin (1972) offers a trenchant and standard critique of the methodology of content analysis.

This passage invokes and anticipates several of the classical leftist critiques of soap opera: the elevation of the individual over the social, the private over the public, figured particularly in the hyena/campfire metaphor, which also conceals a collectivist political vision of 'the community' against the law of the jungle. In the same analytic frame there is the perceived displacement of social structural inequality by individual evil and weakness. But it is the figure of the listener that is most striking. She is constructed as weak, self-deluding, irresponsible, ignorant, vain, prejudiced, and full of resentment. This figure—this character in the drama of soap opera reception—who is clearly feminine, proves profoundly troubling to Arnheim. Her ignorance and weakness could be transformed, but it is her vulnerability to flattery, prejudice, and irresponsibility which leads him to speculate on the grounds of her dissatisfactions and resentments. Because he hypothesizes that a form of identificatory wish fulfilment structures the involvement of women listeners with the serials, he is led ineluctably to speculate on 'the social situation of women confined to an unsatisfactory kind of home life' (Arnheim 1944: 79), finally arguing:

> If it is true that the woman in the home has no satisfactory function to fulfil, why not present the problem bluntly, if possible on the basis of factual material? Why not show its causes and developments, and indicate feasible ways out, instead of conjuring up day dreams? (1944: 82)

Like many subsequent commentators, Arnheim's critique is here focused on the fictiveness of serial drama, its provision of compensatory escapism. The 'factual' and the 'feasible' in this passage partner each other in a documentary world in which things can be put 'bluntly' and on a firm 'basis'. These sentences display a discursive gendering, an argument about fact over fiction which is not unlike Professor Higgins's desperate plea in *My Fair Lady*, 'Why can't a woman be more like a man?' However, as with Betty Friedan's later investigation of 'the problem that has no name' (1963), Arnheim is led to construct an analysis of women's position through a symptomatic reading of, in his case one aspect of, everyday life. These proto-feminist questions to some extent become submerged in Arnheim's more general conclusion, which pleads for an integration of education and entertainment, but they are nevertheless striking comments to emerge from a scholar who considers that 'the content analyst is in a position somewhat similar to that of the psychoanalyst who by interpreting the dreams of a patient, reveals the mechanism and the meaning of strivings of whose existence the patient is unaware or which he even wishes to contest' (1944: 35).

While Rudolf Arnheim had started his research with a concern about the ways in which escapist serial fiction pandered to the worst of stereotypically feminine characteristics, one of his conclusions stresses the difficulties in the position of American women in the home. We have here an early example of the way in which soap opera as a genre has been read symptomatically. In this instance, perhaps slightly against the researcher's original intentions, soap opera is understood to tell us primarily about the condition of US women and the contradictions of contemporary femininity.

(ii) Herta Herzog   Herta Herzog conducted research on soap opera while working for the Bureau of Applied Social Research headed by Paul Lazarsfeld. Like many of those associated with the Bureau, she was a Jewish refugee from Europe, and it is perhaps this history which underlies a dimension of her work that is rarely commented on: its topicality. The essay is, quite clearly, in terms of tone and the sense of urgency created by the entry of the USA into the war, a kind of war work. Read symptomatically, this is an essay about the necessity for political engagement, shadowed by a sense of both the fragility and the luxury of a life absorbed in the private world of home and family. There is considerable suppressed passion in her sense that US housewives should have a civic sense. Thus her penultimate sentence is, 'We live in a world where the ultimate criterion is no longer what we like to do, but what our duty is' (Herzog 1944: 32–3). These very particular historical circumstances contribute to, and perhaps explain, the exhortatory project in relation to serial listeners evident in the essay, and it is this sense of urgent global duty which underlies the project in more than one sense, and which offers very distinct contrasts to the rather more introspective concerns of some of the second-wave scholarship.

Robert C. Allen, in his consistent concern with the history of US communications research, where the term 'effects' has particular resonances, argues for the significance of Herzog's concern with the psychological and social needs soap opera listening fulfilled, rather than with the effects of listening on the audience (1985: 23). It should, however, be pointed out that Herzog herself does initially characterize her project in terms of 'effects':

> From the standpoint of social research, we should like to know the effects of these serials upon the women who have for years listened to them regularly. (1944: 3)

The other point to note here is the straightforwardness of Herzog's assumption that it is in/on women that these effects can be discerned. She is here reproducing the focus of the four surveys she analyses, all of which were conducted only with women, using content analysis, notions of audience profile and structure derived from comparisons of listeners and non-listeners, and interpretations of 'gratifications received' from interviews. Herzog uses a structuring comparison between listeners and non-listeners and is interested in whether avid listeners are (1) more isolated; (2) of 'smaller intellectual range'; (3) more concerned with personal problems than public affairs; (4) more beset with anxieties and frustrations; or (5) just heavy radio users (Herzog's numbering). For our purposes, it is the third area of enquiry which is the most interesting, in that we have here specified for investigation what is often seen as a characteristic of femininity: a concern with personal life and the private sphere rather than the public. Indeed, this is in some ways an example of the tautology of femininity, wherein a defining attribute of difference is also simultaneously potentially pathological. What is to be investigated is, in some senses, the subjectivity of hegemonic femininity, of the little woman who stays at home and depends on her husband for news of the world of public affairs. Herzog finds the most significant differences between listeners and non-listeners in areas 2 and 5. That is, listeners do tend to have less formal education than non-listeners, and listen to more radio—as Herzog expresses it, listeners have a 'general radio-mindedness'. It is the latter finding which is more conspicuous, although none is very distinctive. Herzog makes an interesting comment in her discussion of levels of education when she writes, 'If a woman listens extensively to daytime serials although her education gives her access to a wider range of alternative experiences, then she exhibits the 'typical' characteristics of the serial listener in a more pronounced fashion than the listener with relatively little education' (1944: 20). The interest lies in the notion of the 'typical' characteristics of the serial listener, which are never really established in the article, although there is a sustained effort to discover whether serial listeners have a particular personality profile. But what emerges as the typical characteristic of the listener is Herzog's sense of a habit of listening: 'women who have for years listened to them regularly', 'if a woman listens extensively'. At one level, it is the habitual listening as such which is cause for concern. Apart from the fact of listening, the distinctiveness of serial listeners is not really confirmed—serial listeners tend to be very slightly less self-assured and energetic, but do not think of themselves as worrying more. Herzog herself is extremely cautious about the 'quantitative measure of personality traits', although obviously intrigued and interested in further investigating frustrations and anxieties of listeners.

It is not, historically, the relatively indeterminate findings of the surveys that should now concern us, but the proposition that there is a typical listener, and the features of that typicality. Particularly, given that the nexus of future investigation is seen to be in anxiety and frustration, while the typical listener is seen as having less assurance and energy, we have once again the image of serial listening as symptom of personal inadequacy and social frustration. In this context, the fate of research area 3 is interesting. Herzog understands an interest in public affairs as 'in part a matter of general intellectual interests' (1944: 12), and therefore, following her findings in area 2, expects that listeners will be 'somewhat laggard in this respect'. However, as there was no marked difference in social participation between listeners and non-listeners, another contributory element in an interest in public affairs, she does not expect this difference to be marked. Her data supports her inferences—but her conclusions display what will become the familiar desire to increase the participation in the public sphere of the serial fan. The particular way in which this is figured for Herzog is through participation in elections. Thus she concludes her discussion of area 3 with:

> By emphasising, during the pre-election period, the obligation of every American women to go the polls, the daytime serials could undoubtedly make a valuable public contribution. (1944: 15)

It is only in the last section of the paper that Herzog moves to 'listeners' own reports of their listening experiences' (1944: 23). She justifies this move away from 'effects' on the grounds that she is researching a little known field in which

> preliminary evidence suggests that the gratifications which women derive from daytime serials are so complex and so often unanticipated that we have no guide to fruitful observations unless we study in detail the actual experiences of women listening to these programs. (1944: 23)

It is this sentence which marks the significance of Herta Herzog's contribution to the study of the soap opera audience, this granting of complexity and autonomy to the listeners' experiences. She records that listeners find three major types of gratification: emotional release (through compensatory pleasure or identification), a site for wishful thinking, and a major source of advice—a finding which she describes as 'striking' and 'unexpected'. Those who listen more and those with less formal education were more likely to mention this gratification. As so often with audience research, the quotations from the respondents offer a vivid contrast to the surrounding material, and there is certainly here a real sense of unhappiness eased: 'It helps you to listen to these stories. When Helen Trent has serious trouble she takes it calmly. So you think you'd better be like her and not get upset' (Herzog 1944: 28).[3] Herzog's surprise at the use of the programmes

---

3 Helen Trent, as described by both Kaufman (1944) and Arnheim (1944), is strikingly similar as a character to Meg in *Crossroads*. See Ch. 4, below.

for advice, and her stress toward the end of the article 'that there can be no doubt that a large proportion of the listeners take these programmes seriously' (1944: 31–2), indicates that these detailed audience interviews have altered her perceptions of the ways in which the programmes are consumed, if not of the programmes themselves. Although she accepts what the listeners say she doesn't think it right:

> The overall formula for the help obtained from listening seems to be in terms of 'how to take it'. This is accomplished in various ways. The *first* of these is outright wishful thinking. The stories 'teach' the Panglossian doctrine that 'things come out all right' . . . A *second* way in which the listeners are helped to accept their fate is by learning to project blame upon others. (1944: 28–9)

In contrast with some later audience research which tends towards the destabilizing of the position of the researcher, this documentation of the way in which listeners 'use' the serials serves to confirm the researcher's original judgement.[4] Herzog opens her conclusion by saying 'These data point to the great social responsibility of those engaged in the writing of daytime serials' and finishes by arguing for the use of the serials as a vehicle for war messages: 'We shall have to tell how personal losses should be borne and overcome by work and understanding of higher purposes instead of being submitted to passively as undeserved suffering . . .' (1944: 32). This is a plea for the entry of women listeners into the public sphere, for gratifications to be deferred, and for personal identity to be reconfigured within a meaningful sense of national identity.

This early research on radio soap opera was conducted twenty-five years before the earliest of the (second-wave) feminist research which is the main concern of this book. However, in this early work can be found tropes, themes, concerns, and characters that recognizably return in the feminist work. Arnheim offers reflections on the position of women drawn from analyses of the serials, and pioneers a certain kind of symptomatic reading of the genre. All the writers are interested in the soap fan, and Herzog explicitly points to what I have called the 'tautology of femininity', in which a defining feature of difference—in this case a concern with the private world in preference to the public—is seen as potentially pathological. The context of the Second World War offers a specific urgency to the desire of all the writers to increase the participation of soap opera listeners in public life, but this desire too is very striking in the early feminist work, as we shall see in the next chapter.

4 Hermes (1993: 99) e.g. recounts an unexpected problem in her research into the reading of women's magazines when she discovered that most readers understood magazine reading as an activity about which there was nothing to say. Walkerdine (1986) and Seiter (1990) (both discussed in Ch. 5, below) offer differently self-conscious accounts of ethnographic work as destabilizing for the researcher.

3
Feminists Taking Soap Opera Seriously: The Work of Carol Lopate, Michèle Mattelart, and Tania Modleski

As we have seen in the first chapter, early feminist analysis of soap opera, within the general framework of hostility to media stereotyping, was dismissive or denunciatory. Soaps, not without reason, were seen as a privileged site for the reproduction of the housewife stereotype, and were particularly loathed for their perceived address and appeal to women viewers. In this chapter I make analyses of the first extended feminist discussion of soap opera by non-interviewees to appear in academic and professional journals.[1] My concerns are twofold. First, to outline the parameters within which soap opera was first seen as being of interest for feminist scholars, and to survey the theoretical and conceptual frameworks used. This is a relatively conventional approach to the establishment of a new academic field of study. Secondly, less conventionally, through detailed textual analyses of the language of the articles, I want to progressively trace the discursive construction of significant positions within what I would argue to be the structuring paradigmatic set for this research: woman–feminist–housewife–viewer. The fifth member of this set—'intellectual', 'academic', or 'scholar'—as I will argue below, does not at this stage appear as an explicit speaking

---

1 These were *Feminist Studies* (Lopate 1976) and *Film Quarterly* (Modleski 1979) in the USA. Mattelart's article discussed here appeared first in English in 1982 in *Media, Culture and Society*. Mattelart dates it to 1981, written first in French (Mattelart 1986: 3), although it is clearly written in relation to the earlier experience of residence in Chile, which she left in 1973 (with the downfall of the government of Popular Unity). Dyer, Lovell, and McCrindle (1977) presented their pioneering paper on soap opera to the Edinburgh Television Festival in 1977—see McGuigan (1992: 142–4) on the reception of this. Gray and McGuigan (1993) reprint this article in the section 'Some Foundations' in their popular reader on Cultural Studies. The article, and its reception, is discussed in Ch. 8, below.

position, although there are clear moments of an address to this as a reading position. My argument will be that through the analysis of the shifts of authorial voice in relation to these positions, which are variously identified with each other, we can trace the contradictory and difficult articulation of the identity 'feminist (intellectual)' with her troublesome task of simultaneously addressing a women's movement and an academic community. Similarly, the opposition between the feminist subject and housewife object of research fluctuates, revealing the historical construction of these identities, the ways in which they are, and are not, constructed against each other in feminist research. In each case, using Janice Radway's formulation, we can see the construction of the person 'worrying responsibly'— but the worries have differences as well as similarities.

(i) Carol Lopate Carol Lopate's 1976 essay ' "Daytime Television": You'll Never Want to Leave Home' offers the first US revisionist discussion of soaps. Although she cites research by Arnheim (1944) and Downing (1974) as well as the more popular work by LaGuardia (1977), the article makes no attempt to locate itself within the mass communications paradigms of the US, and is more directly related to other early feminist analyses of media such as those by Germaine Greer (1971), and the radical critiques of Hollywood cinema associated with magazines like *Jumpcut*[2] in its combination of sharp observation, intuition, and radical common sense. This is clearly position-taking, polemical writing. The political impulses behind the work are signalled by the places of publication, both academically marginal—first, in 1976, *Feminist Studies*, and secondly, in the following year, the more widely available *Radical America* (Lopate 1977). The political impulses are primarily articulated in a discussion of the family, an institution which she sees soaps as eroticizing, while family members, particularly women, are simultaneously infantilized. She supports this account of the constitution and representation of the family with textual analysis of daytime serial drama, showing that life outside the family is consistently shown to be dangerous, while incest and quasi-incestuous relationships become a dominant theme through the dramatic logic of this focus on the family:

> Daytime television creates the eroticized family and offers its romances as the solution to the life journey. It promises that the family can be everything, if only one is willing to stay inside it. (Lopate 1977: 51)

---

2 *Jumpcut*, an American left-wing film magazine, specialized in political reviews of Hollywood cinema in the 1970s.

The discussion of soaps occurs within the larger framework of an examination of US daytime programming. This was, in 1976, a relatively innovatory project—Raymond Williams' classic formulation of 'flow' had first been articulated in 1974 in response to US television—and this innovation is marked by Lopate in a paragraph which resonates through much of the subsequent more academic work:

> It is difficult to talk about daytime television. Those who know it
> are experts who cannot be surprised by new bits of information,
> and only nod with a knowing look at any insight or analysis.
> On the other side are the people who have never turned on
> the television before the six o'clock news, or who only switch
> channels rapidly in disgust when searching for their children's
> daytime programs. For them, daytime television is a world of
> screaming women and MCs or murky family scenes. That is all
> they want to know. (1977: 34)

With this paragraph Lopate points to a recurrent issue in the study of popular culture, particularly in the 1970s and early 1980s, in which the unselfconscious expertise of fans exists in a quite separate sphere from that in which more legitimate cultural pursuits and competencies are discussed and analysed. The opposition of these two spheres, the sphere of fandom/consumption and the sphere of analysis (political or academic, or some mixture of both), provides a fundamental binary opposition which structures nearly all the work on soap opera, as I will show. Within this binary opposition we can locate the figure of the researcher, a solitary figure ('It is difficult to talk about daytime television'), who in one way or another moves between the two fields, bringing material from one to bear on the other and vice versa. This purveyor of out-of-place knowledge constantly risks the dismissive nod, the characterization of the cautious work of cultural translation and analysis as banal, obvious, and unnecessary.[3] Or, as Gillian Skirrow has observed, the role of the researcher can be voyeuristic unless she too has a place in the pleasures:

> In investigating popular culture the only way not to feel like
> a snooping health visitor, sniffing out whether someone's
> environment is fit to live in, is to examine some aspect or form
> of it which evokes passionate feelings in oneself. (1986: 115)

---

3 Clifford Geertz offers an eloquent account of this problem for the anthropologist in a postmodern era: 'The basic problem is neither the moral uncertainty involved in telling stories about how other people live nor the epistemological one involved in casting those stories in scholarly genres—both of which are real enough, are always there and go with the territory. The problem in that now that such matters are coming to be discussed in the open, rather than covered up with a professional mystique, the burden of authorship seems suddenly heavier' (1988: 138). Williamson (1986) and Morris (1988) offer differently inflected critiques of the cultural studies engagement with the popular.

I will return to Skirrow's passionate solution, but here would locate Lopate's pioneering essay within the rhetorical structure of much of this work which constitutes the cultural researcher as explorer in the dark continent of popular culture. In this way, the researcher is always other to the work, and indeed frequently receives instruction in its pleasures and procedures. Thus Lopate, at the end of her article, acknowledges the help of her friend Irena Klenbort in the following terms:

> I should like to thank Irena Klenbort, whose insights were invaluable in helping me develop some of the ideas in this paper, and who furnished me with examples from her more extensive soap opera watching. (1977: 51)

This explicit denial of any history of soap opera viewing was anticipated in the article with a disavowal of the skills of this viewing: 'Until I got to know the stories, the afternoon felt like one long, complicated saga of family tragedy and romance, punctuated, of course, by frequent and repetitive advertisements' (1977: 41). We see clearly here the tension between claiming authority as an intellectual and possessing too great competences in the sphere of popular culture.[4] Lopate indeed, in the biographical note which appears after her article in *Radical America*, declares that she has 'stopped watching television and is now writing fiction' (1977: 51).

It is Lopate who first formulates the correlation between the rhythm of daytime programming and housework which is developed with such influence by Modleski in 1979. Lopate too first suggests that the commercials which interrupt soap opera can be understood to offer commodity-based solutions to the narrative dilemmas of the serials, a point later developed by Flitterman (1983). Lopate argues that it is the game shows scheduled in the morning which are paced to allow housework:

> The tone and format of the game shows and serials fit the daily rhythm of the housewife. The noise of the game shows' shrieks and laughter injects the home with the needed adrenaline for getting up in the morning and doing the heavy chores. The heartbreak, confusion, restrained passion, and romance of families in the soaps provides the anaesthesia to fill out the hollows of long afternoons when children are napping and there is ironing or nothing at all to be done. (1977: 34–5)

She repeats this point later in the essay in a way which also reminds us that she is not a habituée of daytime television when she observes, '[o]n days when I have tried to sit through morning television, I got a splitting headache. It is not meant to be sat with' (1977: 41).

---

4 See Allen (1985: p. ix) for a similar disclaimer.

In contrast, the afternoon serials have a less frantic pace. Lopate points to the expansion of narrative time which allows narrative (real life) interruption, but also has specific emotional consequences: 'Everyday life, which often induces boredom and restlessness when taken in its own time, becomes filled with poignancy when the moment can be languished upon' (1977: 47). Although Lopate herself is ambivalent about this dwelling on everyday life, we see here the reformulation, after Herzog (1944), of one of the key themes in the analysis of soap opera. Everyday life, and its appropriate concerns and competencies, is a representational domain with which revisionist work on soap opera becomes increasingly occupied. And in this discussion of women's everyday life, and the role therein of 'women's genres' like soap opera, one of the key dilemmas of contemporary feminism is articulated. The question, as we have seen in Chapter 1, is that of the attitude to the feminine sphere. Crudely, is it good because it is women's culture, or is it bad because it is a culture of oppression? Lopate argues that there is, within daytime serials, a utopian gendered division of labour which is produced by this extension of time: 'The daytime serials present a world where everyone—not just women— has time to deal with the personal and emotional problems of those who are dear to them' (1977: 47).

This formulation captures precisely the ambivalence of the attitudes towards the labour of personal life. On the one hand, there is the recognition that there is an important labour in dealing with the personal and emotional problems of dear ones, but on the other, the recognition is devalued because only women 'have time' to do it. Hence the way in which the emotional hothouse atmosphere of daytime soaps, in which both women and men sweat, can be seen to be utopian. So Lopate distrusts, but also recognizes, the lure of the emotional excess of the serials. As an emancipatory alternative, she proposes a developmental model in which women leave 'this infantile world' (1977: 48), learning about silence and solitude (implicitly by turning off the television), and thereby gaining a grown-up self. So on the one hand Lopate is arguing that these shows construct women as infantile:

> To the viewer at home, the message reiterates the closed-in
> sensibility of traditional family morality. The family . . . is the
> only place where one will be understood and trusted and where
> one can try to understand and trust. (1977: 49)

On the other, she is accepting/proposing that femininity, or the femininity of these 'viewers at home', is indeed in some ways infantile, and must be transformed or transcended:

> While the soap operas are clearly peopled by adults, the characters
> do not have to suffer the isolation and aloneness that is part of the

adult state as we know it. But they also do not gain the power and autonomy that are its rewards. (1977: 50)

Lopate's elevation of the 'adult state' as a desirable goal casts doubt on Ann Kaplan's characterization of this essay, using her adaptation of Kristeva's schema, as 'stage two feminism', the rejection 'of the male symbolic order in the name of difference', or radical feminism (Kaplan 1987: 226–7).[5] Lopate, although clearly hostile to the family, as Kaplan points out, is, as I have shown, in fact also much more within a liberal or equal rights feminist paradigm, with the key aspiration for women being adulthood. In this way Lopate's essay contains the implicit acceptance of the inferiority of femininity as addressed by daytime television. This in turn returns us to the peculiar position of the feminist researcher, the equivocations in relation to her own television expertise, the presentation of herself as in some ways a stranger in a strange land.

(ii) Michèle Mattelart

These preoccupations, differences, and difficulties return in the work of Michèle Mattelart, the second author for discussion. The inflections and positions are different, but the discursive nodal points, 'housewives/ordinary women' and 'everyday life', reappear.

Michèle Mattelart, while resident in Chile until 1973, and subsequently from France, wrote a series of articles about Latin American popular media which were collected in English in 1986 (Mattelart 1986). We shall here be concerned with the articles written in 1981 and 1982 which analyse the Latin American *fotonovela* and *telenovela* (Mattelart 1982; 1986: 5–24). As a preliminary, it should be observed that all Mattelart's work of this period is structured through three main concerns: the expanding, transnational quality of media markets; the political/ideological role of media messages; and the specificity of feminine experience and the address to women within the media. The particular political context in which she was writing, and on which she was reflecting, provides material for a sustained engagement with women as a politically conservative force which is unusual in feminist writing, one of the few other examples being Beatrix Campbell's 1987 study of British Conservative voters (see also Jacqueline Rose (1988) on Margaret Thatcher). It is this much more directly political project—the collection is dedicated to Latin American friends who have died—which informs Mattelart's analysis

---

5 Although both printings of Carol Lopate's article are under the name Lopate, E. Ann Kaplan (1987) refers to the author as Carole Aschur [*sic*]. Carol Ascher has subsequently published a biography of Simone de Beauvoir (1981) and short stories and essays (1993).

and her investigation of the appeal of what she calls the 'order of the heart'. Thus although Mattelart is hostile to 'The ideological functions of these narratives' (1986: 14), she recognizes their appeal to women she works with politically, and her grasp of what is at stake is rather more complex than that of some of the later defenders of serial fiction.

The core of Mattelart's approach, within the triple emphasis outlined above, is through the notion of time. This she articulates first through a reprise of one of the dominating concerns of feminist intellectual work in the 1970s, the domestic labour debate, arguing for the invisible and reproductive necessity of women's work in the home (Bland et al. 1978). She thus proposes, like all female commentators before and after, the centrality of the figure of the housewife in the analysis of media addressed to women. However, it is important to note that Mattelart's concern with the domestic economy is consistently articulated with Marxist-influenced analysis of international capitalism. Unlike both Lopate and Modleski, the housewife for Mattelart is explicitly part of a global economy. She concludes this part of her argument:

> The genre of the women's broadcasts may differ (afternoon magazines, television serials, radio serials); the values around which their themes are structured can correspond to different points in women's relation to capital . . . But they still have in common the purpose of integrating women into their everyday life. (1986: 9)

She sees two dimensions to the integration of women into everyday life. There is first the homology between the repetitive, quotidian serial format and domestic labour, an aspect of the relation between women and domestic serials which subsequent commentators amplify. Secondly, there is the 'symbolic revenge on the triviality of everyday life' (1986: 13) provided by melodramatic coincidence or the unusual adventures of the heroine. Mattelart's political objection to 'the repressive order of the heart' which she sees as the organizing drive of romantic and melodramatic fiction is that it offers only individual, not collective solutions, with its 'two helpmates: Nature and Fate' (1986: 13).

This critique of romance/melodrama is in some ways the traditional Marxist one, except that Mattelart, like Lopate before her, offers a specifically feminist inflection in her concern that heroines should develop into 'independent individual[s]', rather than be swept up by Destiny. Unusually though, for feminist work of this period, Mattelart is concerned with the actual reception of this fiction, and with the contradictory aspects of its appeal. She quotes from analyses of the serials made by politically active working-class women, and goes on to observe:

> We cannot simply ignore the appeal and the pleasure (however bitter-sweet it may be when it goes hand in hand with a social and political awareness) produced by these fictional products of the cultural industry. There *is* a problem here, and one hitherto scarcely tackled. (1986: 15)

It is in answer to this problem that she proposes further hypotheses about temporality and femininity, hypotheses which are closest to Julia Kristeva's notions of women's time, developed in her essay 'Le Temps des femmes' (Kristeva 1979). Kristeva describes female psychic subjectivity as constituted in relation to both cyclical and monumental time, which she opposes to the time of history, linear time. Mattelart uses these oppositions to theorize the fascination of 'These vast stories, delivered in daily instalments and repeated daily': 'By cultivating the enjoyment of this non-forward-looking sense of time, these stories would tend to hinder women's access to the time of history, the time of project' (1986: 16). Mattelart, however, does not stop here with women outside history but goes on to speculate about the positive value of this alternative, non-linear time. This then allows her to move back to a discussion of the value of reproductive work, in which she argues for the importance of restoring value to areas that are not directly productive. It is thus Mattelart, rather than Lopate, who more fully occupies a position that might fleetingly be characterized as radical feminist, in that she argues for a celebration of women's specificity, but of course she does so, at least at the international, macroeconomic level, within a Marxist framework, reinscribing the significance of class.

In her moves from multinational media corporations to the psychic structure constituted by biological reproduction, Mattelart's analysis is more ambitious and more global than any of the subsequent work. She is also most successful in retaining a sense of the contradictory nature of what she is investigating, in her invocation of the 'bitter-sweet pleasure' gained by consumers. Mattelart strongly invokes the figure of the housewife/mother, but this figure is a complex one, with access to understanding and psychic rhythms denied to those more fully in the historical, and thus not simply 'lacking'. Her own relation to this figure is less conflicted than that of many other writers. Perhaps this is because of the Chilean experience when she was involved both in research and policy for the Allende government and in television programming (Mattelart 1986: 3). As witness to, and theorist of, the strongly conservative role that can be played by women in times of social crisis, Mattelart uses a notion of feminine specificity while not at any point assuming, as is sometimes the case with Western feminism, that this is necessarily progressive.[6] She is thus able to occupy the position 'woman' as she writes, while at the same time being very clear about her distance from some other women.

(iii) Tania Modleski

Tania Modleski's 1979 article 'The Search for Tomorrow in Today's Soap Opera' has been referred to in nearly all subsequent studies of soap opera. The arguments most frequently cited are first the suggestion that soap opera, in its repetition and lack of resolution, is a feminine narrative form. Secondly, the article is known for the hypothesis that American daytime soaps characteristically construct a maternal position for their viewers, which is an engagement with Laura Mulvey's influential 1975 argument that classical Hollywood cinema constructs a masculine spectator position. This evocation of the soap viewer as an 'ideal mother' has proved particularly resonant within feminist film and television studies, partly because it is one of the first attempts to specify a feminine viewing position—an equivalent within these disciplines to early formulations in the debates in literary studies about reading as/like a woman (Culler 1983: 43–63). Modleski's other significant argument at this stage is about the villainous figure in US daytime drama, whom she argues is 'an outlet for feminine anger' (1979: 17), but whom she also sees as fundamental to the psychic dynamic of the programmes, as I discuss at more length below.

This 1979 article is later combined with a paper, 'The Rhythms of Reception' (1983), presented to Ann Kaplan's conference on television at Rutgers University in 1981 to form chapter 4 of Modleski's 1982 book *Loving with a Vengeance* (Kaplan 1983a). The Rutgers paper is published alone in 1983, but it is to the combination piece, also called 'The Search for Tomorrow in Today's Soap Operas', to which many subsequent critics make reference.[7] These I will address briefly here, before returning to the 1979 version for a more detailed textual analysis. I am privileging the 1979 version because the earliest formulations of feminist research on soap opera are the richest in the tensions of articulating the project. For the period of this case study, it was the journal version that was most available, since the widely distributed Methuen edition of *Loving with a Vengeance* was not published until 1985.

6 Mattelart's 1975 essay 'The Feminine Side of the Coup', written about the role of women in bringing about the downfall of the Allende government, is in fact included as a later chapter in the 1986 collection.

7 Thus both Seiter et al. (1989a) and Geraghty (1991) refer to the book version, which confusingly has two publishers, the Shoestring Press in 1982 and Methuen in 1985 (which then becomes part of the Routledge list).

Loving with a Vengeance, the published form of what was o1 Modleski's Ph.D. dissertation, includes the discussion of soap opera as the final chapter of a work which addresses a range of fiction aimed at women—Harlequin romances, Female Gothic, and soap opera. As with Lopate and Mattelart, we see that it is the address of the media— fictions for women—rather than genre or medium which is decisive in the selection for study. Modleski, in the preface to her book, points out that

> The present work was conceived and undertaken out of concern that these narratives were not receiving the right kind of attention. I try to avoid expressing either hostility or ridicule, to get beneath the embarrassment, which I am convinced provokes both the anger and the mockery, and to explore the reasons for the deep-rooted and centuries old appeal of the narratives. Their enormous and continuing popularity, I assume, suggests that they speak to very real problems and tensions in women's lives. (1982: 15)

Here again is the voice of the critic who is worrying responsibly, but here also is the clear formulation of a new intellectual enterprise. Thus the concern with narratives which were not 'receiving the right kind of attention' is articulated with notions of hostility, ridicule, and embarrassment which must be overcome in order to understand the ways in which the very popularity of these stories speaks, just as Mattelart also suggests, to 'very real problems and tensions in women's lives'. Modleski's analysis has been extremely generative for both textual analysis and ethnographic investigations. In fact, the empirical projects both complicate and to an extent contradict her analysis, but that is not here our primary concern,[8] and indeed it should be pointed out that Modleski herself claims no empirical verification. My concern here, though, is with Modleski's ambivalent construction of the figure of the feminist critic and the housewife audience, rather than with the empirical audience investigated by later scholars using Modleski's schema.

Modleski's original 1979 article is written mainly in an impersonal third person, exemplified in the opening proposition, 'In soap operas the hermeneutic code predominates'. This voice is maintained for the majority of the essay, with an occasional shift to first person for points

---

8 Seiter and Kreutzner (1989) used Modleski's analysis of soap opera to govern part of the agenda in their cross-cultural ethnography of soap opera viewers. Their research indicated extensive conscious resistance by working-class women, to the position of 'ideal mother' that Modleski described, as well as explicit admiration for the villain-ess. These findings do not substantially undercut Modleski's analysis of the *textual* structuring of soap opera, although they do disprove her hypotheses about how women *watch* the programmes. That is, methodologically, they establish that viewers' readings cannot be deduced from textual exegesis.

of argument and controversy, 'I believe...' (1979: 12). Unlike Lopate, Modleski does not initially differentiate herself from the soap watching audience, and uses the first person plural to refer to this audience in the way which is quite common in both literary and film criticism when the author claims that the text makes certain demands of 'us' the audience, or that 'we' understand a particular device in a certain way. The difference in the 'we' and 'us' that Modleski uses, which again is not marked, is that it is, as the article progresses, clearly revealed to be feminine. This is revealed quite interestingly after the key formulation of the subject/spectator of soaps being constituted 'as a sort of ideal mother' (1979: 14). At the end of this paragraph, Modleski observes: 'Thus soaps convince women that their highest goal is to see their families united and happy, while consoling them for their inability to bring about familial harmony'. This is the first use of 'women' in the article, and also marks the point where Modleski moves out of this identity: 'them'. Here, it seems clear that the separation between 'women' and the author is effected by the author's ability to see the double ideological operation of the soap text on (other) women.

Modleski develops her thesis about the maternal viewing position of the soap spectator into an argument that this multiply identified, and hence ultimately powerless, figure, is the liberal core of shows that are thus constituted as liberal at a formal level. Within this tolerant structure, the figure of the villainess functions as the safety valve for what Modleski terms feminine anger, but also, through transforming traditional feminine weaknesses into strengths, offers a type of monstrous feminine. This character, evoking contradictory hatred and identification in the viewer, is theorized by Modleski to provoke, in Freud's terms, repetition compulsion. That is, through the viewer's identification with both the villainess and her opponents, the viewer becomes psychically caught up in 'internal contestation' and begins to derive pleasure from repetition as such. 'In this way', Modleski suggests, 'soaps help reconcile her to the meaningless, repetitive nature of much of her life and work within the home' (1979: 17). The viewer has here become singular, partly necessarily because it is almost impossible to discuss psychic processes of this kind in the plural. However, significantly, there is also here the thinly concealed proposition that the situation of the housewife is psychically pathological in that it requires adjustment to a routine both meaningless and repetitive. Modleski develops these arguments considerably in the 1981 paper which, as its title suggests, is specifically concerned with homologies between the formal structures of the television text and the domestic day. Although she expresses disagreement with Lopate on the issue of soap construction of the family, and the viewer's relation to the family, her notion of the rhythm of reception and domestic work is very similar. The crux of Modleski's argument in 1979, though, is the linking of the formal qualities of soaps—repetition, interruption, and lack of resolution—with a feminist aesthetics. She makes these links in two sentences:

> Clearly, women find soap operas eminently entertaining, and an analysis of the pleasure that soaps afford can provide clues not only about how feminists can challenge this pleasure, but also how they can incorporate it. For, outrageous as this assertion may at first appear, I would suggest that soap operas are not altogether at odds with a possible feminist aesthetics. (1979: 18)

This passage displays a clear separation between the author and 'women', with the author explicitly addressing herself to feminists. The key words are 'clues' and 'outrageous'. 'Clues' clearly reveals that this is an enterprise of detection, the analysis of soap opera will render information about other pleasures—pleasures that must be challenged. So the justification of the academic enterprise to other feminists is in its gathering of politically useful knowledge. However, within this address to an imagined sceptical feminist audience, Modleski is also making a polemical point: 'outrageous as this asser-tion may first appear . . .'. So this 1979 piece is written against the grain of feminist attitudes to popular television, insisting that there is something here to be taken seriously. Both words disappear in the later version, where the sentences are split:

> Clearly, women find soap operas eminently entertaining, and an analysis of the pleasure these programs afford can provide feminists with ways not only to challenge this pleasure but to incorporate it into their own artistic practices (1982: 104)

and a page later:

> Indeed, I would like to argue that soap operas are not altogether at odds with an already developing, though still embryonic, feminist aesthetics. (1982: 105)

These rewritten versions, smoother, more confident, less embattled, also give much less sense of the author as caught between the pos-itions of 'woman' and 'feminist'. Although this is evidently partly attributable to the author's greater ease with a rewritten argument, I would suggest that the period between the publication of the first and second versions was critical in the changing status of soap opera—not least because of the impact of the original 1979 version.

Finally, I want to point to the way in which the argument about feminist aesthetics is made, for here we see a different audience addressed. Here, what is notable is the way in which the argument is made with reference to modernist fiction by women writers

—Nathalie Sarraute and Ivy Compton-Burnett—as well as to feminist critics such as Claire Johnston and Mary Ellman. Certain levels of cultural capital are assumed here, and we can see the way in which the cross-class category, women, which generates a feminine aesthetic, is constructed by an explicit argument across the divisions of class between women who read Nathalie Sarraute and women who watch *Ryan's Hope*. However, given, as we have already noted, what it is 'outrageous' to suggest, it is to the readers of Nathalie Sarraute and Ivy Compton-Burnett that the article, and the argument, are addressed. The feminist intellectual is present, but not yet fully formed, not yet a speaking part. This 1979 essay, which has normally been approached for what it tells us about soap opera, offers a fascinating glimpse of an emergent speaking position. Modleski, defending serious attention to soap opera from feminist dismissal, calls on a high cultural repertoire as resource and defence. The study of soap opera was at this stage too provocative to stand alone.

Carol Lopate, as we have seen, first formulates many of the ideas that become most significant in the feminist critical approach to soap opera. Arguably, because her work was less academic and more explicitly political than Modleski's, she is less well known as a source. Also significant here may be that fact that she did not pursue an academic career in this field. Similarly Michèle Mattelart's research is not extensively referenced by anglophone scholars, although her work is granted due significance in the burgeoning literature on South American *telenovelas*.[9] Of the scholarship discussed here, it is the work of Tania Modleski to which nearly all Anglo-American writers on both soap opera and popular genre fiction refer.

All of this research is concerned with theorizing relationships between everyday life, television, and the housewife. As becomes clear in the early work discussed in the interviews, particularly that of Dorothy Hobson, the analyses were not determinedly medium- or genre-specific. Radio, game shows, and women's magazines all appear as comparisons and equivalents to soap opera. Instead, the specificity with which this early research is concerned is that of femininity, and particularly, the experience of the housewife. As the detailed textual analysis here offered demonstrated, in the construction of this figure as an interesting audience, there is also the beginnings of the construction of her other, the feminist critic.

This figure, as Janice Radway suggests, worries responsibly about the consumers of serial drama. She does this in ways closely related to the concerns expressed in Chapter 3, particularly by Herta Herzog. Mattelart in particular is concerned by the relationship between viewing and civic involvement, while managing to articulate a quite complex understanding of the contradictory pleasures of *telenovelas*. Each author, in different ways, is concerned with the repetitive routine of domestic labour, and it is to the fantasy of everyday life that we now turn.

4

Fantasies of the Housewife: The Case of *Crossroads*

As we have seen, the history of feminist critical approaches to soap opera condenses and rehearses many of the debates within feminist criticism as a whole, while at the same time re-engaging with personae, like the housewife, who appear in earlier media research. However, this history is also one of the sites whereon the specificity of feminist television criticism is founded and has its own particular contours and emphases. Here, the differences between feminist attention to soap opera and that to Hollywood cinema aimed at women are particularly striking. With some notable exceptions on each side, the criticism of soap opera has tended to be within a realist mode—these programmes do/do not show life as it is—while that of Hollywood cinema has worked with notions of desire, fantasy, and identification, which have their origins ultimately in psychoanalysis. This distinction must be considered alongside the way in which, textually, British soaps have tended to be within a realist/naturalist mode, while US daytime shows, and indeed the exported prime times such as *Dallas* and *Dynasty*, are much more within a melodramatic mode. There are thus a series of overdeterminations on British feminist television criticism, tending to produce it as relentlessly within the realm of the real.

Valerie Walkerdine (1990), in a discussion of girls' comics which she places within a framework of discussion of demands for anti-sexist children's literature, argues powerfully for the significance of fantasy in any approach to children's literature. She differentiates her approach from those which have dominated the field, arguing that the demand for non-stereotypical representations in children's fictions presumes a 'rational' reader, whereas it is precisely the psychic investment in unrealistic narratives which is so powerful for the reader (1990: 90–1). There are clear analogies between Walkerdine's field of study and that of soap opera, most specifically in the contours of the feminist response to the material. So although Ien Ang does use a concept of fantasy to conceptualize the pleasures viewers—and she herself—get from *Dallas* (see Chapter 9), she is unusual in this.[1] The history of feminist television criticism, with its non-generic, contextual origins, has tended to militate against conceptualization of the particular psychic mechanisms of watching soap opera, although, as we have seen, Tania Modleski's formulation of the 'all-powerful mother' as viewing position has been influential, particularly, for example, in formulating routes of ethnographic enquiry (Seiter et al. 1989*a*).

Walkerdine argues for the significance of fantasy in children's investment in *unrealistic* images but I want to use this argument to suggest that fantasy cannot be ignored in *realist* narrative, such as British soap opera. That is to say, if ideas of fantasy allow us to conceptualize one of the ways in which readers/viewers invest in fictional narrative, I would argue that there is an impoverishing literalism in making this investment genre/mode specific. Fantasies of the real and everyday can be as powerful as fantasies of the unrealistic/fantastic, and indeed may be more germane to the constitution of conventional femininity. If, as has been suggested by Elizabeth Cowie (1984) in one of the more extended feminist discussions, fantasy offers a '*mise-en-scène* of desire', then the sites and practices of everyday life, particularly as manifested in the feminine spheres of home and family management, may be most potent in the imagination of successfully achieved femininity. That is to say, the difficulty of 'doing' femininity successfully may demand fantasies of the ordinary as well as the exceptional.[2] It is not only narrative and characters which are marked as 'unrealistic' which can provide a site for fantasy, but precisely figures like the Oxo housewife who appear to manage the multitudinous demands of the housewife/ mother while remaining within the repertoire of ordinary everyday life. Similarly, as Janice Winship has argued, the late 1980s 'activity' women's magazines with their plethora of craft skills and recipes, are best not read as 'simply' offering rehashed 'Kinder and Küche'

1 Indeed, as Jackie Stacey has pointed out, Tania Modleski's book, which deals with Harlequin novels and Gothic novels for women as well as with soap opera, becomes noticeably less psychoanalytic in its methodology when it moves to the televisual (Stacey 1994: 257).

2 Jacqueline Rose, in 'Femininity and its Discontents', remarks that feminism and psychoanalysis share a recognition that there is 'a resistance to identity at the very heart of psychic life' (Rose 1983: 9). This essay proposes some ways of thinking about what I am here calling 'the difficulty of "doing" femininity successfully'. The classical narrative trope for the exceptional in soap opera is provided by the big day of the marriage—in some ways the zenith of the heterosexual feminine career. Soap opera marriages, as Flitterman-Lewis points out, always contain the seeds of their own destruction—often sitting in the congregation (Flitterman-Lewis 1988). See also Rabinovitz (1992) for discussion of the exploitation of the marketing potential of soap opera marriage, and Fig. 4.1.

ideologies for women, but as providing quite complex sites for the elaboration of desire and the fantasy of achieving successful contemporary femininity (Winship 1991).[3] This train of thought allows us also to suggest continuities between the watching of soap opera and, for example, the little girls' imagination of 'the tidy house' documented by Carolyn Steedman in her study of girls' play. What these little girls fantasize is exactly a tidy house, an everyday life of gendered order (Steedman 1982).

Thus I want here to attempt to erode the critical binary which lines up melodrama (film)/US/fantasy v. realism (TV)/GB/stereotypes (no fantasy). I want to do this not by attempting a substantial theorization of the role of fantasy in television watching but by looking briefly but indicatively at one of the central characters in a British soap opera from the period of study in the context of a more general discussion of the housewife in British soap opera.[4] That is, I want to sketch an analysis of what I would argue to be a character site for fantasy and to look at some of the characteristics of the successful housewife/matriarch figure in our period of study. What qualities did the successful housewife/matriarch possess? To what extent can they be seen as exemplary and achievable to a viewer? I do at this point confine myself to British soap opera because it is in relation to these programmes that ideas of fantasy are not used, whereas they have been used, to a certain extent, particularly by Ang and Modleski, in relation to US prime-time and daytime shows. Evidently, as all casual commentators on soap opera point out, the rate and frequency of narrative event in soap opera makes it possible to argue that these narratives are fundamentally 'unrealistic', and therefore the stuff of fantasy. Certainly, I think there are grounds for arguing that there are many formal characteristics of soap opera which may make both fleeting and intense psychic investment both tolerable and pleasurable. These would centre on the interweaving of different storylines and the fluctuating prominence of different core characters. However, it is not this argument that I wish to pursue here. Instead, I want to suggest that it is precisely the type of detail that is often seen to support realist/stereotype/no fantasy critiques of British soap opera which can also support fantasy identifications—a fantasy of ordinariness, of femininity achieved. The internationally generically privileged figure here is historically that of the housewife/matriarch—from

3 Indeed Winship's title is very suggestive in this context: 'The Impossibility of *Best*: Enterprise Meets Domesticity in the Practical Women's Magazines of the 1980s' (1991).

4 Flitterman-Lewis (1987) attempts to discuss the role of fantasy in television viewing, mistakenly, in my view, commencing with the psychoanalytic theorization of cinema viewing. She uses the example of soap opera marriage. A relatively early attempt to theorize the role of fantasy in television viewing can be found in Houston (1984).

Helen Trent to Ms McKenzie to Meg Mortimer to Pauline Fowler to Helen Daniels.[5]

Methodologically I consider this brief discussion important as a way of inscribing within this essay both the concept of fantasy and the third character in the feminist drama of the feminist and the housewife viewer/ordinary woman. This is the textual soap operatic housewife. Then I think we begin to have the full set of characters with which to approach the interviews. We have women in soap opera, women watching soap opera, and women watching and writing about themselves and other women watching soap opera. The very complex interplay between these different positions, and the forging of political and academic allegiances, identities, and discourses therein, is the concern of the following chapters.

Here, I would point out that there may in fact be greater similarities between the feminist soap opera scholar and the soap opera housewife/matriarch than might initially be assumed. For how better can we characterize the housewife/matriarch than as someone who 'worries responsibly'?

Meg Mortimer and the Housewife in British Soap Opera

Nearly all the extant feminist work on British soap opera takes as its starting point the representation of women, and I do not intend to rehearse this research here. From the early piece by Dyer, Lovell, and McCrindle (1977) to a later book like Christine Geraghty's *Women and Soap Opera* (1991), a recurring argument 'for' soap opera has been the strength of the female characters. This, it is proposed, is partly the result of the formal demands of the genre, in that central female characters must withstand repeated buffetings of fate, for if they are not involved in one crisis after another, there is no story. My interviewees talk in different ways about their responses to women in soap opera, but there is certainly a repeated fascination with what can perhaps best be described as watching women coping. Female characters named by the interviewees include Elsie Tanner, Bet Lynch, and Deirdre from *Coronation Street*; Sheila Grant and Annabelle Collins from *Brookside*; and Sue Ellen from *Dallas*. Meg Mortimer (Noele Gordon), the central character of *Crossroads*, whose sensational departure from the show was documented by Dorothy Hobson (1982), is an exemplary—and very long-lived—soap opera matriarch/housewife who, as Hobson has shown, was held in enormous

---

5 Helen Trent was the eponymous heroine of *Helen Trent* (see Ch. 3); Ms McKenzie in *The Young and the Restless*, see Stern (1978); for Meg Richardson/Mortimer see below; Pauline Fowler is in *EastEnders*; Helen Daniels was in *Neighbours*, from 1985–97.

regard by fans. Meg Mortimer displays many of the characteristics of this figure as documented in the critical literature and I wish to offer a brief outline of salient features. This I will do mainly through the textual analysis of photographs of Meg from the enormous quantity of supporting publicity material associated with *Crossroads* as well as through the viewing of all extant early episodes. The use of reproduced publicity material is a choice to offer some evidence to support my readings, which is almost impossible in relation to summaries of archival and long-vanished episodes.[6]

The first point to make, though, is that the housewife qua housewife—unpaid domestic labourer in the home, supported by a husband earning a family wage—hardly exists within British television soap opera in the pre-*Brookside* period. Just as the working class of *Coronation Street* on closer examination turns out to be composed mainly of self-employed small business people, so too the women of *Crossroads*, *Coronation Street*, and then *EastEnders* turn out to be part-time workers or manageresses. As Christine Geraghty (1983) has argued, it was the aggressively realist *Brookside* which in 1982 put women back in the home with the class-contrasted Sheila Grant and Annabelle Collins. Within this context, Meg Mortimer, the motel manager, is particularly interesting.

Images of Meg   Meg Richardson was a widow with two young children when *Crossroads* began in 1964. She had nursed her husband through his last illness in the family home, and it is this home which she decides to turn into a motel on his death. She has some insurance money, and manages to persuade the bank manager to give her a loan. When the series was started, it was planned to focus on the contrasting lives of two sisters, Kitty Jarvis and Meg Richardson.[7] The actress who played Kitty, Beryl Johnstone, died in 1969 and so Kitty had to be written out of the series. This meant that Meg became much more of the central pivot for the show, without any other female characters to challenge her supremacy.

Since Charles Richardson's death, Meg has been married twice. First she married Malcolm Ryder, who tried to poison her in order to claim insurance money after his own business failed. Discovered, he fled to South America, where it appeared that he was killed in a car crash. At this point, Hugh Mortimer, who had previously proposed to

---

6 The British Film Institute has the following preserved episodes which were acquired in the context of my own early research on *Crossroads*; ep.986 tx 5/12/68; ep.1009 tx 15/1/69; ep.1304 tx 12/6/70; ep.2501 tx 3/4/75; ep. 3529 tx 3/1/81; ep.3530 tx 4/11/81.

7 Kitty appears in episodes 986 and 1009 of the extant *Crossroads* episodes.

Meg, reappeared. After a period of wooing, necessitated partly by two previous engagements between Hugh and Meg, both of which had been broken when Hugh got involved with other women, one of whom he married shortly before she died from a brain tumour, Hugh and Meg became engaged again. News comes that Ryder is still alive, and Meg loses her memory in shock. Ryder appears in England and Mortimer arranges for him to be arrested and divorce proceedings start, clearing the way for Meg's third marriage to Hugh Mortimer, which takes place in 1975 and is blessed in Birmingham Cathedral. The city's local paper, the *Birmingham Evening Mail*, prints a special souvenir edition, part of which is reprinted in 1978 to mark the 3,000th episode of *Crossroads* (Fig. 4.1). This marriage ends in 1978, when Hugh Mortimer, captured by terrorists in Australia, dies of a heart attack, leaving Meg alone again.

Fig. 4.1. 'Meg's Memories', *Evening Mail TV Special Souvenir*, Birmingham 1978.

This brief outline conforms to one of the conventions for writing about soap opera, which is to summarize narrative events speedily in a way which emphasizes the melodramatic coincidence and frequency of noteworthy life experiences. However, spread over four days a week of interrupted viewing over several years, these narrative events lose their farcical impact and instead contribute to our understanding of the central character, Meg, as well as exemplifying the generic construction of femininity. Thus the narrative sequence conveys one of the central points about Meg—she is attractive to men, but she has been unlucky in love. Starting the serial with Meg as widow means that she can be a mature, experienced female character, but unlike, say, Mavis in *Coronation Street* in this period, she is not a spinster—she has been wanted. However, as she lost her husband through death, rather than desertion or adultery, she is morally blameless. So she is mature, attractive, good—and available for narrative romance. 'Will this man make Meg really happy?', 'Is this man good enough for Meg to settle down with?' become real narrative questions in a way that would be impossible if Meg were happily settled in a nuclear family. Thus, as has been argued in relation to *Coronation Street* characters of this period like Elsie Tanner and Rita Fairclough, there are two opposing forces at work here (Jordan 1981; Lovell 1981). Conventional ideas about the appropriate destiny for women, indeed about what women can 'do' in life, produce narrative pressure towards narratives of romance and settling down for Meg. However, this is undermined by generic pressure for female characters to be available for things—particularly men—to happen to. Thus Meg, like other strong women soap characters, is generically destined to marriages and romances which, if not unhappy, are short-lived or rather on/off. This generic destiny coexists with the constant narrative inference that women should be partnered, and I think we could suggest offers at a formal level an articulation of the difficulties of contemporary heterosexual femininity.

The other significant character trait which is constructed through the remorseless generic tide of event is capability. Fortune throws one mishap or tragedy after another at Meg, and unlike many of the lesser and more temporary characters, Meg copes.

In this generic and narrative context, the choice of motel-management as Meg's occupation is particularly significant, in that it could be seen as housewifery writ large. Although in fact motel management requires a series of business and management skills, representationally it is amenable to a domestic/familial repertoire. Meg stays with the children—she does not go out to work—and the form her work takes is very often the supervision of an enactment of housework such as checking out the hotel kitchen and chef, or making sure that the personal lives of staff do not interfere with the routines

Fig. 4.2. Meg's integrated workplace family. left to right: Sandy (son), Benny (garage mechanic), David Hunter (co-director of motel), Jill (daughter), Meg.

of catering for the guests. This role also produces Meg as head of a double family—her genetic family and the workplace family. The development of the televisual workplace family throughout the 1970s and 1980s has been increasingly discussed as they have come to dominate many US shows (Bathrick 1984; E. Taylor 1989), but *Crossroads* offered a very early British example in which Meg Mortimer was very literally inscribed as a good mother, loving and efficient to both her families (Fig. 4.2).

This maternal/efficient characterization is constructed partly through narrative and performance, but also, importantly, through dress and extra-textual material such as 'Dear Diary' in *Crossroads Monthly* (Fig. 4.3). Narratively, not only does Meg frequently solve problems and dilemmas for her extended family, but she is always, ultimately, right. Her unflinching moral sense—made reliable through a relatively unvaried performance—in combination with her ability to face disagreeable truths means that even villains frequently end up admitting grudging respect for her. Meg 'wins' by being good, and this must have been one of the great pleasures of watching her.[8] This moral reliability is reinforced by the respectable conservative repertoire of her clothing, as we shall see from the analysis below.

8 Thus in episode 1009, we find the earliest surviving version of a familiar *Crossroads* trope in which the ne'er-do-well Vince has to recognize that Meg knew him better than he did himself.

Dear Diary
A Week in Meg's Life

Today is a bit of a red letter day for me. I've just agreed to allow the printing of selected extracts from my diary and well, all I can say is that I hope everyone has as much pleasure reading my daily scribble as I have had writing it. I suppose I fall into the category of the habitual diary-keeper, stretching back to the great Mr Pepys himself. Few of us, of course, have the opportunity of seeing ourselves in print in our own lifetimes, so I must say I feel doubly privileged.

Saturday...

David Hunter popped over today looking, may I say, very smart indeed in his new blue and charcoal suit. His taste, of course, is just about impeccable and he seemed very pleased that I had noticed this new addition to his wardrobe. His reason for dropping by was to discuss the forthcoming re-decorations to the motel. It's several years now since the last work was carried out and I for one shall be very happy to see a nice new shiny coat of paint.

We had a little difficulty agreeing about colours, though. David was insistent that we ought to experiment and perhaps change to strongish shades of red and blue. Maybe I'm a bit old-fashioned, but my taste ventures more towards whites and pastels. Anyway, after chewing it over for a few minutes, we decided to compromise. To maintain our air of 'respect-ability' we're going to keep the exterior looking fairly conservative, mainly blacks and whites, but inside I'll let David carry out some of his more extrovert ideas on decor! The painters are due to arrive in a week or two's time, so no doubt there'll be more written about this soon.

Monday...

I managed to snatch a few hours away from the motel this morning to pay a visit to 'Birmingham International', our

quite an historic occasion really, because Hugh tells me ~~it's the first British Rail station to be built this centur~~ the first, in fact, since London's Marylebone was complete 1899. I must say I think it's marvellous the way they've b it all up with the main line trains thundering past at all h of the day and night. Of course, as Hugh pointed out, great thing as far as we are concerned is that the new stop been built to serve that seventh wonder of the Midlands, National Exhibition Centre. No one has to tell me National Exhibitions mean just one thing... more gue

Wednesday...

Jill and I popped into town to do a bit of window shopp (although I must secretly admit to having more than hal idea along the lines of a new evening dress). Well, I've he of love at first sight (though I must say it's never yet c my way), but my heart skipped a beat when I saw IT. sort of pale turquoise-green creation with billowy sleeve tried it on and — oh! — it was beautiful, and almos perfect fit. Then the assistant told me it was seventy th pounds fifty. I could have cried with disappointment. tried her best to console me and kept telling me of all wonderful clothes that had never reached her front door, it didn't really help. I suppose like all the others, the d will just have to remain locked away in the wardrobe of dreams.

Thursday...

All of a sudden winter comes to King's Oak. A bit surprise really: I don't remember the weather foreca mentioning snow. Anyway, here it is, like it or loath Mind you, one of the few things for me that makes bel grandmothe~~r~~ bearable is having a new generation of young to get silly about. Children really are adorable little creat and the sight of them all dressed up in their little boots, pullovers and pom pom hats takes me right back to my childhood. I can still remember the trouble I used to into. Things weren't easy in those days and sopping clothing had to be taken off, dried and put straight I on again.

When I come to think about it, what with one thing another, winter for a lot of people isn't really such a time. There is something very cosy about blazing fires you're lucky enough to have an open fire), hot drinks, e nights and the sound of the wind whistling round chimney pots. I suppose this is a very old fashioned sentir in these days of television and central heating, but I believe there is something to be said for that way of

Saturday...

Lord knows if I shall ever get the time this year, but, fir crossed, Hugh and I are determined to start thinking ab holidays. Our dreadful inflation is the guilty culprit whe comes to going abroad. Even the prices of package holi seem to have shot up over the last year or two, so it begin look like a stay-at-home holiday. Of course we are lucky here. I've always been the first to boast that, whe comes to beauty and splendour, Britain can take on the b The weather is, of course, sometimes a little unpredicta but if this summer turns out to be anything like as hot as year's we won't have a lot to worry about.

Well anyway, to start with Hugh was very keen on idea of us going to Rumania. He never tires of telling about the time he had there some years ago. Apparently Carpathian Mountains are quite spectacular with their slopes, lakes and green valleys and forests. He stayed mountain resort called Poina Brasov and was quite ta aback by the overwhelming hospitality of the people. A

Fig 4.3. 'Dear Diary' from
Crossroads Monthly,
1 (1976), 14.

So I am suggesting that this character, rather noticeably, in the time of my study, occupies a position which can be characterized as that of a fantasy housewife. In this she is generically related to earlier key soap characters, such as Helen Trent as described by Rudolf Arnheim in Chapter 3. Meg is a woman apparently in the domestic and all her concerns are domestic familial. However, the domestic sphere here is expanded to include the public sphere—the motel and the workplace family function to dramatize the private sphere, while at the same time being colonized by the representational concerns of personal life. Meg copes—she is in charge, meeting all the obligations of femi-

ninity—keeping the house clean and food on the table, while nurtur-
ing her children and still proving attractive to a succession of men. I
want to support this argument by discussing four images of Meg, in
which my general argument will be that the detail of costume and in
some cases the *mise en scène* provides a series of guarantees for the
credibility of the character (Figs. 4.4–4.7). These guarantees were
also provided, throughout the long duration of the programme, by
the publicity material and photo opportunities about the actress
Noele Gordon, of which I provide a sample.

These images come from a range of materials, including *Crossroads Monthly*, a publication which was widely available through
newsagents in the mid–late 1970s, a series of one-off publications
including supplements to the *TV Times* and special supplements to

Fig 4.4. Meg at work:
the hotel reception desk.

Fig 4.5. Meg at home:
Christmas with Jill
and Sandy.

the *Birmingham Evening Mail* on occasions such as marriages.[9] Richard
Dyer (1970) offers extensive discussion of the different ways in which
this type of publicity material may be approached in relation to film
stars, and following Dyer, it is here assumed that this material offers
privileged insight into the way in which ATV producers and publicity
wished to promote the image of Meg Mortimer in *Crossroads*. In terms
of my argument about 'everyday fantasy', it is a certain banality and
achievability of the overall look that it is significant. Dorothy Hobson
offers a very interesting analysis of the use of costume in *Crossroads*,
and quotes Noele Gordon on the choices she makes for Meg:

9 *Crossroads Monthly* was published by P. H. Bunch Associates under license [*sic*] from
ATV Licensing Ltd. It is described as 'the official magazine of the television series *Crossroads*', and all surviving copies appear to be from the mid-1970s, commencing with
edition 1 in 1976.

Fig. 4.6. Meg and Hugh
in the sitting-room.

You see, I never wear anything too extreme. You look at some
clothes on television—the light entertainment side of it—and
think, 'Oh, that's stunning, but of course, I could never wear that.'
I've always been very careful not to wear anything too extreme or
to have too extreme hairstyles, you know, so that people think,
'Oh well, I can look like that,' you know, which I think is a great
thing . . .' (Hobson 1982: 89)

To Noele Gordon there is no question that Meg serves as a figure of
identification for viewers. She shows a very acute sense of the boundaries which Meg's clothes must not transgress. However, she also
clearly understands the observing of these boundaries as an important responsibility to viewers, and their emulation of Meg as a positive

practice, 'which I think is a great thing . . .'. Perhaps deliberately—as all material makes very clear how professional Noele Gordon was—she is in a way expressing a very 'Meg' sentiment here. The extended family has been further extended to include the viewers who too can be nurtured.

Figures 4.4 to 4.7 illustrate what the boundaries of Meg's dress mean in practice, and are chosen to illustrate the different key elements in Meg's life, and show her at work, with her children and with her husband. Figure 4.8 comes from publicity material about Noele Gordon herself and is chosen to allow some comparison between Meg and Gordon personae, a distinction regularly blurred in most publicity material.

Figures 4.4 and 4.5 illustrate two central aspects of Meg's character, the cheerful efficient business woman and the loving mother—Meg at work and at home. Meg is dressed in a neat but businesslike manner in each photograph. She wears a jacket both at home and at work, which contributes to an image of efficiency. She is wearing make-up but it is quite discreet, just as her hair is noticeable because of its colour but quite conservatively cut and styled. Similarly, although she wears jewellery in each photograph, the 'home' jewellery is discreet, while the work accessories are a little more obvious and 'public'. Meg looks confident and at ease in each photograph, which is partly because of the practised smile, but is accentuated by her domination

Fig 4.7. Meg in the kitchen with Shughie McPhee.

Fig 4.8. Noele Gordon with her Rolls Royce.

of the image. This domination is constructed through framing, and the use of medium close-up rather than long shot, but also through the use of slightly out-of-focus background. Although in terms of production values, we may attribute this lack of background to a tight budget, in terms of an argument about this character as a site for fantasy, we are offered the slightly disorientating combination of a detailed toilette with a blurry background. Meg both is and isn't offered to us as real.

The low production values that are characteristic of *Crossroads* can be seen particularly clearly in the lighting of the work photo, with the just-missed light source at the top of the image and the telephone wire shadow from the right front lighting. However, what is more significant is the interplay of the general and particular which I would argue provides an opportunity for the regular viewer to 'complete' or 'enrich' the significance of the image. For example, the reception desk in Figure 4.4 is a generic reception desk, signified minimally through the telephone, the diary, and the pigeon-holes. It is Meg who secures the desk for identification as the *Crossroads* reception desk. Similarly, the cropped close-up background of the Christmas tree in figure 4.5

is in some ways a non-specific representation of a significant 'Christmas/families together'. The inset photograph of Meg, Jill, and Sandy with champagne is partly what secures this general *mise en scène* of Christmas/family to the particular history of this family. That is, it is precisely this economical, almost diagrammatic *mise en scène* which offers a space for fantasy, for a negotiation by the viewer of their investment in the image.

This strategy is again perceptible in the two images of the sitting room and kitchen (Figs. 4.6 and 4.7). Meg's sitting room is one of the permanent sets of the programme, and its furnishings show very clearly the class repertoire to which the programme understands its audience to aspire. The aspirational quality of Meg's sitting room is constructed partly through narrative reiteration that this room is Meg's inner sanctum, and partly through contrast within the programme with both the public areas of the hotel and other domestic spaces, such as, in this period, the Brownlow's house. In contrast with the earlier two images, but befitting the significance of this set, the background is here clearly focused. Individual items—the sherry glasses and decanter, the horse brasses, the gilt-framed painting, and the 'old-style' lamp—are relatively easily available. Together, with the reproduction furniture and decor, this represents a certain vision of middle England, an aesthetic of a Midlands department store: conservative, quite comfortable, aspirational—what might be called 'classy', but very definitely not upper or upper middle class.

The most striking feature of this image though, is the way in which Meg and Hugh are dressed. The combination of day and night clothes perhaps speaks more clearly than was intended, and shows the intractability of the Meg-type heroine, the incompatibility of all the competence she displays with conventional ideas of feminine sexuality. Put another way, this image reveals the considerable strains of representing a *respectable* female sexuality. Unusually, in the representation of heterosexual couples, it is Hugh who is ready for bed. Meg's dominance in this image is inescapable. It comes partly from the simple fact that she is dressed while he is not, despite the fact that he has his arms around her. She dominates the frame spatially, but also in her address to us—while he looks at her, she looks at us, and thus we are offered a relation with her as this pyjama'd man embraces her. Hugh may be ready for bed, but Meg is ready to meet the world.

The final Meg image (Fig. 4.7) shows the fantasy of housework done—by others. Once again, Meg is dominant as a character, although the foreground of the image is mainly occupied with cooking pots and storage bins. The chef addresses Meg while the *mise en scène* shows us kitchen work dramatized—both real and fantastic. The size and quantity of the pans and bins indicate that this is an image of a hotel, rather than domestic kitchen. However, these proportions also signify the excess of housework, the job that is never finished—here, apparently, obligingly carried out by a cheery male minion.

Finally, I want to juxtapose a 'Noele Gordon' image with the Meg images. Noele Gordon images, throughout the *Crossroads* publications, are noticeably a little more flamboyant and expensive than Meg images, although recognizably within the same repertoire. While Meg dresses mainly in blues, which are more flattering on television, Noele Gordon wears cream and gold. While Meg almost always poses within the hotel, Noele Gordon indulges herself with the luxury of her Rolls Royce (Fig. 4.8). This is clearly a deliberate flouting of the careful limits that Noele Gordon constructs for Meg—and perhaps the only way that Noele Gordon can distinguish herself after sixteen years in the part.

These images together remind us of the main features of the housewife/matriarch, historically a generic staple, in the period of our study. If we follow Christine Geraghty's arguments about the changing representational terrain of British soap opera, we could suggest that this figure has, from the mid-1980s, become much more troubled and less prevalent. However, for our purposes, a character like Meg is one of the 'stereotypes' against which early feminist television criticism mobilized itself. She is one of the female characters that second-wave feminists repudiated as destiny. However, as testified to by the longevity of *Crossroads* and Dorothy Hobson's research, Noele Gordon as Meg Mortimer presents one of these most popular soap opera characters in my period of study. She was widely regarded as trustworthy, helpful, and generally to be emulated.[10] For example, Hobson quotes from a letter from an elderly viewer:

> The serial depicts a kind of steady life we would all like to see today. Meg Richardson the kind of woman we would all like to be. Quick, steady as a rock to everyone in an emergency. Motherly enough to comfort people in trouble and a happy person to laugh with any funny situation and firmly to be committed to family life and keeping families together. (Mrs P., quoted in Hobson 1982: 142)

Meg's dress, her performance, the *mise en scène*, and related publicity contribute to the image of a woman in control, but still within femininity. The contradictoriness of this image—or the contradictions of 'competent sexual femininity'—are hinted at in the image of Meg and her husband, but, as a tasteful, early evening programme, these issues hardly arose on air. It may, however, have been precisely the extent of

---

10 This of course repeats the attitudes discovered by Arnheim, Kauffman, and Herzog in the 1930s. See Ch. 2, above.

this fantasy of competence which made the sacking of Noele Gordon so very shocking to *Crossroads* fans (Hobson 1982: 137–55). For our purposes, what is significant is that Noele Gordon as Meg Mortimer offered a certain embodiment of a figure who recurs in soap opera internationally—Helen Trent, Jill Archer, Miss Ellie come to mind. She is a site of the fantasy of 'ordinary femininity' successfully achieved: as Mrs P. put it, 'Meg Richardson is the kind of woman we would all like to be' (Hobson 1982: 142). But I think she may also have been formative in the constitution of the feminist imagination of 'the housewife' she did not want to be, as well as 'the housewife' whom she wanted to claim for feminism. The soap opera housewife, like the soap opera viewer—as we have seen in the writing analysed in Chapter 3—offers a site of profound ambivalence for the emergent figure of the feminist studying popular culture.

3

Talking Soap Opera

5
Autobiography and Ethnography

THE third part of the book approaches the institutionalization of soap opera as a feminist object of study in a different way. Here the story is told through interviews with five of the women who were involved in the 1970s feminist research on soap opera. In these interviews I asked each participant to tell me about how they started doing research on soap opera, and how their relationship to this field of study had developed. We approach the same history as that traced through the different discursive contexts of the earlier parts of the book, but the history is produced in a different register, the personal voice of memory. Each woman tells the story of her engagement with soap opera in a different way, and each story is different—but there are recognizable axes of significance, both historical and personal, around which these stories swirl. Before presenting the analysis of the interviews and attempting to trace, as history, these axes of significance, I want to address the equally important generic and methodological issues of the form of enquiry developed here. For what is interesting about the extended interviews presented here is the way in which they hover between autobiographical and ethnographic modes. This is a function both of the status and identifiability of the interviewees and of the way in which the material is analysed. Put simply, the project tests the relationship between autobiographical and 'ethnographic' subjectivities, subjecting the testimonies of the 'autos' to the procedures more normally reserved for the 'ethnos'.

(i) The Selection of the Interviewees The selection of the interviewees was governed by three main criteria. First, evidently, as the project was to explore the retrospective accounts of key figures in the study of soap opera and their understanding of their contribution to what is now the academically identifiable field of 'women's genres', the possible field was delimited to those who had published in English on soap opera in the late 1970s–early

1980s.[1] Secondly, given my particular interest in the formation of the identities feminist/woman in this period, it was important that the writers should be women, and that there should be some engagement with feminist concerns or women as an audience in the work.[2] Thirdly, and with the other two criteria in place, the decisive factor: I considered it a prerequisite of the enquiry that I should know the participants personally with some degree of familiarity. The methodological significance of the pre-existing friendships between myself and the interviewees is discussed at more length below. In terms of authors who meet the first two criteria, but who are excluded by the third, the most significant other possible candidates are Tania Modleski (1979; 1982) and Carol Lopate (1976). Michèle Mattelart (1986), was excluded more on grounds of original language of publication and the linguistic difficulties of an extended interview. Early work by each of these authors has been discussed in Chapter 3.[3]

The use of these criteria in the selection of the interviewees, and the relatively unstructured format of the interviews themselves, produces a corpus of data—long tape recordings and transcripts—which analytically demands skills and competencies not found in any one discipline. In this, my research clearly follows other cultural studies research, indebted to disciplines such as English, history, and sociology, a raider in the fields of linguistics, social psychology, and anthropology.[4] It also echoes the interdisciplinarity of much feminist research, which in a manner now well documented, often occupies intellectual spaces at the margins of, or 'in-between', disciplines.[5] While recognizing the incompatibility of different disciplinary paradigms, and the perils of importing concepts from one field, where they have a particular historical and syntactic significance, to another, where these may be misleadingly less apparent, I do at the same time wish to insist on the appropriateness of an interdisciplinary approach to what is in some ways 'meta'-disciplinary material. The interviews are long, reflective, semi-autobiographical,

---

1 Key contributors to the constitution of 'women's genres' as a field of study such as Pam Cook (1983), Rosalind Coward (1984), Angela McRobbie (1991), Janice Radway (1984), Helen Taylor (1989), and Janice Winship (1987) were thus excluded on grounds of 'object choice'. See part one for a broader account of the constitution of the field.

2 Thus excluding early male pioneers such as Robert Allen (1985), Richard Dyer (1977), Richard Paterson (1981), and John Tulloch (Tulloch and Moran 1986).

3 Other contemporary work includes Stern (1978), Swanson (1981), and Flitterman (1983).

4 On this see some of the accounts of constructing the field of cultural studies, such as Hall (1990: 17) with its question 'What was the bibliography of a cultural studies thesis? Nobody knew' or Johnson (1991).

5 Franklin, Lury, and Stacey (1991a) offer an account of the negotiations of feminism and cultural studies, while the title of their collection, *Off-Centre*, captures precisely the relationship they describe.

semi-theoretical meditations by women in different countries and rather different circumstances, drawn together by a shared object of study, soap opera. Only considerable theoretical and methodological flexibility can do justice to the richness of the material.

(ii) What Kind of Interviews are These?

As will already be evident from the importance of the criterion of 'friendship' in the selection of the interviewees, the project is not, in any simple sense, an ethnographic one. That is, it is not an ethnographic project if we interpret that to mean, in Clifford Geertz's phrase, 'the representation of one sort of life in the categories of another' (1988: 144). In my interviews, the knowledge of each other's work, as well as the knowledge of each other, ensured that there was at least a mutual familiarity with 'one sort of life'. It is clearly not an ethnographic project in any terms of the othernesses involved, although the very familiarities could be argued to offer the extended knowledge, gathered through different sources, that much ethnography aims for (see Gillespie 1995 and Tufte 1995 on the attenuation of the ethnographic project within media studies). However, it is a project designed partly *in response* to recent ethnographies of the media audience, and it is also explicitly *about* ethnography of the media audience. The project is in response to recent ethnographies mainly because of the increase in this type of work in the 1980s outlined in Chapter 1. As suggested there, the significance of feminist paradigms and research in this 'new ethnography' is striking as is the frequency with which women—particularly soap viewers—were selected as research subjects. As I have argued elsewhere, the discursive analysis of this material suggests that we can here locate a primary site for the constitution of the key personae of feminist television research: the feminist and her other, the housewife (Brunsdon 1993).

My interviews were designed both to directly enquire about memories of the history of the constitution of these two characters and to be between participants who could not be so designated. The research was designed to avoid differences of status and understanding of the academic field between interviewer and interviewee. The project is 'about' the ethnography of the media audience partly in a quite simple sense because the interviewees were significant actors in the development of the relevant debates and these are discussed. All the interviewees had written about women and television, and in some cases they were also empirical researchers into female audiences.

Autobiography has been a privileged genre for second-wave feminism, and there is now an extensive and sophisticated literature, ranging from founding texts such as Simone de Beauvoir's four-volume autobiography (1959; 1963; 1965; 1977), Sheila Rowbotham's autobiographically inflected *Woman's Consciousness, Man's World* (1973*a*) and Maya Angelou's *I Know Why the Caged Bird Sings* (1969) trilogy, to interrogations of the genre such as Carolyn Steedman's *Landscape for a Good Woman* (1986), Jo Spence's *Putting Myself in the Picture* (1986), and Annette Kuhn's recent work (1995*a*). There are also many collections of essays which are strongly personally voiced including the work of Rosalind Coward (1984), Nancy Miller (1991), Michele Wallace (1990), Valerie Walkerdine (1990), Ann Oakley (1984), Trinh T. Minh-ha (1989), as well as a developing body of analytic memoir, such as Alice Kaplan's *French Lessons* (1993), Gillian Rose's *Love's Work* (1995), and Marianna De Marco Torgovnick's *Crossing Ocean Parkway* (1994).[6]

The privileged status of autobiography has several origins and supports and while this project is not concerned with the autobiographical as such, it is dependent on two types of autobiographical narrative—my interviewees' stories and my own story—which are necessarily told within the broader context of the recurring feminist interest in autobiography.[7] For while the originating circumstances of the interviews—the very fact that they are interviews, arranged by a second party (me), in pursuit of a history that I have delimited—militate against considering them as autobiography, at the same time, they have qualities which makes it possible to see them as generically cognate.

All autobiography negotiates the formation of the speaking/writing self, usually telling a story, or many stories, of the move from 'then' to 'now', of how this speaking subject comes to speak in this way, about these events, formed through these experiences. Each of these interviews negotiates this terrain, often moving very fluently between 'then' and 'now', and constructing 'then' as an intellectual time, a time when we thought, for example, that we could make Marxist and feminist categories fit together, as well as a personal time, when the speaker had just started graduate work or left home. This is

---

6 Autobiographical writing by women has also been a popular object of study for feminists working within the academy as testified by e.g. the work of Benstock (1988), Jelinek (1980), Lury (1991), Miller (1991), and O'Neale (1985). Marcus (1994) offers an astute discussion of key debates.

7 The first significant use of autobiographical forms by second-wave feminism was in the process of 'consciousness raising' in small groups. This process, which is repeatedly described in early Women's Liberation Movement Literature (Mitchell 1971; Bruley 1976), was understood as primarily political rather than therapeutic. It involved the recounting, usually in closely monitored 'turns', by individuals in a group, of chosen experiences; perhaps of the time since the last meeting, maybe that of being a daughter or doing housework. This experience telling would provide the data for the group to work on collectively to attempt to establish the gender paradigms of the experience. To attempt to see the individual experiences—e.g. of being fed up with always being the one who cleaned the bathroom—as both representative and symptomatic of a gendered rather than simply a personal experience. These discussions were the workshop for the slogan 'the personal is political', a slogan which has, as we have seen, particular resonances for the study of soap opera.

important, if one wants to think of these interviews as partaking of the autobiographical,[8] but equally significant are the relatively open-ended structure of the interviews, the fact that we knew each other quite well, and the way in which the material is subsequently dealt with. Also relevant is the way in which feminism's historical invest-ment in the autobiographical makes the project appear mutually comprehensible and worthwhile to participants. This meant that there was in all the interviews an assumption that they were of some mutual value in themselves, a point which is made explicitly several times, for example when Dorothy Hobson says, 'Well doing this interview is making me think about the connection between that and my later work in a new way' (DH: 60), or Ien Ang declares, 'Yes, in fact this is the first time I am saying that, I mean, it's very good, this inter-view in that respect' (IA: 15).

That is, it is partly formal, methodological, and contextual issues that are decisive in considering whether material can appropriately be considered autobiographical. As Gayatri Spivak has pointed out, it has been mainly through the intermediary of missionaries and anthro-pologists that the subaltern has, until recently, been allowed to speak (1986: 229). The material gathered from informants in many socio-logical, historical, and anthropological research projects is mainly auto-biographical material, but, produced in contexts not of the informants' choosing, to ends of which the informant is not aware, it is repre-sented as part of another story, generally severed from its originators.

These interviewees are immediately identifiable because they are already in the public domain as scholars of soap opera. Their pub-lished work is easily available and stands as witness and reference point to my analysis. As intended by the original research design, it is impossible to transform my interviewees from being particular people to being data. Although the project has many of the structural features associated with ethnographic interviewing—crudely, I the interviewer with a research agenda interview informants in long open-ended semi-structured interviews—the choice of the partici-pants and the prior relationships between us produce a real strain in this categorization. What they say is in some ways much more easily assimilable to an autobiographical, rather than an ethnographic, generic home. What I hope this does is to focus some light on the epis-temological category of the autobiographical, rather than on the well-worn difficulties of the ethnographic.[9] As Elspeth Probyn has argued, these two genres of 'speaking the self/other' have rather closer

8 Julia Kristeva (1987) and Denise Riley (1992) offer sophisticated accounts which, while nearly contemporary, endeavour to knit the personal with the wider intellectual climate.

9 In relation to issues of interviewing women and the ethnographic more generally, debates can be traced across e.g. Oakley (1981*b*), Finch (1984), Clifford and Marcus (1986) and Stanley (1990*b*).

connections than is always recognized (Probyn 1989). Indeed, an implicit argument of the structure of this book, with its move from surveys of feminist ethnographic work in the first part to the interviews in this third part, is that at a meta-level we do need to understand these two genres in relation to each other. As Gertrude Stein would have pointed out, everybody is to themselves the subject of an autobiography (Stein 1973: 6).

There is a beguiling and obvious complementarity in the relationship between the two selves of feminist media scholarship in the present context—the narration of the feminist self, the 'I', and the investigation of the female consumer of popular culture, her other, the 'she'. However, as the research design and the substantive content of the interviews reveal, things are rather more complex than this. I was, to an extent, using analytic procedures on persons who, through their own scholarly work—which in three cases was ethnographic—might be seen more commonly as the subjects of autobiography. My own hypothesis, that the construction of the identity 'feminist' necessitated the construction of a non-feminist other, whom I labelled 'the housewife', seems to be both confirmed—and the institutional compulsion for female academics to attribute femininity to an other should not be underestimated here—and far too crude, in that all the interviewees display and discuss very complex identifications.

However, the fact that my interviewees were published authors on soap opera, as well as being known to me personally, inflects the project in a range of ways. It means that there are in some ways affinities with the intellectual celebrity interview in which the 'thinker' is cued and prompted by someone of the same or lesser status.[10] This type of interview is an interview for an audience, in which the interviewer aids the explication of the interviewee's ideas and arguments. However, this is an inadequate model, in that those celebrity interviews are generally conducted and published in ways which present them as more accessible vehicles of the thinker's ideas, or opportunities to press areas of conceptual ambiguity.[11] They are constructed as, in some sense, transparent, allowing access to the ideas themselves. While my interviews can clearly be read in this way, and indeed offer very interesting theoretical and historical reflections on the shifts in intellectual concerns in the 1970s and 1980s, I have also chosen to analyse their discursive features, to see as significant the how, as well as the what, of the account. So while at one level the interviews tell us how each individual came to do the research they did, at another level, attention is paid to how this story is told.

---

10 Radway (1989) discusses interestingly the problems of interviewing those of equal or superior status.

11 For example, the Institute of Contemporary Arts in London sells both audio and video cassettes of speakers 'in conversation' at the ICA.

This is not, however, to suggest that my enquiry was governed by the project of probing 'the woman behind the ideas', in that other model of the interview the revelation of personality. The constant attention to the language of the stories is an attempt to retain a sense of the materiality of the telling, in a belief that the deployment of phrases such as 'women's culture' or pronouns such as 'we' might be particularly significant in a historical understanding of how people regarded as feminist academics/intellectuals understand this identity for themselves. The project is rather more contingent than any 'revelation of personality' model might suggest, focused on the particular autobiographical stories that five women tell about research which was in most cases conducted to ridicule by colleagues, but which has subsequently 'made' their careers, as well as contributing significantly to the syllabus of media/cultural/women's studies. Their research was more or less explicitly feminist, but was in each case concerned with notions of the female viewer and women as an audience which had their origins in feminist work discussed in Part I. I was interested in how the researchers, also women, working in period when feminist ideas were becoming more legitimate within parts of the academy, understood and retrospectively formulated the relationships between themselves and these viewers, within the broader frame of reflection on the original research. So in a way, the object of my enquiry is how particular individuals negotiated, or remember/reconstruct themselves as negotiating, the often slightly uncomfortably exclusive identities of 'woman', 'researcher', 'feminist', 'housewife', and 'viewer', and how these identities were inflected—through factors such as social class, education, ethnicity, age, and nationality.

However, this personal register, the friendships and collegiality which gave me easy access to the interviewees, has had certain consequences in the writing up of the project. Janice Radway describes a related dilemma in her report on her research into the Book of the Month Club, 'Ethnography among Elites' (1989). She points to the strong internal and external pressure to what she calls 'relativism' in writing up her findings because she wants neither to betray those who have been so helpful to her, nor lose access to them. While I was not dealing with an institution like the Book of the Month Club, but with friends and colleagues in that more dispersed international formation 'feminists who have written on soap opera', I too have found inhibitions in the writing. People have told me things that I have found very moving and I have had real doubts about the appropriateness of discussing this material in print. My resolution here has been to show each interviewee her chapter in manuscript to gain her response and approval. No one asked for any changes or withholding. Rather more difficult has been negotiating the position of even limited mastery that any writing involves. I have found myself unwilling to compare or disagree with my friends—I haven't wanted to appear to criticize their experience, or their narrating of it. It would seem unfair—an exploitation of conversations held under one aegis, in a series of one-to-one encounters—to exploit the insight given through the scrutiny of the tapes and transcripts, and the power of the arranging and writing up of the analyses. This has particularly been the case when I have been thinking about the way in which 'women' are inscribed in the interviews (material collected in Chapter 11 (iv)), where I was explicitly reading the material symptomatically. This I have tried to make explicit in my account of these readings, and discuss a little further below.

Less predictable—or maybe, just less predicted—was the ethical dilemma posed by my position of power in relation to what wasn't said. Listening again and again to the tapes while scrutinizing the transcripts, what was not said—sentences started, hesitations, pauses, circumlocutions—grew in prominence. I did on occasion find myself thinking, 'Well, she's saying that, but doesn't she really mean the opposite', or, 'We're spending a lot of time avoiding saying that we don't agree about this'. Generally, these thoughts remained thoughts. It was difficult to think of an ethical way to present this type of hypothesis. When I have presented this type of reading of material—often through the discussion of change of track in a sentence —I have tried to provide substantial contextual material as well as detailed justification. But I wonder to what extent this ethical inhibition was powered both by my sense of my friends/the interviewees reading my account in the future and, in the even more distant future, the prospect of an unknown other reading my account of them. That is, to what extent was what I experienced as an ethical dilemma merely a normal part of ethnographic procedure, highlighted by my choice of sample and their identifiability?

The research design I had used to inscribe equality into the interview worked in contradictory ways in the writing. On the one hand, my friends hovered above the computer, preventing me from making wild generalizations and very out-of-character assessments. Our past —and I hope future—together offered a longitudinal interpretative framework of some complexity. On the other hand, I didn't want to upset anyone. Just like Herta Herzog's critique of 'Panglossian' soap opera in 1942, I have found myself wanting to make everything come out all right—in the end, to be for the best.

(iii) The Conduct and Analysis of the Interviews

All the interviews were structured as intellectual autobiographical narratives, with my opening question a variation on 'Can you remember how you started doing the research on soap opera?' I was particularly interested in exploring the following issues:

   (i) how they started doing research on soap opera;

  (ii) what they remembered as their motivation for, and understanding of, the project;

 (iii) what their own viewing history and habits were in relation to the research material;

 (iv) reaction from others to the doing of the project, and how the research was received;

  (v) how the category 'Woman' is constructed in their account of their research, and how they themselves figure in relation to this category and other cognate categories (feminist, housewife, etc.);

 (vi) how their current research relates to the research into soap opera.

Each individual told her story in a different way, stressing different elements. For some, theoretical debate was given greater significance than family, while for others these priorities were reversed or related to career decisions or political beliefs. Different women stressed different elements and I did not press the interviewees in an attempt to homogenize either the issues addressed or their understanding of my own project. That said, I, as initiator and interviewer, am the constant factor in these conversations. However, this 'I' is differentially constructed both in the history of each friendship and in each of the interviews. Nevertheless, there are continuities, since it is my agenda—the desire to return to discussion of soap opera, wanting to hear about the way ideas about women figure in the research, asking about viewing—which flickers through the discussants' more narrative accounts. They, without exception, tell stories of their research lives which bring us from *then* (when they started doing research on soap opera) to *now* when they may or may not still be doing it.

    If we thus conceive of each interview as formed in the pull between the different structuring factors of the writer's autobiographical narrative and my research agenda, we must also recognize the inscription of our relationship and its history—most obviously perhaps, when the interviewee, or I, refer to something we did together, but also present in the more conversational sequences that occur in all the interviews.

    It is in the context of these minimally described determinations that I would then place the claim for granting each interview an integrity and autonomy, arguing that this spoken and then written material is most usefully approached in the first instance as a narrative text, which can be analysed for its themes, rhetorics, structures, and absences. The recognition of the particularity of each encounter and the contingency of narrative patterning and emphasis, as well as the determinations exercised on these particularities by a very wide range of factors, lead me to argue that we can best produce some understanding of the origins of the feminist work on soap opera from this corpus through analysis of the detail of these accounts.[12] Only through an emphasis on the textuality of these interview conversations can we construct an object of study which inscribes the contingency and the historicity of the accounts into the analysis.

My procedure is to present an analysis of each interview which is explicitly constructed through what has seemed most significant to me in each account. My primary analytic procedure was to work on transcripts of the interviews while listening to the tapes, understanding myself as a skilled reader as well as a participant. Ien Ang offers a pithy defence of what in social science methodology is a very 'soft' method, although of course it is an accepted procedure in literary studies:

> I do think like in cultural analysis intuition is a very good thing. When you know a culture and you live in it yourself and you're sensitive enough you can see those kind of things. That's the problem with a lot of the hard-core social sciences that they would never, never use that whereas I think that's where—that brings you further. They won't accept that fact unless they have hard statistics a little bit, and that seems like calculated ignorance at times on their part. (IA: 7)

My first concern in each case was the analysis of the interview 'in its own terms'—an attention to how each story was told, and what was considered part of the story.[13] Thus, for example, 'family' was an important and recurrent issue for Ellen Seiter, as was 'teaching/pedagogy'. Neither made any significant appearance in Dorothy Hobson's account. Although I experimented with coding across all interviews using concepts such as 'defence of soap-opera discourse', 'being a feminist', this led to a flattening out of the differences between the accounts, while at the same time not delivering much in return.

That is, my method explicitly depends on my own research, training, knowledge, and what Ang calls 'intuition'. The provision of some unedited transcript as an appendix to this book offers some control so that readers can see what the raw material originally looked like. Similarly, the account of each interview uses lengthy quotation in order to provide some context for any particular conclusion. This use of qualitative methodology should not, however, be interpreted as a

---

12 Here, the body of work to which mine is closest is Hollway's enquiry into the discourses through which subjectivity is constructed (1982; 1989), although I don't share her reliance on a Lacanian framework.

13 In this process, the close analysis of texts in a wide range of fields has been relevant, e.g. Atkinson (1990); Frankenberg (1993); Hammersley (1990); Hollway (1989); Lull (1991); Montgomery (1991); Parker (1992); Passerini (1990); H. Taylor (1989).

repudiation of the desirability of a larger study. With a bigger sample and corresponding socio-biographical data, it might have been possible to make quantifiable claims, and to investigate, for example, the number of scholars in this field who were first-generation university-educated women in their family (see, for example, Pierre Bourdieu's discussion of the French academic field, 1988). But even a larger study, perhaps dependent on more apparently scientific methods of analysis because of the possibilities of quantification, is also in the end—or at some key early point in the research process—dependent on interpretation. There is always a moment—as Liesbet van Zoonen has recently argued with specific reference to the field of feminist media studies—in which the researcher has to make a qualitative decision about the material for analysis, even if this appears only to be 'this statement belongs in this category' (van Zoonen 1994: 143).

(iv) The Presentation of the Interviews: The Use of the Portrait Format

The initial presentation of the interviews in this study is in a 'portrait' format. I discuss the structure and main concerns of each interview in detail, individually, in turn. I use this procedure rather than the more common one of regarding all the interview material together as one big corpus from which the researcher can distil the most significant themes and issues. Each portrait has three elements: a biographical sketch of the interviewee (from material supplied by the interviewee); an account of the interviewee's published work on soap opera, with some analysis of the way in which this work has contributed to, and is informed by, key debates; and finally an analysis of the interview in the manner outlined above.

Existing work within cultural studies which has made use of the semi-focused or open interview, such as that of Gray (1992a), Hobson (1990), Jennings (1998), Morley (1986), Radway (1984), and Seiter et al. (1989a) has tended not to use the portrait method of presentation, instead organizing interview material under what have been discovered to be, or were theorized as, significant categories. Gray, for example, gives very brief sociological descriptions of each of 'her' women before beginning the research report proper, and provides as an appendix a more traditional description of her sample by socio-economic category. In the substantial discussion, she groups and regroups the women by topic, using categories such as 'Viewing and reading preferences' and 'Use of the time-shift facility'. Hobson (1980) organizes published accounts of her MA work through her interviewees' accounts of different media, radio and television, and distinctions made within television output. Radway (1984) uses topics, as does Hermes (1993), although Hermes also includes a detailed portrait chapter, 'Portrait of One and a Half Readers', which is interesting in this context because the reader is her mother. Morley uses portraits—'Family One, Family Two, etc.', but he pre-groups these families: 'C1 families' etc. In later work, he and Silverstone use quite extensive portraits, but the context is a quite specific argument of the significance of (particular) family relationships to the pattern of use of domestic technology (Silverstone and Morley 1990).

Generally, though, scholars who have used portrait, such as Ellen Seiter (1990) and Valerie Walkerdine (1986), have done so in order to problematize methodological issues and particularly the role of the researcher. Seiter, in 'Making Distinctions: Case Study of a Troubling Interview', returned to an interview on which she had already worked in the 'themes and issues' manner to discuss 'how the power differential between us as academic interviewers and Jim and Larry as subjects related to the playing out of class difference during the interview' (1990: 62). She begins her conclusion by arguing:

> In writing up this interview, I have done extensive editing. I have attributed intentions and feeling to others. I have bolstered some generalizations I wanted to make with the authority of the real empirical subject. I have emphasised a couple of points, the role of gender and the role of cultural capital, which I would like to pursue here. Before doing so, let me also argue that audience studies might be helped at this point by the publication of unedited transcripts along with analyses. In a partial fashion, I hope to have demonstrated here how certain statements, if taken out of context in a discussion of something like 'genres' or sitcoms might create quite a different impression when the interview is taken in sequence. (Seiter 1990: 68)

Although Seiter is to some extent self-critical in this case study, she insists very firmly that many of the problems of the interview are not avoidable because they stem from the playing out of actual and antagonistic class differences in the interview. As the quotation above illustrates, Seiter is here concerned with both the significance of these differences in the actual interview and with the way in which they can be obscured by a 'thematic' writing up. So, in addition to the publication of transcripts, she advocates more explicit attention to these structural inequalities, and a recognition 'that the differences we find will [not] be sympathetic or ideologically correct or even comprehensible from our own class and race and gender positions' (1990: 68). This sentence, with its call for the explicit recognition of real difference in the ethnographic enterprise, alludes to something else, the aspiration or fantasy of its opposite, the finding of a certain unity in that enterprise—'sympathy', 'ideological correctness', 'comprehension'—and thus poses the very difficult issue of fantasy in the research process. It also refers to the tendency within some cultural studies to conceptualize the audience for popular culture as resistant or oppositional. However, for our purposes, most significant is the way in which Seiter's use of the portrait format draws attention to difficulties often obscured in the writing up of interview material.

Valerie Walkerdine, in one of the most challenging uses of the 'portrait' format, tries explicitly to deal with the issue of fantasy. In her analysis of watching a *Rocky* film with a working-class family she tries to deploy not just the impact of structural class, gender, and generational difference in her analysis of the interaction, but also the multilayered presence of fantasy. The role of fantasy is, quite evidently, notoriously difficult to establish empirically.[14] Walkerdine wants to insist on the role of fantasies of family life, of fighting to escape this family—Rocky's, her own, and the Coleses'—in the interaction between herself and the family she is studying. She is also insistent on the way in which what we might call the researcher's fantasy—that of knowing the other—activates the situation. For the discussion of this fantasy, of knowledge and surveillance of the Other, she is mainly dependent on a Foucauldian schema. However, this characterization of herself—the researcher as surveillant—is complicated by the ambivalent, but perhaps stronger, identification of the piece, which is of herself as 'still' working class. She includes a lengthy discussion of her own relationship to her father, and his image of her—to the extent of offering a detailed analysis of a photograph of herself—within her account of watching *Rocky II* with the Coles family. Indeed, it is arguably this contradictory desire—to be recognized as 'one of them', the surveyed, while in the position of the surveyor—which is the dynamic of the argument.

These two articles which use, and investigate the use of, the portrait format in the reporting of ethnographic work raise a series of issues. The most important for the current study include the particularity of each interview—the way in which there is always a contingency to each interaction; the significance of contextualization in the approach to interview material, and the extremely problematic issue of what constitutes contextualization (the interviewer's childhood, etc.); and finally, the role of fantasy in the ethnographic context (which to some extent returns us to the discussion of the housewife in Chapter 4). My choice of sample was partly designed to minimize fantasies of otherness—indeed in some ways a motive for the project was to investigate the extent to which the researchers thought that dynamics of this type had been involved in their research. Whether I produce the opposite fantasy, that of identity/unity, is to some extent discussed in Chapter 11.

---

14 Stacey (1992) makes an impressive attempt, while Radway (1994) reflects on the issue in relation to her own earlier ethnographic study.

The main reason for using a portrait format is to try to record, and thus create for the reader, a sense of the particularity of each interview. This particularity inheres not so much in what one might call the anthropological specificity of each encounter—how I made contact with my informant, my journey, the rituals of greeting, the domestic environment—as in the narrative specificity. By this, I mean the sense in which anything that can be abstracted from the interview comes from a particular conversation between two people who have known each other for some years. These conversations are explicitly autobiographical, and tell the different stories of the constitution of feminist intellectual work through and against an engagement with conventional feminine culture. They are, finally, stories of the production of a speaking position, one which, in its articulation of femininity with intellect, is particularly troublesome, as suggested by Michèle Le Doeuff in her writing on women and philosophy (1991). While we might insist at a general level of the significance of major structural factors such as class, ethnicity, age, and gender in the shaping of individual identity, only attention to the specificities of particular stories allows us to understand the complexity of particular interplays, and the periodicity as well as the performativity of identity. Thus presentation in a portrait format permits the narration of identity as history and memory, and reveals the differently, but distinctively, mediated relation between self and object of study in the developing scholarship on soap opera. Although I do proceed to draw out commonalities of these stories in Chapter 11, my aim, in the prior presentation in portrait format, is to constrain, limit, and contextualize these commonalities.

6

'I Don't Think We Thought about It as Studying Soap Operas': Christine Geraghty

THE interview with Christine Geraghty took place between the proof-reading and publication of her 1991 book *Women and Soap Opera*. This book was the culmination of many years work on soap opera, inaugurated, as described below, both by a history of watching *Coronation Street* and by membership of the London Women and Film Group. At the time of the interview Christine was working as full-time trade union officer for NALGO (National and Local Government Officers Association). She had started working for NALGO in 1978 as an administrator, but at the time of the interview was a national negotiator for Health Service members with specific responsibilities for equal opportunities and pay. Of all the interviewees, Christine Geraghty is the only one with no involvement in full-time academia at any stage of the work on soap opera. However, throughout the 1970s and 1980s she was involved in British film culture. In the first instance, this was as an evening class and British Film Institute summer school student, and subsequently as teacher on both. She continued teaching a film evening class until 1995. Paralleling this was involvement with the Society for Education in Film and Television (SEFT), of which she was for a brief period chair, which necessitated involvement with both the British Film Institute and the magazine *Screen*. She was also a school governor at a local school in Lambeth for some years in the 1980s.

Christine comes from London and describes her background as 'conventionally middle class. Mother stayed at home to care for five children of which I am the eldest. Catholic, though not oppressively so.'[1] She adds—and this is typical of many British middle-class homes in the 1950s—'No television until the mid-sixties'.[2] Christine began

1 Author questionnaire.

2 Author questionnaire.

working for NALGO after taking degrees in History and American Studies and then American Literature.

Her earliest published work on soap opera appeared in the British film Institute *Coronation Street* television monograph (1981), and was an essay offering a broader definition of the continuous serial as a context for a critical approach to *Coronation Street*. Christine outlines characteristics of the genre, concentrating on narrative and characterization, while also giving special attention to the role of gossip both inside and outside the text. While the essay concentrates on *Coronation Street*, she also uses examples from *Emmerdale Farm*, *Crossroads*, and *The Archers*. Although there is discussion of female characters, and of the special role of gossip (often considered a feminine preserve), there is no discussion of 'women' as such in this article. This does appear, though, in a 1983 article on *Brookside* where Christine argues that the new realism of this serial paradoxically leaves women in more isolated housebound positions than is the case with *Crossroads* and *Coronation Street*. Christine has also written on the second of the new 1980s British soaps, *EastEnders*, where she concentrates on the repeated failure of the programme to successfully include black characters and families (Geraghty 1989).

Although Christine has published and spoken on soap opera in a range of contexts since the early 1980s—indeed, it is perhaps most characteristic of her engagement with soap opera, as we shall see below, that she has felt a desire and an obligation to address non-specialists and non-academics in both her writing and speaking—the book dominates the conversation analysed below. *Women and Soap Opera*, first published in 1991, offers a certain culmination to feminist research on soap opera in the way that books by Hobson (1982) and Modleski (1982) can perhaps be seen to inaugurate it (if we use books, rather than articles, to mark periodicity). Much of the core of the book is already present in condensed form in Geraghty's 1981 article, although the serial reference is massively expanded with extensive discussion of *Dallas*, *Dynasty*, *EastEnders*, and *Brookside* in addition to the serials discussed in 1981. That is, if on the one hand, the book summarizes and incorporates feminist scholarship on soap opera since the late 1970s, it does so partly through enormous textual familiarity with the programmes. It is the culmination of a decade's scholarship, but also of a decade's viewing. On the other hand, the book draws on a much wider field than soap opera alone, and utilizes, in particular, material from film studies, such as Richard Dyer's influential 1977 'Entertainment and Utopia' article and the feminist material on melodrama and the woman's picture, as well as drawing on analysis of romance fiction. The book is situated very clearly in the domain of 'women's genres' outlined in Chapter 1, although it also draws on narrative theory and uses film studies concepts like 'production values'. So if this book brings together much of the relevant scholarship since the late 1970s, with a consistent argument away from consideration of the unconscious and the use of psychoanalytic paradigms, the change in focus in terms of Geraghty's own work since 1981 has been the explicit focus on women. This is epitomized by the title, and indeed, in the interview, it is discussion of the title that is most extensive, leading to a lengthy exploration of what it is, as a woman, in 1990, to write a book called *Women and Soap Opera*.

(i) Starting Work on Soap Opera: The Women and Film Group

Christine Geraghty, like Terry Lovell, traces her initial analytic interest in soap opera to the London Women and Film Group which became the *Coronation Street* Group. Thus as with Terry, the first discussion about the genre takes place in a non-academic context in a group which is first constituted within a feminist framework: 'Women and . . .'. Christine is very firm about the fact that she watched *Coronation Street* for pleasure from before the group work started:

> And I certainly watched *Coronation Street*. I mean I didn't have a television until I was 15/16 at home, so I didn't have a history of watching *Coronation Street* for all those years, but when I came back from university and lived with my parents for a bit we actually—I started watching *Coronation Street* . . . (CG: 1)

I will return to the family story which is clearly embedded in this affirmation, 'And I certainly watched . . .', but first I want to work closely with the description of the Women and Film Group and their decision. Not only does Christine's account offer a specifically non-academic origin to the work on soap opera, it also offers a certain social aspiration:

> Well I think it was the Women and Film Group that got me into it, because that started off as a film group and was full of people who were—well, women who I thought were very important and very impressive, and I was kind of lurking on the edges of it, and always actually rather ambiguous about the project. But as it turned out, nobody was much going to the cinema, because, largely because of children, so then we discovered that we actually watched *Coronation Street*. (CG: 1)

This is a clear description of a desirable social group in relation to whom Christine feels marginal. She presents herself as on the edges of a circle which she clearly genders, 'that started off as a film group, and was full of people who were—well, women who I thought were very important and very impressive, and I was kind of lurking on the edges of it'. The correction or specification, 'people who were—well, women who . . .', indicates that the gendering of this group is significant, not just to their work, but also to the constitution of the identity to which Christine feels marginal.

There is here a relation of desire, 'women who I thought were very important and very impressive', and a strongly visual representation of herself, 'I was kind of lurking on the edges of it', somehow illegitimate, in the shadows on the edges of the full beam on these 'very important and very impressive [women]'. But there is also ambivalence, which is expressed specifically in relation to the project of 'film theory', but perhaps more generally in relation to the group as a whole: 'and I was kind of lurking on the edges of it, and always actually rather ambiguous about the project'. The 'always actually' is temporally unspecifiable. Geraghty does use 'actually' quite regularly in speech, so it is impossible to tell, contextually, the extent to which this is a retrospective articulation of a critical position that was self-censored —in the half-light—at the time.

However, ambiguity about the project of 'women and film' in 1974 remains unvoiced, as it turns out that the cinema will not be the focus of study:

> CG: But as it turned out, nobody was much going to the cinema, because, largely because of children, so then we discovered that we actually watched *Coronation Street*.
>
> CB: How interesting—what time was that? Seventy—?
>
> CG: Seventy-four, something like that. And I met xxx, who must just have had her first baby, and there were kind of various others, and so basically we switched from discussion of film theory to working on *Coronation Street*.
>
> CB: Did you watch television—did you watch—how many people do you think watched soap operas anyway?
>
> CG: Well, you see, at the time I don't think we thought about it as studying soap operas. We were looking for something that we wanted to look at, and I guess we were looking for something that had something specifically around women that would enable us to justify doing it in a 'Women and Film' group, as opposed to any other group. And I certainly watched *Coronation Street* . . . (CG: 1)

This passage, with its complex imbrication of different types of causal factors, points to the density of historically specific and contingent determination on particular 'facts'—here the decision of one of the London Women and Film Groups to research *Coronation Street*. We see the role of the local and specific ('I met xxx, who must just have had her first baby . . .') in the making of events which can also be seen within a much broader sweep.

So first we have a quest clearly conceived within the concerns of second-wave feminism, the search for a site in which to investigate the specificity of women:

> I guess we were looking for something that had something specifically around women that would enable us to justify doing it in a 'Women and Film' group, as opposed to any other group. ·

Christine's phrasing, although apparently casual, is theoretically very careful—not in fact attributing a specificity to women, but holding open that possibility, however it might be understood theoretically (biographically/culturally, etc.): 'something specifically around women'. However, there is also the slightly defensive note, 'that would enable us to justify doing it . . .', which in the use of 'justify' records the whole history of the arguments about women-only groups which were such a feature of 1970s leftist culture (Evans 1979). Coupled with this concern with specificity though, this commitment to 'Women and . . .', is a certain randomness—'We were looking for something to look at'. The scope of the 'Women and . . .' project is, at some level, content-free, much larger than any particular 'something'. The political project of 'Women and . . .' wings its way over the mid-1970s British cultural landscape, seeking something on which to alight.

However, even the designation of the 'something', when chosen, has a historical specificity. My question uses the term 'soap operas' and it is partly this Christine picks up on when she answers. 'Well, you see, at the time I don't think we thought about it as studying soap operas.' 'Studying' has not so far appeared in the interview—my question was about 'watching'—and so I think Christine is making two modifications to my formulations here. First the verb change is clearly a move from passive to active, from 'watching' (easy) to 'studying' (more difficult). But it is the use of the term 'soap operas' that is the focus of Christine's negative here, and which she is saying is anachronistic. This interpretation is supported a bit later when she says: 'See, we didn't write—we didn't use the term "soap opera" in *Coronation Street* [the book] except perhaps Terry. So I think perhaps we accepted more the Granada kind of version of a continuous drama, a continuous serial . . .' (CG: 12). So here, Christine is remembering the stigma attached to the term soap opera in the 1970s, and the way in which Granada, in particular, was always most insistent that *Coronation Street* wasn't a soap opera. When 'soap opera' has these connotations—well documented elsewhere—then the notion of studying it has a particular incongruity, and Christine registers this too: 'but I'm sure we didn't, or certainly, I didn't think of it, as being studying soap opera'. Here, the double gerund, 'being studying', serves both to hold together what is almost being offered, reminiscently, as the oxymoronic 'studying soap opera', and to locate its anachronicity.

The other way in which the stigma of soap opera emerges is through the verbs used to describe watching *Coronation Street*. These are verbs of confession and revelation: 'then we discovered that we actually watched *Coronation Street . . .*', 'and then xxx confessed that she'd been watching' (CG: 2). Christine returns to this issue later in the interview, when she observes:

> I mean *Coronation Street* was interesting because it wasn't looked down on, like *Crossroads* was, it was accepted as being good of its kind, and—but I don't think it was accepted as something that you could/would particularly study, and that its relationship— what it offered women hadn't been looked at. So there was, there were some moments where you felt you were doing something that was considered odd by the general—you know the people working in film theory or TV studies at the time. And, I mean now, I think that has been almost entirely reversed, and what makes me feel slightly ambiguous about it now is that it's—you hardly have to argue anymore about the importance of looking at soap opera, it's just assumed, so that the only place I ever argue about that is at work with people who aren't, you know, in film studies, so that, I mean I think there is an irony in the kind of cultural studies work and what have you—in the very particular sort of field of people—has meant that soap operas are considered much more seriously by them than by anybody else in the population. (CG: 3/4)

Here Christine outlines changes in attitudes to soap opera in a way which puts in a broader context her terminological particularity above—her sense that, although it might be quite difficult to specify what the group did think they were doing, they did not, in the main, consider themselves to be studying soap opera.

The other point to note in the original 'decision' account is the role played by familial and domestic patterns. Thus, for Christine, her own viewing patterns, within her family of origin after her return from university, mesh with those group members with young children who have abandoned cinema-going for television watching at home. Women in different homes and families, of different ages, and at different points in individual biography 'meet' in front of the television screen on Mondays and Wednesdays at 7.30.

Thus we have the personal, both in habits and families, and the broader contexts of 1970s feminism and cultural attitudes to a particular television genre meshing to produce the particular decision to look at *Coronation Street*. As with the later accounts of Terry Lovell (of the same group) and Ien Ang it is perhaps also worth stressing that this is an account of work—research—on soap opera being started by a group of people who came together for political/cultural, rather than academic, reasons. However, this group clearly has as part of its agenda an exploration of identity, of 'Women and . . .'.

(ii) Why the Interest in Soap Opera?

Although Christine clearly contextualizes the work in relation to women, both as object/subject of study ('Women and . . .') and socially, in that these 'Women and Film' women appeared as people to be emulated, she stresses throughout the interview that it was narrative rather than gender which was most interesting to her in an approach to the television programme. Thus she says:

> I think we accepted more the Granada version of a continuous drama, a continuous serial and that was certainly what I was writing about then was not about, particularly about, the appearance of women. I was writing about the conventions of a continuous serial, or a continuous narrative, and what engaged and what didn't. (CG: 2)

This point recurs throughout the interview: for example,

> I think since the thing that involved me first was an interesting narrative, and that I do think soaps handle narrative differently from other formats . . . (CG: 12)

However, her particular interest in the narrative structure of soap opera is articulated through a concern with what audiences—in which she includes herself—do with soap opera narratives:

> I was interested in the narrative side of it before I was interested in what women could get out of it—because it may have been— particular things may have been happening in *Coronation Street* at the time that made people talk about it, but I do remember long conversations at work which was where that notion of people talking about it as if it were real yet knowing perfectly well it's not. (CG: 4)

So within a clearly gendered account of the origins of work on soap opera, Christine Geraghty clearly stresses both formal qualities of the genre ('the conventions of a continuous serial', 'what engaged and what didn't') and the way in which audiences—wide, socially differentiated audiences—engaged with it ('that notion of people talking about it as if it were real, yet knowing perfectly well it's not'). She consistently inscribes herself as one of these people:

> I don't think I was interested in it because millions watched it, I was interested in it because I watched it, my Dad watched it,

the people at work watched it and seemed to get different things out of it. So I don't think it was a kind of abstract thing about 'it has audiences of 20 million therefore it must be important' so much as this actually is what people are talking about. (CG: 4)

This inscription of herself as a *Coronation Street* viewer—which has already been made earlier in the interview ('and I certainly watched *Coronation Street*')—is a structuring feature of this interview, and is indeed an identity claimed much more unproblematically than that of either woman or feminist as I will discuss below. Christine claims, with emphasis, the authenticity of the position from which she began to think about serial drama, and that her interest in the narrative structure of the genre is partly because she, as a viewer, is caught up in its delays and promises. She locates her own viewing in a vivid description of watching *Coronation Street* regularly with her father and sister for a particular period:

> CG: [I]t was a particular thing at that particular point—and we [CG, sister, father] used to watch it together and occasionally my Mum would watch. So that it was a particular family thing at that point, I mean he doesn't watch it now. It lasted for about two years. I remember watching when Bet Lynch nearly committed suicide, we were all three of us sitting there with our hankies out. My Dad of course despises television, you see, so it was something of a shock to him to discover he could actually get involved in this programme that really he oughtn't to like. So that was quite—it was to do—he would say things like, 'Well, of course it just hooks you'.
>
> CB: Did you tease him about it?
>
> CG: Oh yes, we'd say, 'Come on, it's twenty-nine minutes past seven, time you got into your place'. [*laughs*] I don't know quite, perhaps it was also, well again, a similar thing perhaps with work: as a family we don't discuss things very much, so the notion of spending half an hour on you know Mondays and Wednesdays watching other people's major traumas where they endlessly talk about them is quite intriguing for us. And then once I'd left and [sister] got interested in other things that kind of stopped. So it was just one of those kind of 'moments' of how your viewing kind of changes. (CG: 5/6)

This description evokes the precision of television watching rituals ('it's twenty-nine minutes past seven'), each person with their regular 'place', the father and two daughters very involved in the narrative ('we were all three of us sitting there with our hankies out'), the mother in and out of the room. Also vivid is the father's resistance ('My Dad of course, despises television'), his understanding of the appropriate attitude for him to have towards television in general, and soap opera in particular ('a programme that really he oughtn't to like'), and the constant negotiation of his position ('he would say things like "Well, of course it just hooks you" '). Also present I think, is a very clear sense of the enormous pleasure that this viewing ritual brought to this family, the way in which it permitted them to be together on a regular basis.

This portrait, this use of television within a particular family at a particular time, is clearly reminiscent of some of the usages discussed by both Morley (1986) and Lull (1991) when it becomes clear that 'watching television' is often a way for some or all members of a family to come together and be close. Christine speculates on the particular interest and value for her own family when she says, 'as a family we don't discuss things very much', and thus offers an hypoth-e'sis that the pleasures of viewing soaps to this particular family lay in the contrast, the continual talking about emotional things, that is specific to the genre.

This issue of the 'usefulness' of soaps to their viewers, first pointed out, in surprise, by Herta Herzog (1944), and recurring much later in some of Dorothy Hobson's work (Hobson 1990), has already been noted by Geraghty in her comments about the discussion of soaps at work:

> And I do think that soap operas have a rather peculiar function at work of allowing people to talk about things at one remove. You kind of spend half your life with these people with whom you're extraordinarily intimate and yet have no intimate relationship with. So soap's quite useful for discussing love and death. So I think that that was probably where my first kind of interest in it came. (CG: 4/5)

This strong inscription of an active audience carries with it another significant feature of Geraghty's account, which is the commitment to a democratic project:

> Yes, I mean the project was to take the stuff seriously. It was that whole high/low culture, popular/avant-garde divide, and to look seriously at what you enjoyed, I enjoyed, as well as what other people enjoyed, and I think part of that was being—was having some respect for what other people like. (CG: 18)

Here we see clearly the way in which the investigation of the origins of the work on soap opera brings us back to broader currents in the British political scene of the 1970s, here the passionate debate in which the origins of Cultural Studies itself can be partly located, on the value of popular culture (Hall and Whannel 1964; Williams

1961). Christine Geraghty's approach has two elements, both of which involve an attention to the connotational feminine gendering of soap opera. First the validation of the skills and tastes involved in soap watching, 'that was part of what I was interested in, was to say actually that soap opera watching involves skills, intelligence, fun, that are as demanding anything else you kind of take seriously in terms of leisure' (CG: 19), or in an earlier formulation, 'It's that kind of attitude that thinks that because people watch soap operas they can't do anything else, that I think we've got to try and get at' (CG: 18). The second element is rather more complex in that it involves an attempted redefinition of the political, again a feature of 1970s politics.[3] Here Christine very firmly sets herself against the classic leftist critique of soap opera, that they reduce structural features to personal relationships, wanting instead to stress the importance of what she calls the quality of the engagement they elicit:

> soap operas are like taking entertainment seriously and putting some energy into it and being involved in them. Those are qualities that you can use in whole loads of areas. So I think there is a kind of political engagement with it, it's not the kind of overt 'soap operas would be alright if they talked about serious issues like unemployment', it's more like getting that quality of engagement into other areas as well. (CG: 20)

Christine is here characterizing the involvement that soap operas demand of their viewers—an involvement commented on by nearly all writers—as a transferable, rather than a substitute, civic skill: 'Those are qualities that you can use in whole loads of areas.' She is arguing that the engagement of viewers is indicative of other potential engagements, rather than a disabling distraction. However, she is also very clear about the way in which she wants to argue that personal life is important, as against the classic 'male' position of the 1970s, which saw only structural cause as significant, refusing to acknowledge the significance of experience as well:

> I mean poor Carl Gardner had the misfortune to write that throwaway remark in *City Limits* which I've been using ever since which is this business about '*Coronation Street* reduces serious issues like unemployment to the level of melodrama'. You know, I mean absolutely, it might even have been 'to the level of personal life'—it sort of summed it up, that was real seventies' kind-of diagnosis—work, social issues on one hand, that could only be dealt with in fairly abstract ways, you dealt with them in—all of a piece, and the other important things were even if you did get

---

3 A key formulation in British politics was that offered in *Beyond the Fragments* (Rowbotham, Segal, and Wainright 1979).

a social issue it was basically reduced to how it affects somebody's personal life. (CG: 20)

(iii) 'Women' I now want to rework some of the material that I have already discussed in a different context. I want to address the construction of 'women' in this interview, a topic on which Christine explicitly reflects at several different points. It is also, of course, a topic that can be explored when it is not the explicit subject of conversation, given the history that is being recounted.

Close analysis of the conversation suggests, as with other of the interviews, that the use of the term 'women' is extremely complex, and that its particular significance in any one usage can only be arrived at through contextual analysis. This complexity of significance I would understand to be directly related to the particular discursive claims that feminist discourse has made on the category woman, the way in which feminists have variously, and sometimes simultaneously, wanted to speak as, for, to, and on behalf of women. Thus sometimes 'women' appears coterminous with 'feminist' and sometimes it appears to signify 'not feminist'. This issue is highlighted in this interview because it is one to which Christine repeatedly returns, as she tells a story of consistently feeling rather cautious about the *feminist* invocation of women—but also raises the question about the difficulties of *feminine* identifications.

Let us return to the very opening of the interview, and the description Christine offers of her relation to the 'Women and Film Group': 'that started off as a film group and was full of people who were— well, women who I thought were very important and very impressive, and I was kind of lurking on the edges of it, and always actually rather ambiguous about the project' (CG: 1). I have already argued that the specification of gender 'well, women' suggests that gender is a significant element in the feeling of exclusion, and Christine makes explicit her admiration for these 'important and impressive [women]', by implication suggesting that she herself at this stage felt quite unlike this. In my earlier discussion, I suggested that the ambiguity could also be interpreted in relation to the implicit 'film theory' project of a group calling itself 'Women and Film'. Certainly, historically, the period under discussion, which is approximately 1974–6, was the period in which semiotic and psychoanalytic film theory was first becoming available in Britain through the journal *Screen*. Here, I would want to suggest that the ambiguity is also attached, however contradictorily, to the very project 'Women and . . .'. So a certain kind of femininity is a lure, but also a difficulty. The project 'Women and . . .' is off-putting as well as attractive. This is picked up a bit later in the interview when Christine reflects on the title of the book she has just finished, *Women and Soap Opera*.

> I always—I mean I—it does slightly surprise me that I end up writing a book about women and soap opera, because I was always a bit ambiguous about women and anything. So it kind-of —it is a cause of some surprise to me, and slight alarm, that I end up writing a book, you know, with that kind of a title, and which does, because you have to, it does a kind-of—well I don't think I assume a particular position that women take up. I think I'm arguing more that particular positions are offered to women which women are more able to, or more likely to, more readily can inhabit. But I still think that's a rather odd argument for me to be making. [*inaudible: one word*] it with how I see myself in relation to other feminist work or activity I don't know. (CG: 2/3)

Here I think we have a quite clear theoretical exposition of what is at stake in a certain kind of feminist usage of the category 'women', the problem of the assumption of particular positions by people because they are women.

However, what Christine offers is not only this reflection on assumptions she doesn't want to make about women, but also a very interesting discussion of the way in which soap opera may play to the enormous difficulty of feminine identifications:

> I think one of the reasons why I watch soaps, but it only just occurred to me right at the end of all this, was that the soaps assume that women are good at your personal life, and can handle all these things and they kind of value the way in which women do things, and I think that is true. On the other hand also they are— they assume that that is the case and I think maybe that the guilt that women feel about watching is not so much tied up with the fact that men will mock you but that actually they don't themselves always feel terribly good at—so that while on one hand soaps do value what women do, they also are I think a bit problematic for women because they make assumptions about how well you can do it, and if you actually aren't terribly good at it or feel yourself at that particular point not to have been, then the pleasure is rather more complicated than I think I've described it as. (CG: 8)

The second Birmingham Popular Memory Group formulated a distinction between 'safe' and 'risky' stories in their analysis of British identities and individual memory which I think is most useful here (Johnson, n.d. [*c.*1993]). Baldly, 'safe' stories are easy to tell and pleasant to remember, and can be told of individuals or various kinds of collectivities like families and nations. They can, when investigated, turn out to involve forgetting and repression of difficult moments.[4] Risky stories—which often emerge in the interstices of safe stories, are more problematic, troublesome—in Johnson's terms, 'knotted'. The Popular Memory Group saw these stories as 'unfinished business' as opposed to 'Golden Memories'. Although these categories were formulated in the context of a rather different project, we can I think use this distinction in relation to the histories of identity discussed in this interview. Because, as discussed in Chapter 5, I had known all the interviewees for some years, I suggest that there is a superficial contextual 'safety' to all the interviews, which made possible the telling of more or less risky stories. Contextual safety is one issue—what I think this interview raises is the historicity of what is safe and what is risky. Christine Geraghty tells some very risky stories in this conversation, but they are, I think, much less risky than they would have been in the late 1970s. She makes this point herself, I think, when she says, 'I'm not sure I would have joined a "Women and Film" group in 1978, let's say. Or not—I don't know—maybe—but anyway it would have been something different joining in '78 than it was in '74' (CG: 11). Christine is here talking about the different political and intellectual meanings that a 'Women and Film' group would have had to her in 1974 and 1978, and the way that she might have seen herself as one of the women in 1974, but would have been less likely to do so in 1978. My point is to do with the historicity of categories such as 'woman' and the different degrees of safety and riskiness in identifying with it in particular contexts and periods. Christine's story, which is one of a very cautious identification with, and suspicion of, the political category 'woman', has, in a sense, come into its own in the 1990s, when the hegemony of self-evident identity politics has been shaken. What was once risky is now safer, and, concomitantly, this allows Christine to open up some new risky stories about women and soap opera.

4 This argument is very similar to the structure of argument in the work done by Jo Spence and Patricia Holland on the family photograph album. To rephrase their findings, a family album would be a 'safe story' par excellence of the family—rare indeed are the photographs of rows, of illness, or funerals.

7

'What about the Rest of the Audience?': Dorothy Hobson

DOROTHY HOBSON was completing a book about the first five years of Channel Four and working as a writer and freelance media consultant at the time of this interview. Since the 1982 publication of her book on *Crossroads*, she has acted as consultant to, for example, the British Film Institute, the Canadian Broadcasting Corporation, and Channel Four. She was the producer of Television events at the Birmingham Film and Television Festival from 1985–91, and since this interview served as director of the Birmingham Media Development Agency between 1990–2. Dorothy Hobson, who describes herself as of respectable working-class background and a 'Butler baby' in terms of the provision of post-war secondary education,[1] studied English as a mature student at Birmingham University for her first degree, and then went on to complete an MA by thesis at the Centre for Contemporary Cultural Studies.[2] It was while she was conducting research for her Ph.D. at CCCS that she made the decision to write her book on *Crossroads*, which was published shortly after Noele Gordon had, with considerable publicity, involuntarily left the show in 1981 (Hobson 1982). Methuen marketed the book outside their academic list as a trade paperback and it sold extremely well and was reviewed very widely, with national press and television coverage. Although Dorothy Hobson has not pursued an academic career, her work with female audiences has been recognized as inaugural within the cultural studies/ethnographic audience tradition, and she was, for example, invited to the 1987 Tuebingen conference on the audience, and to contribute to Mary Ellen Brown's collection 1990 *Television and Women's Culture* (Hobson 1989 and 1990). Both of these contributions concerned the currency of soap opera as an

1 Author questionnaire.

2 Although this MA diss. remained unpublished (Hobson 1978*a*), Hobson's early articles presented the major findings of her research. See Hobson (1978*b*; 1980; and 1981*b*).

everyday topic of conversation in the workplace. She continues to work as a freelance consultant, writer, and lecturer.

In *Crossroads: The Drama of a Soap Opera* Hobson writes sympathetically and polemically about soap opera as a genre as a context for reporting the dramatic response from the public to the sacking of Noele Gordon in 1981. Her first published research had been on the lived experience of young white working-class women (Hobson 1978*b* and 1980). This ethnographic study incorporated some discussion of media usage by these young women which had led Dorothy to the formulation of the hypotheses of her Ph.D. which she describes in the interview. In original conception, as was characteristic of many *CCCS* research proposals of this period, the project was based on Stuart Hall's 'Encoding/Decoding' model, and therefore involved both a production study and audience research (Hall 1973).[3] Although the *Crossroads* book departed from the original Ph.D., it too is subtended by the encoding/decoding model, offering illuminating and detailed accounts of the production process as well as analysis of watching with viewers, and viewers' letters to the *Birmingham Evening Mail*. Perhaps because the MA research was not media-specific and *Crossroads* has now finished—or perhaps indeed, because *Crossroads* was a soap opera—the originality of some of this early audience research has been underestimated. Thus for example, Liesbet van Zoonen (1994) refers mainly to Hobson's two later essays in her recent survey of feminist media scholarship, although Shaun Moores does give Hobson substantial recognition in his *Interpreting Audiences* (1993: 35–9). It is Dorothy Hobson who first insists, with empirical evidence, on the difficulties and complexities of television viewing for women in families, particularly those who are simultaneously preparing tea for children and husbands. She offers the first ethnographic investigation of what is entailed in the idea of women being 'available to view'. Hobson also offers a pioneering account of one of the most neglected of audiences, the elderly, although this aspect of her work has been completely ignored.[4]

The *Crossroads* book, then, has its origins in a particular research environment, and is a development from Dorothy's MA thesis (1978*a*) which includes methodological discussion of research procedures and defence of her naturalistic method. In relation to early and proto-feminist writing discussed in the early part of this book, Hobson's description of isolated days measured out in self-imposed

3 For example, Morley's 1980 audience study was a much reduced version of a research project for which Connell, Hall, and Morley repeatedly failed to win SSRC funding in the 1970s. Hall (1980) offers an account of media work in CCCS in the 1970s.

4 Cook (1990) and Tulloch (1989) offer sympathetic engagements with elderly audiences and survey available work. Neither mentions Hobson (1982).

deadlines of 'Our Tune'[5] has clear antecedents in both Ann Oakley's work and the domestic labour debate (Oakley 1974; Malos 1980), while the similarities between the backgrounds of Hobson and her interviewees give substance to my suggestion that one of the pre-occupations of feminist research was the investigation of 'the woman she (the researcher) had not become'. In terms of discussion of research methodology, the *Crossroads* book clearly bears the marks of a publication aimed at a non-academic audience, although it does engage with popular criticism about the researcher's presence affecting findings (1982: 107). The two later essays also offer precise, if limited, methodological specification (Hobson 1989: 150; 1990: 62). In each case, the finished text itself bears witness to Dorothy's skills as a researcher, in that she is clearly able to make people feel very much at ease with her presence, and is, in a fundamental way, able to 'join in' discussion about *Crossroads* in particular, or television in general. This is discussed further in the interview. However, Dorothy is also very attentive to the difference between the research encounter and the extrapolation from this of transcribed material. In this connection, she specifically observes:

> Extracts from transcripts of interviews can appear very bland and unexciting. To *listen* to tapes is an entirely different experience from *reading* short extracts which lose, above all, the intonation and laughter of the speakers. The enthusiasm which some of the viewers have shown in their own recounting of storylines of the programme and incidents involved in the programme can only be realized by the reader if my words are able to recreate the atmosphere of the times when I have watched the programme with them. (Hobson 1982: 106)

The attempt to recreate, for the reader, the individual voices of her respondents is indicative both of Hobson's awareness of *the writing* of ethnographic work (a topic which has recently much occupied post-modern anthropologists—for example Clifford and Marcus 1986) and of the democratic impulse which underpins it. One of the strongest lines of arguments in the *Crossroads* book concerns the unfairness of the disregarding of viewers' opinions in the sacking of Noele Gordon—a gesture perceived by most interviewees and letter-writers as likely to spoil the programme. Hobson's purpose is partly to give voice to those fans who felt themselves betrayed by ATV/the producers in this act. As she observes: 'Everyone is a television critic but most of us do not get paid for making selections and commenting upon them for the rest of the population' (1982: 106). So her book is

---

5 'Our Tune' was a short regular morning slot on BBC Radio 1 in which the DJ Simon Bates recounted the stories that lay behind the designation of a particular pop record as 'our tune'. It ran through the 1970s and 1980s on national radio.

partly written to empower those 'everyones'. However, it is also written to defend soap opera the genre, and *Crossroads* in particular. Hobson offers a serious defence of the genre on mainly populist grounds, for which she has subsequently been criticized (for example, McGuigan 1992: 144–5). She manages to be sympathetic to producers, cast, and audience, arguing that the show needs more resources, the actors do a good job, and the audience is undervalued. The relative unfamiliarity of this argument in the early 1980s, in combination with Dorothy Hobson's considerable performance skill and evident sincerity, contributed to the media impact of the book, and the constitution of Dorothy Hobson, as she describes below, as a 'soap expert'.[6] The interview below traces some of the complexities and contradictions of this journey.

Although both Ien Ang and Ellen Seiter, of the other interviewees, have done work with audiences, Dorothy Hobson is by far the most experienced interviewer participating in this study. This is an interview with someone who has researched for an MA and a Ph.D. using participant observation and ethnographic interviewing, and who, as part of this research and the later Channel Four commission, has interviewed a large number of senior television personnel. This experience—Hobson's clear knowledge of the many uses to which unguarded opinion or personal revelation can be put and the way in which this knowledge imperceptibly structures what appears to be a seamless and fluent account—is exemplified in an unusually explicit form in an exchange quite early in the interview when Dorothy responds to a question I ask her by saying firmly, 'You're saying that . . .'. Although she characteristically omits the forceful, negative implied partner to this clarification 'I'm not saying that . . .', I clearly got the point, and qualify my next statement by starting 'Yes, I'm saying that, and it sounds to me that you're saying . . .' (DH: 37). The other aspect of this professionalism is that some of the most interesting material comes when Dorothy analyses her own skills as an observer and interviewer, and reflects on why it was that people did, and do, confide in her. This discussion of the hidden skills of participant observation provides an implicit but substantial recognition of the way in which these very skills are likely to inflect the current interview. Significant for the same reason is the radical absence of any familial reference from this interview. There are here no sisters or fathers watching television, although there is considerable personal voice in

6 For example, if we take the period just after the publication of the book, Dorothy Hobson gave a 'Lunchtime Lecture' at the national Film Theatre on *Crossroads* (2 June 1982). Much later, in the *Observer* of 29 Aug. 1994, she is quoted and referred to as 'Dorothy Hobson, a soap expert who has written an academic text on *Crossroads*' by Andrew Billen in an article about the forthcoming launch of a satellite channel showing US soaps (Andrew Billen, 'Lather of soaps to bring tears to viewers' eyes', *Observer* 29 Aug. 1994).

the mainly professional story. Although the interviews were designed as relatively unstructured, precisely because I was interested in how people constructed their accounts of soap opera research, which circumstances and contexts they saw as relevant, it is noticeable that this interview is the only one without even fleeting mention of family circumstances in autobiographically explanatory sentences.

Apart from being the longest of the interviews, this was also the most profoundly narrativized. All the interviews took the form of storytelling, but this interview, as the analysis below will reveal, was like a set of Russian dolls in that each major story turned out to have minor stories within, and within these were embedded micro-stories and anecdotes. It is in this context that I offer a detailed analysis of one of the embedded anecdotes in Section (ii) below, 'A Tale of Chance and Skill', where I also suggest that 'luck' may be a peculiarly significant player in feminine narratives of achievement, one that recurs in other interviews.

This interview is discussed in three main sections, which correspond to the central narrative dynamics of this interview. However, overall, there is also, rather more strongly than in any of the other interviews, a sense of the current conjuncture in the changing legislatory context of British broadcasting (the interview took place in the period following the publication of the White Paper *Broadcasting in the '90s: Competition, Choice and Quality* (HMSO 1988). That is, also unlike most of the other interviews, and for reasons which are discussed below, this interview takes as its primary context and referent British television, rather than either the academy or socialist/trade-union/feminist debate. This is Dorothy's definition of the field—but it is one to which I very noticeably contribute because I was at this stage very interested in debates about 'quality' in television. The end result of this is that although this is one of the longest interviews, the final third is not very relevant since it is a lengthy discussion of legislative possibilities and predictions about the shape of British television in the 1990s. Although most of this part of the interview is not used below, it is important to mark its presence, as it shows the direction of Dorothy's work since the study of soap opera. She, of all the interviewees, is the one whose career has developed into a more general concern with television. Indeed, the interview as a whole is marked by a recurrent concern with television as a popular medium and attention to the contemporary debate about the nature of 'quality' television.

The analysis below focuses on the three overarching narrative dynamics of the interview. First, there is the story of beginning to work on soap opera, which is told partly through the narration of the concerns of Dorothy's earlier academic work, but which very quickly becomes the narration of a changing/changed professional identity.

This story, which in a way is *the* story of the interview, is the negotiation of a move from identification with one professional culture, that of the academy, to another, television. In the second section—and this distinction is a complex one—there is what I am calling 'a tale of chance and skill', which is the primary narrative device through which Dorothy constructs her own persona and agency in the interview, particularly when she is recounting how she got started on the *Crossroads* work. That is, analytically, in the second section I will rework some of the material in the first section, where I will concentrate on referential narrative, to look at the use of micro-narrative and anecdote in the elaboration of this narrative. These stories are echoed chronologically by another story, told in the third section, which is the account of the way in which the status of soap opera as a genre has changed in the period under discussion. This account brings in a recurrent theme of the interviews, which is the very contradictory feelings of many of the television people involved in the production of serial drama towards their product. Thus there is a way in which all the stories told here are imbricated with each other, and each of the key participants—soap opera, Dorothy, and television professionals, working on popular genres—have a more assured place by the end of the tale.

(i) Starting to Work on Soap Opera: Researching Women at Home

The origins of Dorothy's work on soap opera lay in her MA research. This research explicitly took 'housewives' as its subject (not a word Dorothy uses in this interview, although it does appear in the title of her 1978 and 1980 articles), and used primarily feminist paradigms in the analysis of data (Hobson 1978a; 1978b; 1980). What is interesting in the account in the interview is the mobilization of this feminist knowledge in a way—extremely rare in the 1970s (see Chapter 8)—that it is recognized by those outside these paradigms (television professionals) as *real* knowledge. The early research was not specifically about television:

> DH: I did . . . my MA was about women at home with children, how they made the transition from being 15–16, leaving school, and then being 21, and living with two/three children sometimes, in various houses and flats on a council estate, and that covered—
>
> CB: Oh it was the radio wasn't it?
>
> DH: No, it was television as well, you see, overall, it was about their perceptions of how they had felt their lives might be, whether being married and being a mother was different from what they expected. One small part of that was actually about what I thought naively was their leisure time, so one

straight naive question was, 'What do you do in your spare time?' to which of course they answered they didn't actually think they had any spare time. (DH: 2–3)

This research focuses on the lived experience of femininity, a kind of femininity which is class-specific ('15–16, leaving school', 'council estate') and local. Dorothy Hobson's first research project was on young white women from backgrounds that were not, initially, unlike her own, about their expectations of their lives as young mothers after getting married. In this account of it, I would argue, she uses 'naively' to signal her distance from these young women. 'Naive' immediately follows this first usage, and it is this repetition which warrants some close attention to the two usages. The recounting of this research project involves the construction of a series of positions. First, Dorothy uses a certain ironic retrospect, a constructing of herself as the researcher who 'naively' thought that these young women had leisure time, in which she invites me to be complicit. She invites me to join her in the less naive present, when, 'of course', we all know that women like these don't have leisure time. This is a generous rhetorical strategy, which may give some indication of Hobson's skills as an interviewer, because of course, it was through research such as hers that the gendering of leisure became apparent. The 'naively' is ironic, but it is also modest, making no pretence that she had anticipated what is retrospectively one of her major research findings, inviting me to join her in feeling superior to this naive researcher. However, it is also a claiming of a position, academic researcher, who does not know about this life, who asks naive questions about it. I think it could even be suggested that the position Hobson constructs for her naive self is implicitly masculine—certainly academic—in that the question she asks is partly a question informed by the sociology of leisure, which was, in the 1970s, a relatively unselfconscious masculinist field, as this interaction indeed indicates. For our purposes, what is significant is the claiming of an identity which is clearly separate from, while familiar with, the lives of the young women she visits. Only those who do not belong to the category under investigation can ask this type of 'naive' question. At the same time, Dorothy points out in her questionnaire, 'As my son was at school during the period of my research this gave me access to many interviewees.'[7] Later on she comments, 'My family and living situation was never solely connected to the academic world and this has considerably helped my knowledge of audiences and their views on television.'[8]

It is the interviews that she does with these young married women that lead Dorothy Hobson on to the formulation of her Ph.D. project,

---

7 Interviewee questionnaire.

8 Interviewee questionnaire.

which is constituted round a distinction between 'the two forms of television', which is a gendered distinction, formulated by her interviewees:

> their interest in television was specifically what started me on the path of my own television research, because, until then, media issues had not been at the forefront of my own interests, my interests had been much more about people's lived experience and the way they related that, and how they understood that. The television part of it was interesting because they—completely without me setting up that—difference between the two forms of television—they told me the different forms of television which they liked. And it came in two clear patterns: one which they did like and watch was, drama series of any kind, plays, films, soap operas, quiz shows—what we would term popular television. What they didn't watch was news, current affairs and documentaries, unless the documentaries had a topic which was of specific interest to them. (DH: 4)

It is this gendering of genre in Hobson's early research which has subsequently been picked up by later researchers into women's viewing patterns, and more general research into family use of television such as that of David Morley (1986). However, despite the significance of this research finding to subsequent television audience research, it is not one which Hobson pursues in this interview at an intellectual level, although her use of the pronoun 'we' ('what we would term popular television') invokes, in the interview, a recognition of an academic community of which she and I are at that moment a part, and which uses different categories to her interviewees. This is evidently partly because the *Crossroads* project eventually rather overtakes the Ph.D. research, and through this project Dorothy developed a different relation to television. So instead of claiming her place as one of the very early investigators of what we might now call the gendering of genre, Dorothy tells another story. She recounts the way in which these early research findings gave her value to television executives, and functioned to give her an entrée to senior broadcasters and schedulers.

There are two significant encounters here, the first when Dorothy makes an intervention from the floor at a conference, in which she uses a common feminist strategy, drawing attention to the use of the male pronoun, but with a rather different twist:

> Someone I spoke to at a conference—from the floor, News and Current Affairs people were on the platform—and I pointed out this feeling about the audience [DH's analysis of women's feelings about why they didn't watch news], and they were actually very

interested to know this because of course they don't really want half the audience, even though, you know, the particular speaker talked about 'his' audience [*laughs*]—the audience—and used the male pronoun, and I actually said, 'I'm not criticizing you, you're quite right to use that pronoun because that is your audience, but, you know, what about the rest of the audience?' And they were interested to talk about it, because, I know—I was coming to television from the perspective of the audience, that's why I never had any problem getting to watch productions getting made, because the programme makers didn't ever see me as going in to criticize them, but to be relating to what they were interested in anyway, so that was why I was very lucky in terms of having access right from the start, but I'm sure that was part of the reason, because of that interest they of course were interested in audiences and they didn't get that sort of feedback from the audience research that was done by the broadcasters at that time. (DH: 6)

It is the repertoire of second-wave feminism which enables the focus on the use of the male pronoun, but Dorothy's intervention rather elegantly pre-empts being dismissed as a feminist ('I'm not criticizing you, you're quite right to use that pronoun because that is your audience, but, you know, what about the rest of your audience?'), while also offering the promise of information about 'the rest of your audience'. An encounter with Jeremy Isaacs before the start of Channel Four has similar elements:

The real breakthrough in terms of what developed to be the work I was going to do, was again quite a fluke really, because I was speaking at a—Jeremy Isaacs was speaking at a RTS [Royal Television Society] meeting about the beginnings of Channel Four, and he'd just been appointed, and said that he was going to have programmes specifically for women. Again I stood up from the floor, and said I was delighted to know you'd be having these programmes, have you thought about scheduling, because what was important was not just to have these programmes but to schedule them at times when women were available to view. And he hadn't actually thought of that at that point, but said that it was a point of great interest not just to him but to the whole network and said that you should talk to Charles Denton about this because ITV are as much—have this—problem as much as we do. And Charles Denton, who I didn't know at all then, was at that meeting, and I went and spoke to him afterwards, and he said well, give me a ring, and come in and have a chat. Which I did, and it was. (DH: 14)

Again, we see that Dorothy's entry to the debate is through a recognizable feminist site, programmes for women on Channel Four, but also that her research allows her to say something else, something which is 'a point of great interest'. However, it is also noticeable that Dorothy herself is thinking—either now, or in retrospect—in the language of television professionals, as evidenced by the phrase 'available to view'. So although she was bringing material from another place, the academy, to television, she was doing it in a way that was comprehensible to television professionals. In strong contrast to the reception of the *Coronation Street* paper at the Edinburgh Festival discussed in the next chapter, Dorothy Hobson's research was perceived, mainly through considerable effort on her part—she is speaking from the floor at both these events—to have a clear use value to television professionals from the beginning. This she converts into an exchange value. She gained entry into television productions because she was perceived as bringing with her news about a female audience. This she clearly recognizes in this retrospective account: 'And they were interested to talk about it, because, I know—I was coming to television from the perspective of the audience, that's why I never had any problem getting to watch productions made, because the programme makers didn't ever see me as going in to criticize them' (DH: 6). Although 'women' hardly appear again in this interview, it is significant for our enquiry that it is with a gendered project that Dorothy first essays entry into the world of television, and it is this news from elsewhere that she brings which first gives her access.

(ii) A Tale of Chance and Skill

The story Dorothy Hobson tells in this interview is basically how she transformed one section of her Ph.D. research into a widely and well-received book. Following the success of this book, and her related journalism, she was commissioned by Jeremy Isaacs to write the history of the first five years of Channel Four. In the narration of this story, particularly the early days (1978–81) Dorothy frequently comments on the role of luck and fortuitous encounters. Indeed, as I show below, agency in this narrative is repeatedly assigned to chance, but in a quite contradictory manner. I want here to analyse the discursive inscription of chance in her narration, looking particularly at the interplay of 'luck' and 'skill'.

First, I want to extract sentences from sequences that have already been quoted at length in the first section of this chapter:

> that's why I never had any problem getting in to watch
> productions getting made, because the programme makers didn't
> ever see me as going in to criticize them, but to be relating to what
> they were interested in anyway, so that was why *I was very lucky*

in terms of having access right from the start, but I'm sure that was part of the reason because of that interest they of course were interested in audiences and they didn't get that sort of feedback from the audience research that was done by the broadcasters at that time. (DH: 6; my emphasis)

The real breakthrough in terms of what developed to be the work I was going to do, *was again quite a fluke really.* (DH: 14; my emphasis)

I have already suggested that these early accounts of meeting broadcasters should be understood in terms of the construction of an exchange, in which Dorothy gained entry through offering, as she puts it here, 'feedback' that they didn't get 'from the audience research that was done by the broadcasters at that time'. Also, I think it reasonable to infer that speaking from the floor at, for example, a Royal Television Society meeting, when you are an unknown postgraduate student, probably required considerable courage. Thus, I would want to argue that the very context in which this phrase, 'I was very lucky', occurs, testified not so much to luck as to considerable effort on the part of the speaker. This is, to some extent, recognized within the passage when Dorothy says, 'I'm sure that was part of the reason'.

The next passage for analysis is crucial, in that it formulates what is at issue in this notion of luck. This passage comes very shortly after the explanation of the idea of 'the two forms of television' already quoted:

Anyway that, when, I finished the MA, I then decided to pursue that particular line of interest into the Ph.D. research, and for that purpose I decided to look at the two forms of television [watched and not-watched by women in DH's MA research], and go to the productions, and actually try and tie up going to watch, to view, with audiences the very programmes I'd watched made. That was only possible for certain programmes of course, for things that were pre-recorded. And there were elements of luck there. I mean, it's partly luck, but it's partly knowing when to move in, to be quick and have the nerve to say to somebody 'Would you mind if I could do that', and persuading them really. (DH: 9–10)

In this key passage, Dorothy restores 'luck' to a more subsidiary role, where it has to take its place alongside more human skills such as a sense of time, a recognition of what is important, and 'nerve': 'I mean, it's partly luck, but it's partly knowing when to move in, to be quick and have the nerve to say . . .'. So here, luck is brought to fruition through labour, luck is reduced to something more like 'opportunity'. With this recognition, 'luck' does, however, remain a very significant narrative element, as in the following passage:

And then the real break happened, because Wendy Craig was
actually a guest star on the programme, I went, I went and I asked
her if I could talk to her about the specific *Butterflies* programme
which she was—there had already been one series—she was very,
very nice and said to me really I'm the actress, and you should talk
to Carla Lane. If you ring Gareth Gwenlan, who's the producer,
and say that I gave you his number, and suggested you rang,
he may let you go down and talk to her. And then I rang him up,
and as it happened again, this was what—I would call it an act of
God—he answered his own phone because he just happened to be
walking past his phone, so I didn't have to go through anyone to
ask him this. He in fact didn't say who he was when he answered
the phone, he let me go through the whole thing, he said yes,
come down, actually they start filming—told me the date—and
I went down the next week to the production where nobody was
expecting me, but they knew I must have been there genuinely
because otherwise I wouldn't have known where to go at 7.00 on
a Monday morning . . . (DH: 11–13)

In this sequence there is first of all 'the real break', which is very much
an instance of 'opportunity' in the sense discussed above, in that
while it is clearly necessary for Wendy Craig to be there, it is also necessary that Dorothy seizes the time, and does so in a way which is
sufficiently engaging to interest Wendy Craig ('she was very, very
nice'). Then there is the by-passing of the producer's secretary, and the
direct contact with the producer. On the one hand, I would tend to
agree with Dorothy that this was quite lucky, but on the other I would
want to argue that she must have been interesting enough 'to persuade them really' (the same would apply to the 'fluke' with Jeremy
Isaacs). That is, this narrational mode systematically undervalues her
own role. This is a very skilfully told story, and a story which is told in
ways which would cue any listener to understanding the significance
of this surprising access to Gareth Gwenlan. So we have the lead-in
through Wendy Craig, which sets up Carla Lane as the desired object,
and it is made clear that it will not be easy to reach her ('he may let you
go down and talk to her'). Then Dorothy acts ('And then I rang him
up') and then the narrative is suspended while she explains in advance
to her audience the significance of what she is going to say next. First
of all it is placed within the dominant characterization of this whole
chain of events as extraordinarily fortuitous ('and as it happened
again') and then we have the hyperbolic, but also, to anyone who has
tried to get hold of a television producer, very expressive, designation
'I would call it an act of God'. The punchline is the producer answering his own phone, which is both funny because of the build-up,
but also an act which any listener to this story would now understand

to be very unusual. Thus the skill of the telling works against an attribution of skill to the teller.

These stories of luck and chance are intercut with other passages when, usually with some prompting, Dorothy reflects on the extent to which she is using skills, and the type of skills these are. That is, the narrative is partly constructed through a very accomplished disavowal of skill which coexists, when pressed, with what is in fact a very acute sense of the fine judgements necessary to carry out successful fieldwork. Thus Dorothy points out that in the observation of television production, much depends on timing:

> any time you're in a television studio/production you have to negotiate finding out what you want, but at the same time, pulling back, I mean the skill is knowing the moment to be unobtrusive, not to say a word, you know—to maybe think people are getting a bit fed up of you, to say 'I won't be in tomorrow, I've got to go to the dentist' or something. It's a very careful game you have to play, to be in and out, and not be obtrusive, but also to be able to join in with them, so that they don't feel you're observing and not giving anything to them really. (DH: 16–17)

'It's a very careful game you have to play' points to considerable recognition of the balance of demands that must be juggled, while the naturalism of the excuse example, 'I've got to go to the dentist', offers once again a deskilling of this exercise of judgement, a self-presentation that disavows these fine judgements. The skills of interviewing senior television personnel are slightly different:

> what's quite difficult is to get people to talk to you anyway when you get to the top level and you're actually asking them to trust you not to name them, but to speak openly, and when they have said, sometimes afterwards, they've said, 'Actually, that was very interesting, I never would have dreamt I would have said so much as I've said to you, because usually I don't talk so much in that sort of way.' Or they've said, you know, someone actually said to me, 'you're actually very good at doing this because you've made me say things that I probably wouldn't have thought I would be talking about any way', and they've just been, it's been about their professional work, and another person said to me once, 'Do you know why you do get people to say so much?' and he said, 'I think it's actually because you do make people feel, one, you're very interested in what they're saying, but two what they're saying is very interesting.' And he said 'it's almost like you adopt a professional naivety, and really, you know, if you logically think about it, you know that she knows the answers to these questions, but the trick is to make people feel you don't know, because then

they will reveal things that you don't know, but you've go to be', he said 'you're wary with interviewers who you feel really know, they're just out to catch you, they're not really wanting you to talk a lot and expand', so I think that way of operating is important because otherwise, from my point of view, it's only if people tell you things that are interesting that you can actually do your own work. (DH: 71–2)

In this passage, most interestingly, Dorothy incorporates her inter- viewees' comments on her interviewing techniques. One of these proposes that 'It's almost like you adopt a professional naivety', which Dorothy then goes on to consider in terms particularly of making interviewees feel relaxed and interesting. In the following passage, I press her further about the issue of skill and she talks about the naturalization of skill as instinct:

DH: Really to whatever level you're doing research half of your skill is to make people feel they're just talking, they're just talking to you I mean in the way you and I are doing this now, but we know each other, the skill is as well that can have that same effect with people you don't know and that's that's a lot harder to do—

CB: Do you have when you're doing it—do you sort of think oh, I must do this, or does it or do you experience it more unconsciously than that?

DH: You don't think—you're only conscious of the professional skill you're using if the interview is difficult, if it's an easy interview it just all comes instinctively, but it's the instinct you know is the professional skill you've developed, if someone is difficult that's when you start thinking in your head you know you've got to do some work here, you've got to consciously think how can I help this person, what can I do, and it's things like particularly eye contact and phatic language you use to them, and keeping them assured and because certainly you've got to be careful you've got to not load what they're talking about, and you've got to keep that, and to reassure them, because sometimes people become most ill at ease when they think they don't know anything and again particularly men who you interview, women who—this is a vast generalization—but—are anxious to help you—tell you what they can, but sometimes, if people are nervous that they don't, that maybe they don't know as much about what you're going to ask them, they can become defensive which can come over as clamping up and not saying anything and that's when you've really got to work hard to make them come out and actually, you've got to make them feel what they do know is important, they do know it anyway but just get it out of them and that's I suppose when you more consciously work on those things. (DH: 74–7)

Dorothy offers an explicit, if qualified ('this is a vast generalization'), distinction between male and female interviewees here. Female interviewees are 'anxious to help you', while male interviewees seem to demand much more careful handling. Read carefully, this passage explicitly offers a scenario in which senior male interviewees are reassured and coaxed into relaxation, into feeling that they are experts, that they are significant, that 'what they do know is important'. That is, Dorothy describes, with senior male interviewees, an interviewing technique in which gender is inscribed, in which she occupies a traditionally feminine, supportive position. This skilled practice of interviewing—and it is, I think, indubitably skilled ('and it's things like, particularly eye contact and phatic language')—must be juxtaposed with the disavowal of skills in the tales of luck and chance with which this section started, but also with a deep uncertainty about her work which also appears in the interview. Without wanting to be essentialist about the analysis of this data, what I want to suggest is that this account, in its contradictoriness, offers one very clear instance of specifically feminine positionality in relation to intellectual work:

I suppose what is interesting to think about is how what you're asking me is how you perceive what you've done, how one perceives one's work, and that's something that, I don't know whether this is to do with me personally or if it's a trait of women, or if it's just a personality type, but I almost never think what you've done is that significant unless someone else tells you, and you think, oh, thank you very much, but you still, the breakthrough is when someone, the thing that really pleases me is if someone I don't know at all says, 'Oh, I've read your book, it was very interesting' or 'I think what you say is interesting', because I suppose, deep down, you still believe that when people are talking to you and are positive about what you've done you're almost never quite sure it's because they know you, or they quite like you as a person, or are they just being nice, and I mean someone said, someone introduced me and they said, 'Oh you're the author', and was kind of a real [*inaudible*] because you don't actually think of anyone thinking of you in that way really, so you all the time, you don't, you don't perceive what you've done has been important. On the other hand, you do know it's been important because you know these changes have been made. (DH: 60–2)

So while on the one hand this interview offers a confident and nuanced account of the skills of managing an interview through specifically feminine performance, on the other there is no sense of achievement except through the testimony of strangers.

(iii) The Status of Soap Opera

Dorothy Hobson is extremely clear within the interview about the changed status of soap opera since the period of her main research in the early 1980s, offering an analysis which holds together both the international impact of *Dallas* and *Dynasty* (not quoted below) and then the impact of first *Brookside* and then *EastEnders* on the soap landscape:

> And then of course the whole genre of soap opera has expanded during that period so rapidly [*inaudible*] really the two major soaps which were *Crossroads* and *Coronation Street* . . . but *Brookside* broke the mould in terms of not just bringing in new issues and handling them more openly, like particularly early on—issues they had had on other programmes certainly in *Crossroads* . . . [*long discussion between CB and DH about the comparative treatment of male infertility on* Crossroads *and* Brookside] but crucially the reason they've been held in more regard was that they have brought a new audience to television, those two programmes [*Brookside* and *EastEnders*] brought in a new audience and this reflects the way they were seen. Before they were seen as programmes predominantly watched by women even though they were watched by the whole television audience, but because that has more women in it at the upper end of the age scale—it is more women—but in terms of the overall audience it's watched by men as well. What *Brookside* and *EastEnders* brought was crucially the new young audience and particularly a male audience, which in advertising terms are what the advertisers want, these are the people—young people with money are what were wanted because they weren't heavy television viewers before that, so its status has changed in terms of the respect in which it's held by programme makers because they do bring in more of an audience that is needed to bring in money, so it's that combined with the added money that's been put into the soaps so production values are higher, they're given more time. (DH: 52–4)

Here, as we see, Dorothy is thinking 'industry' rather than 'academy', but she is remobilizing her own research, and that of others, about the low status of the female audience into this analysis. The changed status of soap opera in the period of discussion is a recurrent theme in the interview, given resonance by her own experience when she was starting her research. Early on in the interview she identifies defensiveness on the part of the television professionals working on soap opera as the main reason that she found it difficult to gain access to the *Crossroads* set in 1981. She was trying to do this as part of the Ph.D. research introduced in Section (i) of this chapter, in which part of her research involved production observation. She had already had access to *Pebble Mill at One*, *Weekend World*, and *Butterflies*.

> But the hardest programme to get into was in fact *Crossroads*. And that was what particularly I'd been trying to get in and couldn't, but I then had an appointment with Jack Barton [producer of *Crossroads*]—and this comes then to the nub of what soap operas were about at that time, this is back in 1981, and the reason that it was hard to get into soap operas—I mean you would think it would be hard to get into news or current affairs work, newsroom or current affairs production but it was not, it was because of the whole way that soap opera was seen at that time, and all that they were used to was press criticism, so if someone wanted to go and actually spend time there not only were they worried that it was just going to be another rip-off, but also they were concerned that—they were concerned about storylines obviously, so you'd got a double-convincing job to do there. And I know that the reason that Jack Barton did agree to me going there, was because I did know such a lot about the programme, so he knew that it was not going to be a criticism in the conventional sense, and so he agreed that I could go along . . . (DH: 16)

Dorothy is here very clear about the way in which she is recounting a historical story. She weaves together her evocation of a common-sense expectation about access to the most pressurized and prestigious productions ('I mean you would think it would be hard to get into news or current affairs work') with a very specific temporal reference ('and this comes then to the nub of what soap operas were about at that time, this is back in 1981 . . .'. '[T]he nub of what soap operas were about at that time' is their low critical standing: 'all that they were used to was press criticism'. But what she manages to do— through the considerable skill already discussed in this chapter—is to finally gain access as some kind of insider: 'because I did know such a lot about the programme, so he knew that it was not going to be a criticism in the conventional sense'.

Perhaps ironically, given that Dorothy's primary interest was in the production culture of the programmes, she gained access when storylines that were of national interest were in development. So although she, I think quite correctly, characterizes the opposition to her access as primarily related to fear of 'another rip-off', in fact, her secondary reason, about early knowledge of storylines, was particularly apposite. Through this, audience reaction to the news of Noele Gordon's sacking, a series of other contacts, and with the consent of ATV, Dorothy, as already discussed, signed a contract to write about audience response to 'the drama of a soap opera'.

> DH: And then another thing that pushed the work into the forefront was as the storyline broke about what would happen at the end to this character—everyone was speculating—all the newspapers—and someone—again, who I knew—was a friend of the Features editor of *The Times* and said to this man I know the person who'll write the best story you'll get on what's going on in *Crossroads*, and he rang me, and said could you write this piece, and again, a little story that highlights the interest into soap operas at that time was apparently at *The Times* editorial meeting on— they phoned me the night before and they said—I had to write it for the next day—and on the morning that they had their meeting they said to this guy what's the page today and he said there's an article by a woman from Birmingham about *Crossroads* [*laughs*]. At which he told me afterwards the response was a lot of mumbling and muttering from the editor who said 'Where is Birmingham?' 'What is *Crossroads*?' and 'What is a woman?' [*laughs*]. That story, of course, was a real coup, to have a piece in—to have a piece in *The Times* about *Crossroads* [Hobson 1981*b*] I think it was probably the first time that anything had been written in a serious newspaper of that kind about it . . .
>
> CB: I remember it—I've got it cut out. (DH: 20–2)

Although Dorothy tells this story as a funny anecdote, she has no doubt about its significance. She frames this story with reference to 'the interest in soap operas at that time', and then recounts the story of the three unknowns. She finishes by expressing pride about her own achievement: 'That story, of course, was a real coup'.

Dorothy Hobson's story is one of substantial success. What started as a Ph.D. turned into a book which sold well and offered the opportunity to earn her living as a media consultant. She has written for *The Listener*, *Broadcast*, and a range of daily papers as well as taking part in radio and television programmes. She has become a media figure, just as the soap opera landscape, as she suggests above, has been completely transformed in the same period. The interview suggests the significance of 1970s feminism at the start of this journey, while Dorothy herself has always been careful to stress the significance of class as well. But the interview also points to the disavowal of skills and contradictory sense of achievement which will recur in other interviews. As Dorothy herself puts it:

> So all the time, you don't, you don't perceive what you've done has been important. On the other hand, you do know it's been important because you know these changes have been made. (DH: 62)

8

'Slightly Guilty Pleasures':
Terry Lovell

TERRY LOVELL teaches Sociology and Women's Studies at the University of Warwick where she has been a full-time lecturer since 1972. She was one of nine children born to a Surrey family. Her mother was Irish, her father English ('a factory manager/ farmer'), and in answer to the question 'How would you describe your family background?' she responded 'How would I characterize it? Odd!!'[1] Terry went to grammar school after her 11-plus but left school at 16 to work as a bank clerk, from which she went on to work as a librarian. She was a member of the *Screen* editorial board and the London Women and Film Study Group in the 1970s, from which she wrote two influential early articles on *Coronation Street* (Dyer, Lovell, and McCrindle 1977; Lovell 1981). During this period she also contributed substantially to the debates within Marxism, arguing, against the dominant Althusserian and discursive currents, that Marxism was, epistemologically, a realism. This work was published as *Pictures of Reality* in 1980. Her subsequent publications have included a gendered sociology of the novel, *Consuming Fiction* (1987), and an edited collection, *British Feminist Thought* (1990).

For the purposes of this enquiry, initially the most significant aspect of the interview with Terry Lovell is the relative insignificance she accords the work on soap opera. As she says in the interview, 'I think it was probably an episode in terms of my interests, really' (TL: 18). However, it is also clear that, episodic as it may have been, the research on soap opera condensed many of her political and theoretical interests. The issues she pursues—concepts of ideology, the inscription of gender in the pleasures of consumption, cultural fictions of femininity—recur throughout her published research, whether its primary focus is Marxist epistemology or the English novel. Thus of the two articles, the first, co-written with Richard Dyer and Jean McCrindle (1977), 'Soap Opera and Women', with its defence of the utopian element in the pleasure of soap-viewing of women, anticipates some of the critique of Althusserian theories of ideology

---

1 Author questionnaire.

found in *Pictures of Reality*. It also contains, in a very compressed form at the end, a clearly 'Lovell' argument which suggests that commercial television may be more ideologically 'leaky' than 'the more state-controlled BBC sector' (Dyer, Lovell, and McCrindle 1977: 28).[2] That is, Terry is particularly associated with an argument (present in each of the soap articles) that, within a Marxist paradigm, analysis of the commodity, and particularly of 'cultural' commodities, must recognize that it is to some extent market demand, rather than ideological command, which will in fact determine what is reproduced, and that in this ambivalence of 'use-value' can be found unpredictable representations. However, this first article, as well as launching this argument, and other arguments which have become more familiar such as the distinctive representation of strong women in soap opera, is also clearly the product of joint authorship and the necessary negotiations this way of working demands. In the interview, Terry draws attention to the different attitudes of the writing group, and explicitly separates herself from some of the views expressed.[3]

The second article, published in the *Coronation Street* monograph, develops and extends the argument about ideology and the commodity form while using determinedly gendered examples and closing with a discussion of *Coronation Street* (Lovell 1980). This article, in its justification of study of a gendered genre, also begins to anticipate the articulation of gendered concerns with those of class in Terry's study of the novel *Consuming Fictions* (1987). As Terry Lovell points out, soap opera was of interest to her—could be 'an episode' in her interests—because as an object of study it posed questions within the sociology of culture that she was already addressing and would continue to do. It was one instance through which one of the more general analytic problems which has dominated her work since the 1970s could be explored, a problem I would characterize as: 'How is the pleasurable consumption of (mass) cultural production to be theorized?' Significantly, though, in her own trajectory, the soap

---

2 The named authors for this article are Dyer, Lovell, and McCrindle. It should be noted that they give acknowledgements to twelve others who between them constituted most of the members of the *Coronation Street* groups in Keele and London, and many of the key movers in relation to feminism and television in the 1970s. As discussed above in Ch. 6 and below in this chapter, the London group had its origins in a Women and Film group. The Keele group was partly formed under the aegis of the Society for Education in Film and Television (SEFT). Those acknowledged are (in original order) Angela Martin, Christine Gledhill, Sylvia Harvey, Helen Baehr, Joy Leman, Sue Honeyford, Christine Geraghty, Gillian Dyer, Nicky North, Marion Jordan, Richard Paterson, and Stephanie McKnight (Dyer, Lovell, and McCrindle 1977: 26).

3 'Women and Soap Opera' was recently reprinted in the Gray and McGuigan cultural studies reader *Studying Culture* (1993: 35–41) which I would argue to be an appropriate recognition of the historical significance, in the 1970s, of this short article. Confused and contradictory as it may now appear, it really was one of the very first attempts to think about women and soap opera in a way that was not simply condemnatory. In this sense, it stands alongside the articles discussed in Ch. 4, above.

opera work comes precisely on the cusp of the gendering of the question. The move is given tangible presence in the theoretical shifts from *Pictures of Reality* (1980), where it is the Marxist problematic in general that is addressed, to *Consuming Fiction* (1987), with its clear recognition of the inadequacy of the Marxist paradigm to address the effectivity of sexual and gender difference in the production and consumption of literature and the literary institution.

The structure of the interview reproduces this relative balance of concerns, in that the discussion of soap opera is framed within wider theoretical reviews of debates within Marxism in the 1970s and 1980s, the significance of ideas from psychoanalysis, and the general issue of value and the canon. Within this, soap opera as 'women's culture' is both incidental—'I did get involved in a—as a—I mean it was coincidental' (TL: 10)—and central, in that an analysis of soap opera does indeed condense all these issues. Thus Lovell's story is partly particularly interesting because of the dialectic in which the soap work is both marginal and appropriable to a central interest; and partly because of the temporal, biographical placing of this work, and its theoretical signified, gender, in the evolution of her own consuming interests. It is additionally her participation in the paper presented to the first Edinburgh Television Festival (1977) which is decisive to her inclusion here, in that this very hostilely received paper marks the first 'public' point in the turn of feminist attitudes to this type of 'women's culture'.

This interview covered what can retrospectively be seen as three main thematic areas: soap opera and 'women's culture'; theoretical problems of the 1970s (Marxism, consumption, feminism, and psychoanalysis); and questions of the literary canon. I investigate the first at length, and deal rather more briefly with the second. Questions of the literary canon which partly arose through discussion of ideas of quality in television are not directly relevant and so analysis of the interview presented here is mainly focused on the first two-thirds of the conversation.

(i) Soap Opera and 'Women's Culture'

Terry Lovell, early in the interview, introduces the formulation 'women's culture', and it is within this wider context that she consistently places soap opera. I want first to examine the way in which this phrase is introduced, for there is a considerable amount of non-verbal 'business' which signals a series of relevant issues. The phrase 'women's culture', obviously a key signifier in terms of my general enquiry, appears several times in the interview, used by Terry twice in rapid succession at the beginning of the interview, and returned to by me at the end in an attempt to summarize some of our discussion.

There are cognate usages at various points in the interview, but these three framing instances require special attention precisely because of the way in which they themselves are framed. The first occurrence is at the end of the 'introductory' section of the interview, shared referential narrative, where Terry and I are together trying to date the formation of Women and Film groups, tracing origins and naming participants. Terry tries to recollect whether two or three groups eventually appear from the initial formative lunch coordinated by Sam Rohdie[4] in 1974 in Soho:

> and I think that the second group was an offshoot of that and
> we—and the group I think of as the *Coronation Street* group
> had a discussion about what we wanted to do, and we took a
> decision then that we really wanted to be looking very definitely
> at popular forms and at what—and we took a decision to
> look—at soap opera really as a kind of—I mean partly out
> of the interest of some people like Christine Geraghty who
> were very interested in soap opera already and partly in terms
> of actually saying that it was important to be looking at you
> know—kind of the bulk of stuff that was actually part of
> day-to-day um women's culture really.

The emphasis in this extract is partly contextual, in that Terry is comparing the concerns of what became the *Coronation Street* group with the initially more theoretically focused group from which it was an offshoot. Thus the stress of 'very definitely' which introduces 'popular forms' as an object of study, which in context is posed in contrast to the more abstract concerns of the earlier group. 'Popular forms' is the first of three substantives which concludes in the rather blocked introduction of the phrase 'women's culture'. The definition of the object of study moves from 'popular forms' to 'soap opera' to 'you know—kind of the bulk of stuff that was actually part of day-to-day um women's culture'. This series is then resolved into the decision to watch *Coronation Street*, which in Christine Geraghty's rather more narratively referential account—as opposed to the theoretical choice for the popular stressed here—emerges partly because the aspirant Women and Film Group discover that few of them can get to the cinema, mainly because of young children or pressure of work. My interest in Lovell's account, though, is in the rather delayed introduction of the phrase 'women's culture'—'you know—kind of the bulk of stuff'. The pattern is one of delay—the phrase 'women's culture' is postponed, padded out. The significance of this slight awkwardness round this phrase is not deducible from this instance alone. The

---

4 Sam Rohdie was editor of *Screen* at this point. It was during his editorship that the first cine-semiotics were translated and published in the journal.

second usage, which occurs only a few sentences later clarifies what is at stake.

In this instance, to considerable laughter from both of us, Terry tries to establish that the phrase 'women's culture' is in quotation marks. The laughter is caused partly by the excessive signification with which she does this, in that she both says, 'um, in quotes, women's culture', and makes the customary gesture used to signify quotation marks in an academic lecture:

> TL: . . . I think some of the impulse behind that decision [to watch and study *Coronation Street*], I think is still one I would stand by now in relation to attitudes towards um in quotes [*gesture*] 'women's culture' [*laughter*]. I'll put the quotes on tape so you'll remember them.
>
> CB: So we'll remember that, in quotes, 'women's culture' [*laughter*].

We both laugh quite a lot in this sequence, and I respond to the manifest anxiety on Terry's part that I should not represent her as saying 'women's culture' without quotation marks by verbally reiterating her point—'So we'll remember that, in quotes, "women's culture".' The conversational quality of these interviews, and the pre-existent friendship of the participants is significant at moments like these, for there is no felt need by either of us to spell out *why* 'women's culture' should be in quotes. There is no explicit discussion of the significant theoretical issues in the difference between '*women's culture*' and *women's culture*, but we clearly both see this difference as significant.

This moment, which is to some extent dependent on friendship and familiarity with each other's work, is also self-reflexive in terms of the interview, in that Terry's insistence on the recording of the quotation marks, 'so you'll remember them', is a clear marking of a recognition that the substance of the interview will be used 'elsewhere', when she will be absent, unable to remind me of what she meant. So here we have a combination of both private and public speech which is quite characteristic of this interview as a whole. There is, throughout, a certain attention to the specificity of the situation, sometimes in a way which is like talking on two levels, for both referential and theoretical narrative—an enjoyment of the intimacy, but also always a consciousness of the public aspects of the situation. Thus there are several points in the interview where Terry and I gossip about other people who enter the narrative, and in each instance she or I signal that the material won't be used substantially in the research. Similarly, at a theoretical level, Terry displays a clear sense of a politics of position, observing at one point, 'So, yes, there are certain things that, you know, you will only say in certain circumstances [*laughs*]' (TL: 16).

There is, in this way, a distinctive inscription of context throughout this interview, both in this micro-manner, where the context of the interview, and its future recontextualizing elsewhere, is invoked, and at a broader level, in the careful placing of her own research concerns within broader intellectual debates. It is partly in this way that the placing of 'soap opera' within the broader 'women's culture' is significant, for this references the series of debates within feminism about attitudes to conventional cultures of femininity which have already been discussed in Chapter 1. This type of contextualizing is conducted both discursively and theoretically in this interview— hence the final reference to 'women's culture' that I want to discuss.

The final use of 'women's culture' comes at the end of the interview, when I try to summarize the understanding I have gained of the significance of the *Coronation Street* work to Terry Lovell's research trajectory:

CB: The *Coronation Street* work becomes in some ways, in terms of what you've talked—becomes significant as an example of a particular kind of work that was being done at the time, but actually—and with its concerns with popular forms and 'women's culture', blah blah blah—mass-produced women's culture—

TL: Yes that's right.

CB: Is characteristic of interests that you've continued—

TL: Yes, yes.

Here, it is the 'blah blah blah', immediately following 'women's culture' which signifies the way in which 'women's culture' is an issue for the participants in this interview. It is a concept which neither of us can leave alone or suggest is unproblematic. It is invoked awkwardly ('you know, kind of, the bulk of stuff'), pinioned in quotation marks, or signified as the site of familiar debate too familiar to be more than referenced ('blah blah blah'). At this point, for example, the quick gloss 'mass-produced' indicates that I am not attributing to Terry a longstanding interest in 'craft' women's culture. This extreme self-consciousness about the articulation of the phrase 'women's culture' by both participants is a trace, a residue, in Foucault's sense, of historical, theoretical, and political debate. 'Women's culture' is for both of us redolent with meanings that we know we cannot pass over in silence, but with which we do not wish to engage. And it is precisely in these linguistic usages, I would argue, that we see the 'results'—or, if you will, the traces—of the debates about media genres such as soap opera which feminism put on the agenda in the 1970s. But before considering this issue at more length, we need to examine the account of soap opera as 'women's culture' that Terry Lovell gives in this interview.

First, the obvious point is that to classify soap opera within 'women's culture' is to understand it from the beginning as a gendered form. Thus in contrast to Christine Geraghty's initial interest in the narrative qualities of television serials, Lovell's interest is initially constructed in and through gender. Lovell makes two other main points about 'women's culture' throughout the interview. The first is the idea of the strategic and political defence of this culture, and the second is the notion of being personally implicated or formed within it. Both of these ideas are presented, at each point, strongly temporally contextualized, which is another aspect of the repeated 'putting in place' that characterizes this interview so strongly. Thus if we return to the second usage of the phrase 'women's culture', and consider it in within the interview dialogue:

TL: What I mean—the basic impulse—I think some of the impulse behind that decision, I think is still one I would stand by now in terms of a kind of anxiety that has always been present in relation to attitudes towards um in quotes, 'women's culture' [*laughter*]. I'll put the quotes on tape so you'll remember them.

CB: So we'll remember that, in quotes, 'women's culture' [*laughter*].

TL: Which I think, although it's much less prevalent today, it's still—I still get a great deal—I've had a lot of undertow towards those positions actually in some of the students in 'Women and society' [course TL teaches at Warwick] and some other courses, of actually wanting to say, it's all that stuff that keeps us down, you know, that kind of culture of femininity is actually what keeps women into patriarchy—

CB: And it's that that has to be repudiated more than anything else.

TL: Yes, yes, and it's really not ours, it's something that's imposed. And that was an absolutely valid impulse at that stage, and [*inaudible*] really had not been theorized and that was not the dominant understanding of feminist . . . of that within feminism, and I think that was important and right, that impulse to try and understand where women's actual engagement, what the engagement with popular forms and popular soaps, soap opera, actually was, and therefore the question of pleasure, the pleasure of soap opera was very much there from the beginning as a question which would be investigated. (TL: 3)

There is here a very clear statement of the way in which interest in the 'culture of femininity' had to be defended within feminism, against feminism—'It's not really ours. It's something that's imposed'—and it is around this that the temporal marking is made:

> I think some of the impulse behind that decision, I think is still one I would stand by now
>
> A kind of anxiety that has always been present
>
> Although it's much less prevalent today
>
> And that was an absolutely valid impulse at that stage.

What Terry is reconstructing here is the hostility in the 1970s, within the women's movement, to an engagement with forms such as soap opera. '[I]t's all that stuff that keeps us down, you know, that kind of culture of femininity is actually what keeps women into patriarchy.' 'Women's culture' is such an issue in this interview because the term condenses fierce debates within feminism about the constitution of femininity, and appropriate feminist attitudes towards commercial cultures of femininity. Terry characterizes the dominant position in the 1970s by speaking in a gendered voice ('It's not really ours', 'It's all that stuff that keeps us down'), where the speaker is clearly 'we women', but a 'we women' with whom Terry is disagreeing. So in telling this story, Terry, clearly identifying herself as a feminist, is faced with problems of identificatory enunciation, when the 'we women' of feminism is inadequate to the complexity and complicity the narrative demands. And of course, I too, in these moments, assent to being outside the 'we women' that thinks these things. This splitting of feminist identity recurs in the interview, and clearly echoes the concerns voiced by Modleski in the 1979 article already examined, pointing to the way in which feminists undertaking this work met hostility from both inside and outside feminism. Terry Lovell explicitly addresses the hostility from 'outside' feminism, in *Consuming Fiction*, which is partly an examination of why 'woman-to-woman' fiction (in which Terry Lovell includes soap opera) has such low critical status. Here, though, we have the articulation of the consciousness that this is one of the enduring issues in the understanding of women and cultural production ('a kind of anxiety that has always been present'), with a clear sketch of the way in which attitudes within feminism have changed since the mid-1970s. Thus a few seconds later, Terry reflects, 'And as I say, all that is old hat now, but at the time it was quite . . . it was fairly new . . .' (TL: 3). The most vivid example of the converging hostility to this type of research comes in Terry's account of the reception of the paper she, Richard Dyer, and Jean McCrindle presented to the first Edinburgh Television Festival in 1977. This paper, which was the first public British feminist defence of soap opera, was received with enormous hostility by the audience of (mainly) professional broadcasters.[5]

> So we—there probably was a way in that you could read what we'd done in terms of these academics who were precisely not part of women's culture nor are they part of the professional ideo-professionals who are coming and looking at us and giving us a hard time about it and creating all this difficult stuff about it and patronizing it as well. But what I hadn't expected, apart from the ferocity of the attack that they made—and I've never experienced anything like that before or since, I'm glad to say —but also the extent to which the professionals were really caught in a situation where they precisely inhabited some of those attitudes of contempt towards what they were doing and they were compromised in terms of their livelihood and their whole career development and they were actually only doing a professional job in the production of soap opera. But the kind of contempt that they themselves actually had for the punters and for the product in the end which at the same time in professional terms they were wanting to defend . . . (TL: 8–9).

This is a complex passage which both addresses the contradictions of the paper presented and offers an analysis of the situation of those television professionals who attacked it at Edinburgh. Terry suggests that there were two elements of the attack she hadn't anticipated: its ferocity and the contradictions the paper exposed in television professional ideologies. What her analysis suggests is that it was precisely because the soap producers themselves were minimally ambivalent towards, if not straightforwardly contemptuous of, their 'product' that the paper sparked such a reaction. So what was being enacted was not just a defence of television soap opera against what was perceived as an attack by outsiders, for in that very defence a greater contempt was articulated. I now want to look particularly at the way in which Terry locates the inscription of feminism within the occasion:

> TL: . . . but certainly it was quite out of proportion to the thing, the modest thing, we thought we were doing, and where we thought we were being kind of like—
>
> CB: On what grounds did they attack you, can you remember?
>
> TL: Oh yes, they treated us as though what we said was, about *Coronation Street*, was the kind of thing that at that time you would have expected a group of feminists to be saying about a product like *Coronation Street*—

---

5 Jim McGuigan, in an account of this occasion, describes the delivery of the paper as being met with 'uncomprehending disbelief' (1992: 142). See also Rod Allen's report in *Broadcast*, 929 (12 Sept. 1977): 12–13.

CB: Oh I see—which of course you weren't.

TL: Which we weren't at all and so were completely taken aback by this, we were actually saying: 'Look this is actually rather interesting', and they weren't hearing and—

CB: They just didn't listen—

TL: They weren't listening, so they were attacking us for a feminist attack on *Coronation Street* and defending it in populist terms, but at the same time it was quite clear that they were actually rather distant from, and rather, I mean terribly, defensive about it, and quite contemptuous of people who watched soap opera, so it was a very complicated set of things that were going on there. (TL: 9)

The key sentence here is Terry's characterization of the attack that was made—'they treated us as though what we said . . . was the kind of thing that at that time you would have expected a group of feminists to be saying about a product like *Coronation Street*'. The first point to note here is that this story too is told, indeed only makes sense, through a splitting of feminist identity. The central device in this is the invocation of feminist critique in the mid-1970s as having predictable contours and targets, and the placing of the paper-givers in relation to this critique. The sentence assumes that television professionals would in fact have a clear image of what a feminist critique of *Coronation Street* would be, and that this image is what they heard the paper as offering. This is very complicated—as Terry points out—because not only did the paper givers identify themselves as feminist, but the paper itself was deeply contradictory, including both stern dismissal *and* cautious, innovatory defence—both made on feminist grounds. For our purposes, what is most interesting is the positions Terry occupies in narrating this story. For what she does is to identify herself, and by implication the other paper-givers, with this characterization—and dismissal—of 'the kind of thing . . . you would have expected a group of feminists to be saying'. With this move, Terry clearly endorses the 'pro-soap opera' aspects of the paper. In memory and retrospect, it is the innovatory 'modest' defence of the pleasures of soap viewing, and the considerable endorsement of the strength of the key female characters of *Coronation Street*, which seems most significant—but, evidently, with all the contradictoriness that we see in some of the work discussed in Chapter 3. However, it is also significant in Terry's account that she stresses the social identity of the paper-givers ('academics who were precisely not part of women's culture') as informing the judgement of the paper—indeed, in determining what could be heard.

This question of social identity is closely related to the other main issue in relation to 'women's culture', the question of whose culture this is. This problem can obviously be approached through the debates about 'mass' and 'popular' culture which have been so significant to the European left, and which underlay some feminist opposition to 'commercial' culture ('It's not ours, it's something that's imposed') but I think that Terry, throughout this interview, is posing the issue at another level. She clearly points out that her interest is in the engagement with mass-produced culture aimed at female audiences—the use of 'product' in the extract above is significant and polemical here—and in this context, the more interesting question is 'Who are the women of "women's culture"'. I asked a question about how the group understood their work in relation to this issue:

CB: The other thing I was wondering was if you could pick out of that is can you remember if you kept a distance, if you were separate from the pleasures that you were investigating or if you were investigating pleasures that you thought were your pleasures? Can you remember how you thought of yourselves?

TL: They were very much kind of slightly guilty pleasures [*laughs*] but everybody had, um, was ready to recognize— some had a much closer relationship than others, um, xxxx, for instance was very much—saw herself as—you know, it was her culture and not you know, theirs, um, and everybody was involved enough to recognize that it wasn't something we were investigating from the outside. (TL: 5–6)

The 'slightly guilty pleasures' Terry refers to here recur in many feminist analyses of commercial cultures of femininity and signal complex questions about the moral imperatives associated with 1970s feminism. Individual women clearly experienced contradictory pressures and pulls when living/working out this new identity, feminist, and how it fitted with other older identities, such as, for example, *Coronation Street* viewer. Thus although Terry, in the account of the Edinburgh festival, clearly differentiates the *Coronation Street* work from 'what a group of feminists would say about a product like *Coronation Street*', the invocation of guilt here reveals the way in which the repudiation of conventional femininity was a formative element in all 1970s feminism. The laughter too suggests that there are particular attendant tensions, as do the two uses of the verb 'recognize', which point to a certain reluctance, a will not to see. Because Terry is talking about a group of women though, individual senses of contradiction in approaching what was clearly experienced to some extent as forbidden pleasure is less apparent. Difficulty can be dispersed over the group as a whole, so that individuals can occupy different—by implication, coherent—positions, while the group as a whole can 'recognize that it wasn't something we were investigating from the outside'.

Terry continues to answer this question about the group's relation to what they were studying by talking a bit about herself:

> Um, I mean, in my case, um, having left school at 16, and been a bank clerk for several years, um, I quite er belonged to, very much to, a culture in which it was perfectly accep[?]/expected that *Woman* and *Woman's Own* was something that, you know, you just read every week. Of course, once you actually start becoming being a university student and an academic it's simply not respectable reading in terms of—so I mean in terms of periods in one's life when you have been involved there have been—there was all that to actually draw on, and so then to actually starting thinking, well, how does it come about that those shifts are actually made? But I don't think anybody actually saw themselves as being totally outside—it wasn't set up in that kind of anthropological spirit. (TL: 6)

Again, there is the reiteration of all involved in the group being, at least partly, 'women' of 'women's culture': 'I don't think anybody actually saw themselves as being totally outside—it wasn't set up in that kind of anthropological spirit'. The use of 'anthropological' here references a whole tradition of the study of the 'Other' from which Terry firmly differentiates the project of the *Coronation Street* group. However, it is clear that there was in some cases considerable distance: 'I don't think anybody actually saw themselves as being *totally* outside' (my emphasis).

In this passage, Terry speaks of her own history, and her involvement with 'women's culture', in a way which poses, implicitly, an interesting notion of a periodicity of identity, and a transformation of the lived culture from one period into material ('all that to actually draw on'), for investigation in another. She speaks of herself as having been a member of 'a culture in which it was perfectly accep[?]/ expected that *Woman* and *Woman's Own* was something that, you know, you just read every week'. I can't hear from the tape with certainty whether she makes the verbal switch I think she makes, from 'accepted' to 'expected', which does imply a certain coercion in that culture of femininity, but it is clear that this is a period of membership of 'women's culture', of being, in these terms, a woman, which is then superseded by another identity, that of a student. This transition is interesting because of its abruptness. It starts more gradually ('Of course, once you actually start becoming . . .'), as if there was a period of apprenticeship, but immediately 'becoming' is replaced by 'being', a new identity without transition. This abruptness is matched by the clarity of the cultural codes of the new identity: 'it's simply not respectable reading'. The story Terry is telling here is partly a woman's version of the more familiar post-war scholarship boy's story, which has mainly been told as a story of class migration. But in this story of a move out of one class background, there is also a story of the different class constitution of gender identities, so that 'being a student' means stopping being a certain kind of woman. Although class is hardly mentioned explicitly in this interview, I think it is legitimate to argue from this that the women of 'women's culture' are significantly defined through class. In Terry's case, the *Coronation Street* work, then, does, at one level, involve an explicit return to this 'simply not respectable' culture of origin. The pre-academic culture is remembered, and retained both as material for specific reflection ('there was all that to actually draw on') and more general meditation ('so then to actually start thinking, well, how does it come about that those shifts are actually made?').

In *Consuming Fiction*, Terry Lovell repeatedly stresses the way in which female experience and authorship are not valued/transmittable as cultural capital. Terry's account of the beginning of the study of soap opera, can, I think, be read as exactly an attempt to make legitimate the study of 'women's culture', given impetus by the second-wave women's movement, but at the same time often opposed by feminists, and responded to with some anxiety by television professionals. The final element in the discussion of feminine identity and women's culture is the significance of psychoanalytic ideas in the formation of subjectivity, which I will discuss substantively in the next section.

(ii) Questions of Theory

Although the whole of this interview is strongly informed by feminist and Marxist theory, there are points, rather the obverse of the laughter about the quotation marks for 'women's culture', where theoretical issues are directly addressed. At one level, the interview does offer a theoretical narrative, an account of a committed, position-taking engagement with theoretical debate inside British left culture in the 1960s, 1970s, and 1980s. Discursively, this theoretical narrative is quite difficult to analyse, not just because of the complexity of the philosophical issues involved, but also because it moves between different kinds of elements.[6] Thus for example, very early on, one of the ways in which Terry describes the project of what became the *Coronation Street* Study Group is through a reference to Juliet Mitchell's book *Psychoanalysis and Feminism* (1974):

> It was also very much the time when Juliet Mitchell's book was still reverberating, it was very early days in terms of having to

---

6 Julia Kristeva's 1984 piece 'My Memory's Hyperbole' offers an extremely sophisticated reflection on 'theoretical' autobiographical material. She suggests—and I think this also true of some of the histories told here—'What follows, then, will be an autobiography in the first person plural' (Kristeva 1987: 219).

think seriously about psychoanalysis in relation to feminism because of course the dominant position was then against it within the women's movement, when psychoanalysis was still— think back [*inaudible three words*] and that had just recently been challenged by Juliet Mitchell in 1974, and we'd all read that . . . (TL: 4)

Here, we have 'theory as context', and indeed Terry and I then launch into a quite long discussion of what we clearly both experienced as the *Psychoanalysis and Feminism* moment. However, before we do this, Terry continues her discussion of the reverberations of *Psychoanalysis and Feminism* with a much more personal comment, a very clearly retrospective account of her own position at that time, one which, as the telling indicates, she no longer holds:

> and we'd all read that, even those like myself who were very resistant to actually taking it on board were being forced to recognize that this needed to be done, and that actually looking at psychoanalysis was going to have had a direct bearing on these kinds of questions [questions of pleasure, women's engagement with soaps] and related questions, not only the way that women were already formed, as it were, or engaged with popular culture —with 'women's culture', but also the way in which we inhabit our own feminine identity as well. (TL: 4)

This passage moves beyond 'theory as context' to reconstruct particular individual positions ('even those like myself who were very resistant'), and to retrospectively map shifts in understanding. The difficulty of this kind of speech, in which past and present positions are articulated simultaneously, is shown clearly in the rather peculiar tenses here: 'was going to have had'. Together, these two strategies repeat, in the domain of the theoretical, the micro-/macro-contextualizing moves which are characteristic of this interview at several levels, and both are used several times in the interview, noticeably in the discussion of English Literature as a discipline.

The main part of the theoretical narrative comes in the second half of the interview, and has many of the rather peculiar tenses noted above. It is, as Terry tells, it, the continuing story of the gradual shifts in the significance of Marxism in her own work, set within the wider context of the radical impact of structuralist and poststructuralist continental thought on British Marxist, socialist, and feminist thought. So the comment about Juliet Mitchell and psychoanalysis condenses both the beginning and the end of this story—in the beginning, 'those like myself [. . .] were very resistant to taking it on board', whereas by the end, that speaker, recounting that story, wants to stress the significance of that theoretical intervention to an understanding of 'the way in which we inhabit our own feminine identity as well'.

So this story Terry tells, which is in many ways the story of the seventies for many on the British intellectual left, has what could be seen as a dramatic scenario in which the central protagonist, Marxism, is assailed by wave after wave of critique, and eventually found lacking. Terry's account gives a real sense of the theoretical labour involved, of the relentless demand to come to terms with new (often, newly translated) bodies of theoretical work:

> that whole tranche of Theory with a capital T, you know, and all those traumas we went through, and struggling with it, and struggling against it, and swimming with it, and swimming against it. (TL: 16–17)

But she was also seen as someone who was particularly engaged in theoretical intellectual work. She explains that it was her brief, within the *Coronation Street* Group, to write the theoretical chapter ('the problem was also I was in this group marked down as the theorist') as one way of approaching what she retrospectively sees as 'really the most depressing thing, I think, about reading it now—just the extent to which it's not, the heart is really not in *Coronation Street*' (TL: 12). Terry raises the whole question of 'theoretical memory' when she says how surprised she has been on rereading the work (before the interview) to see how preoccupied it was with trying to make things 'fit' within Marxism. This, as publications like *Women Take Issue* (Women's Studies Group 1978), or the 'domestic labour debate' (Malos 1980) clearly testify, was a common occupation for feminists in the 1970s:

> I think what has surprised me about it was the extent—way—in which it very much engaged—and I think this is also true of *Pictures of Reality* and the other piece at this time—very much engaged with, preoccupied with, really, trying to find a space within, in Marxist theory, for inserting things that really are quite/I mean still having a, still wanting to think that Marxism provided the kind of an overall frame that within which you could the, you could rework it. (TL: 11)

What Terry clearly reminds us in this interview is first the way in which much British feminism—including those women who were first attracted to work on popular forms—came out of the socialist tradition which in the 1970s was itself deeply divided over issues of theory and theoretical issues. Secondly, she reminds us how anti-psychoanalytic these traditions tended to be, and finally she shows how early second-wave feminist theory took Marxism as in some ways taken for granted, but still had the ambition to produce a new inclusive theoretical framework. So, in a final contextualizing move in an interview which has been characterized by contextualizing moves, Terry places the *Coronation Street* work in this wider frame of struggles within British Marxism:

TL: ... but nevertheless, I also think that the idea that you can have a kind of totalizing theory which will really provide you with all you—I mean I think that was already, um, I mean in a lot of work people weren't doing that necessarily—but nevertheless, there was still the hope that you would one day have that [*inaudible:? theoretical frame*] which would give you the whole works.

CB: and need to have these terrible long theoretical introductions—

TL: Yes, that's the other thing drives me spare reading that [*Coronation Street* article] now—I keep thinking that it's going to start now, and then it's ended.

9

'The Pleasure of a Programme Like This Is Not Something Simple': Ien Ang

IEN **ANG** was working as a lecturer in the Department of Communications at the University of Amsterdam at the time of this interview. She is not a native English speaker, holding Dutch nationality while of Chinese descent. She emigrated with her family to the Netherlands from Indonesia in 1966 at the age of 12, where she had a classical Western education (including Greek and Latin), and went on to take her first degree in psychology at the University of Amsterdam.[1] Her MA and Ph.D. were also taken at the University of Amsterdam, in the field which would be translated as 'General Social Science'. Her MA dissertation, a study of the reception of the US prime-time show *Dallas* in the Netherlands, was first published in Dutch in 1982, and formed the basis of what was subsequently published as *Watching Dallas* in English in 1985. This book has also been translated into German and is widely used in media and cultural studies courses in the anglophone academy.

Ien Ang's work has consistently been informed by, and addressed to, the Anglo-American cultural studies/mass communication constituency, as she points out several times during this interview, and it is because of her involvement and influence in this arena that she is included here. This very inclusion, though, raises a series of problems about the appropriate understanding of 'context'. For while in terms of her influence in the academic study of soap opera it is clearly appropriate to interview Ien Ang, this move, which contextualizes her work in terms of international anglophone feminist media scholarship, also decontextualizes her from the Netherlands, where she had studied, published, and was employed at the time of the interview. The complexities and specificities of the Dutch context are not

1 Author questionnaire.

substantially addressed here, although Ang herself has written about broadcasting in the Netherlands as both journalist and academic.[2] Instead, Ang's regular visits to Britain and the USA, and her periods of teaching in the USA and Australia are taken to legitimate an approach to Ang within the hegemonic Anglo-American framework. Ang herself, in the introduction to the English version of *Watching Dallas*, states that one of her original aims with the project was to 'introduce the interested Dutch reader to theoretical perspectives on television and television serials . . . which stem mainly from Anglo-Saxon media and cultural studies' (Ang 1985: p. vii). Thus although Ang, like all the other interviewees, tells a local story—what it was like working on *Dallas* in the Netherlands in the early 1980s—she, more than the others, tells it self-consciously in an international context.

Ien Ang was, at the time of this interview, best known for her book on *Dallas, Watching Dallas: Soap Opera and the Melodramatic Imagination*, published in English in 1985, although she has subsequently published a book on television audience research (Ang 1991) and a series of articles on cultural studies, audiences, and postmodernism highlighting, increasingly, non-European perspectives on these areas (collated in Ang 1995*b*). In the introduction to the *Dallas* book, Ang says it was the enormous, international, and controversial popularity of the US serial *Dallas* in the period 1978–81 which first motivated her investigation. Ang is, however, careful to establish her own pleasure in *Dallas*—the fact that she has 'always particularly liked watching soap operas like *Dallas*' (Ang 1985: 12), as well as the symbolic significance of this US serial, which comes to represent for many in this period the worst of US cultural imperialism.[3] While acknowledging the significance of *Dallas*'s popularity, Ang specifies that she will focus, not on the issue of *why Dallas* is popular, but, using limited empirical material, on the process of watching *Dallas* and the pleasure generated therein. Her empirical data is formed by the letters she received from viewers in answer to an advertisement she placed in a Dutch woman's magazine.

Ang's study is innovatory in several ways. First, to some extent following patterns of work developed at the Centre for Contemporary Cultural Studies at Birmingham, Ang moves from analysis of the soap opera text, as in the work of Modleski or the *Coronation Street* group, to the investigation of audience accounts of the processes of viewing. However, she investigates the empirical television audience using the concept of 'pleasure' (which had its theoretical home in

---

2 For example, in Ch. 13 of *Desperately Seeking the Audience* (Aug. 1991), which deals with the Dutch channel VARA; an example of more journalistic writing would be 'De televisier als Kroegmaat', in *De Groene Amsterdammer* 5 Jan. 1983.

3 Vividly realized, e.g. in the title of Christopher Dunkley's 1985 book on the future of television; *Television Today and Tomorrow: Wall-to-Wall Dallas?*

psychoanalytic film studies in this period), as against the mass communications paradigm of 'uses and gratifications', historically more commonly associated with the empirical analysis of audiences. So Ang brings together work from different fields. She uses ideas from film and literary studies—pleasure and the melodramatic imagination—which are historically associated with a textual, rather than an empirical, audience, to investigate the television audience, normally conceptualized within mass communications and 'effects' paradigms.

Secondly, Ang uses the notion of the 'symptomatic reading'—again a concept with origins in Freudian psychoanalysis, although in this period mainly available through French structuralist Marxism—to conceptualize her procedures in relation to the viewers' letters. It is through this concept that she can contextualize the letters, for she suggests that particular statements by individuals about watching *Dallas* are likely to draw on common cultural repertoires. These repertoires she, to a certain extent, infers from the recurrent themes and structures of the letters, grouping her material into three main areas: realism, the ideology of popular culture, and 'the melodramatic imagination'. Under these headings, she discusses the role of fantasy and entertainment in pleasure, as well as the prohibitions internalized by viewers about the value of US serial television. She also examines the way in which prime-time soap opera can be said to inherit a structure of feeling derived from theatrical melodrama using the work of Peter Brooks (1976).[4] It is the melodramatic imagination and what she calls, adapting Raymond Williams, a 'tragic structure of feeling' which she juxtaposes with both feminism and ideas of proper femininity (Ang 1985: 45–6, 121–30).

Throughout her analysis of readers' letters about watching *Dallas*, Ang is concerned with pleasure, and the fans' ambivalence about this pleasure. It is particularly this ambivalence that interests her since it is a feeling she shares, as she had made clear in her original advertisement:

> I like watching the TV serial *Dallas*, but often get odd reactions to it. Would anyone like to write and tell me why you like watching it too, or dislike it? I should like to assimilate these reactions in my University thesis. Please write to . . . (Ang 1985: 10)

Ang has been criticized for the formulation of this advertisement. It has been suggested that the mention of 'odd reactions' overdetermined the responses to the request, providing a script for her correspondents.[5] However, from the perspective of my enquiry it could be

---

4 Ang is one of a number of scholars of the audio-visual who turn to Brooks's (literary) work in the early eighties. In that sense, as she discusses in the interview below, the simultaneous revaluation of film melodrama referred to in Chapter 1 is historically significant in shaping Ang's arguments about *Dallas*.

5 Modleski (1991: 45).

argued that her formulation is exemplary in that it explicitly appeals to other viewers stating the contradiction which is the motor of the project. Ang names herself fan first, 'puzzled/reacted to' second, and academic third. She shows herself particularly sensitive to the role of the researcher in shaping the research:

> Moreover, any study always bears the traces of the subjectivity of the researcher. Doubtless for that reason my own ambivalent reaction to *Dallas* will also have its repercussions. This ambivalence is on the one hand connected with my identity as an intellectual and a feminist, and on the other hand with the fact that I have always particularly liked watching soap operas like *Dallas*. At one time I really belonged to the category of devoted *Dallas* fans. The admission of the reality of this pleasure also formed the starting point for this study—I wanted to understand this pleasure, without having to pass judgement on whether *Dallas* is good or bad, from a political, social or aesthetic view. (Ang 1985: 12)

Here, at the end of the introduction to the *Dallas* book, Ang places herself unequivocally within the research frame. 'The admission of the reality of this pleasure' is posed as the starting point of the study, in which the contradictory identities 'intellectual', 'feminist', and 'devoted *Dallas* fan' are investigated together. The process of investigation leads to a final chapter on '*Dallas* and Feminism'. Here, Ang argues that there is a 'monstrous alliance' between feminist criticism and the ideology of mass culture which colludes in the denigration of the feminine as well as over-politicizing pleasure. She goes on to suggest that soap operas offer 'intuitive' recognition of some of the same dilemmas of femininity recognized by feminism, while not offering the utopian happy ending—social change—that feminism aspires to. This position we have already detected as a prevailing thread in approaches to soap opera in both Chapters 2 and 3. Indeed, of the interviewees, Lovell in particular suggests elements of the same analysis. However, Ang's originality lies in her use of 'the melodramatic imagination' to think both soap opera and feminism. Instead of feminism being the answer to the hankerings of desire finding expression in soap opera, Ang suggests, conscious of her polemic, that feminism too can be seen to occupy that Manichaean universe which characterizes melodrama. Because Ang uses a concept of fantasy, and grants this concept some autonomy, she is able to keep separate the pleasure of watching *Dallas* from the desire for social change. Partly, I would suggest, through precisely the self-inscription in the project discussed above, and therefore the explicit address to contradictory desires and practices, Ang can argue both for enjoying *Dallas* and wanting to change the world, without collapsing either practice into each other. She thus makes a very interesting intervention into the debate about the personal as political by re-establishing a certain autonomy to desire as it is experienced in personal life—like watching soap opera.

As a study of the reception of an American serial in a small European country, *Watching Dallas* is centrally, if implicitly, concerned with issues of cultural identity and cultural imperialism. Ang could be seen to contest any simple understanding of the processes of cultural imperialism—the imposition from above of an alien culture—with her insistence on the pleasures of *Dallas* watching and her deconstruction of 'the ideology of popular culture'. The links she makes between feminist attitudes to soap opera and this ideology also serve to point to the hegemonic aspects of feminist ideology with its origins in 'Anglo' culture. Ethnic identity, as with all the early work on soap opera, is not, however, an issue, except insofar as it is raised by 'American-ness'. Ethnicity is an unmarked term, as it is with most of the writing surveyed here. However, this is here particularly worthy of comment because Ien Ang, like Ellen Seiter, has increasingly written on this topic since completing the soap opera and audience research, and indeed raises the issue of ethnic essentialism towards the end of the interview.

In a series of recent articles, including 'Hegemony in Trouble: Nostalgia and the Idea of the Impossible in European Cinema' (1992) and 'On Not Speaking Chinese' (1994), Ang has explicitly addressed her own migrant origins and the contradictory demands of heterogeneous diasporic identifications. For example, she recorded her responses to reading an account of annual rituals of Chippewa Indians by Gail Valaskakis (1989):

> When I first read Gail Valaskakis' text . . . I was moved because I identified with the subordinate position from which the narrative was told. However, my response was also filled with a slight sense of envy, an ambivalence which reveals the distance between us: sometimes I wish I could speak as strongly and vigorously from so certain a position of 'us', based upon a collective memory and a codified cultural heritage. Yet, as one whose ethnic history is thoroughly mixed up by a multiplicity of geographical, cultural and biographical movements it seems both impossible and unwarranted for me to construct a clear sense of 'us'. For me then, individualism is both a necessity and a solution, and thus ultimately distanced me from the subject position inhabited by Valaskakis. (Ang 1989*a*: 29)

If the *Dallas* book was written from the position of a European, and to some extent offered a cautious defence of the pleasures of a US television programme, Ang's later work has interrogated both the assumptions of 'Europeanness' and the taken-for-granted whiteness of this position, while also refusing to capitalize on her newly desirable difference. She observes in an article in a 1995 collection: 'As a woman of Chinese descent, I suddenly find myself in a position in which I can turn my "difference" into intellectual and political capital, where "white" feminists invite me to raise my "voice", *qua* my being a non-white woman, and make myself heard' (Ang 1995a: 57). Ien used these insights in response to the 'background' questionnaire filled out for me two years after the interview where, in answer to my question 'How would you describe your family background?', she wrote:

> A middle-class family of Indonesian-Chinese background, my parents were upwardly mobile and Dutch-educated and stressed education for their children. Therefore they emphasized integration in Dutch culture during my teen years. In a way, I can now read my response to *Dallas*—and the writing of the *Dallas* book—as a metaphoric articulation of some of the problems and tensions of that desire for integration.

This interview took place between the *Dallas* project and this characterization of it, but is, as we shall see, shot through with meditation on migrant subjectivity. Since the interview Ien Ang has moved to Murdoch University, Perth, Western Australia, and then to Nepean University, Sydney.

The interview took place in 1990 London not long after Ien had completed her Ph.D. dissertation and second book, *Desperately Seeking the Audience* (1991). As usual, some part of the interview was spent in shared referential narrative establishing chronologies and sequences, including when we had first met, but for the most part, Ien concentrated on how she started the *Dallas* work, and the shifts that had led her from there to her study of the conceptualization and measurement of the television audience in Britain, the USA, and the Netherlands.

This interview is analysed in three parts. Each part is dominated by discussion of the *Dallas* research, but in very different ways. The first part offers a series of contextualizations and remembered referential narrative which together explain some of the origins of the project, but which also show the way in which this was a project with a genesis *against* prevailing research paradigms. The second section explores the extent to which the *Dallas* project was about *Dallas*, exploring the other issues which were addressed in the work. In the final section Ien comments in more detail on advertising for, and receiving, the letters which formed her audience data.

(i) Margins and Nomads

In addition to the discussion of soap opera—and even as part of this discussion—this interview has a striking and repeated concern with positions of structural marginality and notions of intellectual not-belonging. Thus I will start the analysis with this material as it appears structuring at both a discursive and an intellectual level. Ang introduces the formulation 'nomadic subjectivity' herself, towards the end of the interview, when she says:

> I can relate very much to this idea of the nomadic subjectivity. I sometimes think, well, I'm the embodiment of it. (IA: 19)

She says this as a gloss to her own comment on a common feature across her work which she describes as 'the autobiographical aspect':

> The autobiographical aspect is the urge always to be at many places at the same time, and nowhere also of course. (IA: 19)

I shall return below to the intellectual urge to deconstruct, and the stress on cultural contradiction which Ang sees as most important in her work. I want initially to trace this 'nomadic subjectivity' through Ang's own account of her own research, where we shall see that her story is, at a discursive level, structured through the repetition of different kinds of intellectual marginality. While the substance of the intellectual disagreements changes over the ten years discussed, Ang's relative position, through a series of shifts, seems to remain at the edges of each orthodoxy.

Methodologically, this analytic strategy is a double-edged move. On the one hand, I take advantage of, take literally, the skills of the interviewee: she can tell me something about the dynamics and patternings of her intellectual biography. On the other hand, the authority of the autobiographer—even of the most intellectually sophisticated one—is of a very peculiar type, and in this context the story told can properly be analysed at a discursive level as well as read referentially. Here, I would argue that Ang's characterization of herself as in some ways embodying a nomadic subjectivity is strongly supported by the rhetorical structures through which she gives an account of the development of her work. That she is, in origin, more nomadic, more of an 'international intellectual' than any of the other women in this study, could clearly also be adduced, either as original evidence, or in some other causal relation. This, on the data I have, is methodologically improper without a reductive leap, a collapsing of different levels of analysis. However, 'the urge always to be at many places at the same time, and nowhere also of course', structures this interview at a deep level, as I will demonstrate below. This discursive enactment/construction of the speaking subject provides legitimate support for Ang's own self-description as a 'nomadic subject', but this subjectivity is in turn inflected in most interesting ways by the interest in 'soap opera' as we see below.

The first instance of the structure of marginality occurs in Ang's account of her involvement with the editorial board of *Skrien*, with which she was associated between 1979–82. Ang was invited to become part of the editorial board 'in order to write specifically about television, and [I] was there with some other people who also did work on television' (IA: 1). It is clear though, from her account, that the editorial board had a rather more ambiguous attitude to television than to film: 'It was quite a stimulating group of people in fact, but they were also quite snobbish about television, as if "this is a very common thing"' (IA: 2). It is in this context with this group that Ang embarked on the *Dallas* project, in which *Skrien* featured an article on different aspects of *Dallas* every month for seven issues. Ang's article, 'the only one that was a bit personal—in terms of "I do like it but . . . what does it mean to find *Dallas* pleasurable?"', begins, against contemporary Film Studies orthodoxy, to ask questions about melodrama and pleasure in relation to television:

> I was quite oriented towards what was happening in this country [GB] and also because one of the other members of the Board in fact who did not write about television but about film, was interested in the question of melodrama and pleasure but he insisted that *Dallas* was not real melodrama and could not be. (IA: 2)

So in this first narrative event, the period recounted as originating the later work, Ang is writing about television in a context where film is more highly valued ('as if [television] . . . is a very common thing'), and she is writing about television in a personal way, in terms of her own pleasure ('*the only one* that was a bit personal [*my emphasis*]'). Clearly one of the constituting factors here, which can be marked, rather than explored, is the particularity of the Dutch broadcasting structure, with the structural representativeness of channel allocation, as well as the ability to receive British and West German television.[6] Continental European intellectual approaches to television have also historically been more distanced than is the case in Britain. Thus Ang is clearly, as she says, 'quite oriented towards what was happening in this country . . .', adopting what is in effect a much more British cultural studies/British Film Institute approach to television than was common in the Netherlands. She expands on the novelty of this approach to television in the period:

---

6 Ang herself is interesting on this: see Ang (1987). A brief outline of the Dutch system can be found in Garnham (1973).

It was a politics also in that board when you write something you have to write about things that you like. For the film people it was quite clear, but for the TV people it was much more difficult somehow. When you write about television you can only write about it from a position of distance, and I was trying to show that that was not necessary, that it was possible to write about it in a more personal way. So that was somehow the politics of it. And I did like it at that time—my writing was in fact especially for those people. (IA: 2)

Here, when Ang is tracing the intellectual argument she is having with the *Skrien* board, she also introduces a key element in the feminist discussion of soap opera, the validation of 'the personal'. The personal here occurs in two forms—first in the argument that it is possible to like television series like *Dallas*, and 'to write about it in a more personal way', and secondly in the specific address to her colleagues, 'And I did like it at that time—my writing was in fact especially for those people'.

The other originating element in the decision to do more extended work on *Dallas* is that as a student (in Political Science) she needed a dissertation topic. Here, a similar structure, although with a different content, is manifest:

I was always struck by the lack of interest among people interested in ideology in issues of media culture. It seems like there it was completely absent—about ideology—it was about political ideology or ideologies as developed in schools or whatever but somehow media culture was not on the agenda, and on the other hand the people who were interested in film and television generally did not ask that many questions about the larger cultural and ideological context. (IA: 3)

Again, we see the affiliation/difference pattern, but also, as with Terry Lovell, a substantial theoretical critique. Ang then moves on to gloss her specific narrative account: in this instance, the way in which the political science version of 'ideology' ignores media culture, while media analysis ignores wider issues, in a more abstract fashion. This is the first exposition of 'nomadic subjectivity' in the interview:

I've always been moving between different positions and like always when I'm here [*thump*] I want to be there [*thump*]—it was always like finding some sort of articulation *between* different positions. That was important, I think, in terms of what makes me motivated to do a certain kind of work. It's always that—that when you're in that position [*thump*] then you don't ask those and these questions and I think that's a problem—and when you're in that position [*thump*] then you forget that [*knock*] and that [*knock*] and that [*knock*]. I'm always trying to find a way of making clear that there is something to be said in the gap between those different positions. (IA: 3)

Here, in quite abstract terms, but with considerable emphasis—Ien is using the table at which we sit as a mapping place for different positions, and so the recording is punctuated with thumps and knocks—she lays out the intellectual experience of never being rooted—at home—in one paradigm. The idea of 'articulation' is here used both intellectually ('something to be said in the gap between') and experientially ('when I'm here I *want* to be there, and when I'm there I *want* to be here [*my emphasis*]'). This passage also begins to suggest, in a way which subsequently becomes more manifest, that it might not have been the project of working on *Dallas* or soap opera *as such* which was attractive, so much as the relative position of soap opera in the intellectual field or the way in which it was only a legitimate object of study for certain kinds of enquiry.

But there were also specific institutional supports, particularly in Britain, in the late 1970s/early 1980s for the serious study of popular television. One key site was the annual British Film Institute Summer School, which was devoted to the study of television in 1981 and 1982. Ien has already pointed out that she was 'quite orientated towards what was happening in [Britain]', and this orientation has intellectual, social, and institutional aspects as we see from the following account of going to British Film Institute Summer Schools in the early 1980s:

IA: I'm sure it was before I did the book, in fact, because I used a lot of the material of those summer schools for writing the book. In a way—of course—maybe this is also a more personal note—of course, I was at those summer schools and it was *quite* difficult, in fact, to be there because my English was not that good yet, at that time, and also there was a certain sense of 'in-crowd' feeling—

CB: Oh yes, very much, a clique—

IA: Yes it's not very self-aware, I think, but it was not that easy to communicate with you and all those people who were there, so I was in the margins, and I wanted to be part of it, and also—and I had something to say. Having something to say—is not—I realized very often that that only happens when you've already proved yourself, then you can say something. That's how this interpersonal politics works somehow, this is a nasty bit of how people function, when you have a status, then people will listen to you. Unfortunately, it works like that. (IA: 9)

Here, Ien talks about herself as being 'in the margins' and points in the first instance to her difficulties in speaking English, to what could be seen as a marking of her 'foreign-ness'. She does this in a way which indicates how colloquially sophisticated her English now is by choosing 'quite' to qualify 'difficult', to carry a meaning which rivals 'very' through its combination of understatement and tone of voice: 'It was *quite* difficult, in fact, to be there, because my English was not that good . . .'. However, Ien then goes on to make a rather more challenging analysis of what was at issue in her feelings of exclusion.

First, she points to the perhaps unconscious exclusiveness of the 'in-crowd': 'it's not very self-aware, I think, but it was not that easy to communicate with you and all those people who were there'. This is complicated, because she is including me in this group, and it's difficult to tell whether the attribution of *unconscious* exclusivity is an analysis of the past, or a politeness of the present. It is certainly partly a qualification of my interjection, 'Oh yes, very much, a clique'. Perhaps it is best registered as both, the speaking of a significant memory of exclusion, in a context which works against the attribution or implication of intentionality. This interpretation is supported by the way in which Ien then moves to generalize from this and other ('I realized very often') experiences, about the conditions of identity in intellectual work. Here she reverses the common-sense notion that the first condition of intellectual 'audibility' is 'Having something to say'—and she clearly sees herself as having had to learn, repeatedly, to abandon this innocent idea ('I *realized* very often [*my emphasis*]')—to propose instead that 'when you have a status, then people will listen to you'. Inscribed within this passage is the social effect of having written a successful book. *Watching Dallas* was most successful in exactly the academic constituency of BFI summer schools, and one of the stories in this passage is the move from 'before I did the book' to 'when you've already proved yourself'. This social effect has intellectual consequences: '. . . then you can say something'. Ien offers this observation in a very general way—almost as a truth about human nature ('this is a nasty bit of how people function . . . Unfortunately it works like that'), in which she makes no distinctions within the category 'people'.

So the structure of exclusion for Ien Ang in this instance echoes the structure of marginality that I have already argued to be central to her account. Congruent with all the other instances is the way in which the grouping to which she perceives herself as marginal is not given an identity through sociological categories such as gender or ethnicity, although national identity can be inferred from the implicit 'English-speaking'. They are here just (British) 'people', who, if they have any other identity, have an identity of 'intellectual'—people who might be expected to listen to new ideas about, in this instance, television. At other points, the people were an editorial board, or scholars of a particular academic discipline, or those organizing politically round particular identities. However, what is slightly different in this instance is the relation of desire towards these people that Ien recalls. In most of the scenarios of marginality that she recounts, she presents herself as in some ways conceptually antagonistic to the dominant/centre. Here though, she says quite simply, 'so I was in the margins, and I wanted to be part of it, and also—and I had something to say'. There are here two different elements: the desire to be included and the desire to be heard. Ien's broader argument here is that, despite the apparent codes of intellectual life, the social can be determinant in the audibility of intellectual work. However, she is also telling a more personal story (which she has signalled as such), about wanting to belong. So there is thus a certain overdetermination on the relation of causality here between these two elements, the personal/social and the intellectual. Ang is arguing that there is 'a nasty bit of how people function', which grants social hierarchy a kind of intellectual gate-keeping function, while at the same time recalling the desire for social acceptance in her own history. This overdetermination is figured in the change in sentence structure at the relevant point: '. . . and also—and I had something to say . . .'. The more difficult subordinate structure implied by 'and also' is abandoned for the simple conjunction 'and', and so the necessity of specifying exact relations is evaded. What might have been a risky story for us two is modified. The elements of the personal/social and the intellectual are just joined together.

(ii) The Topic of Dallas

Ang's complex account of the genesis of the *Dallas* project is matched by a similarly sophisticated understanding of the central concerns of the research. These, as she makes clear, both are and are not to do with soap opera:

> I was much more interested in the tensions that the pleasure of *Dallas* creates at different levels—for the viewers themselves but also in a larger cultural context. I think my book is not so much about the pleasure of *Dallas* but more *Dallas* as something that acquires meaning in many different contexts. (IA: 10)

She returns to the question of whether the book was about *Dallas* later:

IA: So I was wondering, this book, I do still feel that in a way it's about soap opera, but it's also not about soap opera.

CB: Okay, so what's it about?

IA: In fact, it's much more about cultural contradiction. And that's something I think—the bigger theme for me, I think

all my work is about that and it's just—soap opera and
Dallas was a convenient subject, a concrete theme, through
which I can explore this idea of cultural contradiction.
(IA: 14)

The notion of the 'convenient subject' condenses Ang's claim about
her intellectual project ('it's much more about cultural contradiction.
And that's . . . the bigger theme for me') with a recognition of historical contingency. *Dallas*, as we have already observed, was an international topic in the early 1980s—there was, as Ang herself refers to
it, 'a soap opera moment'. However, while claiming in 'convenience' a
certain lack of premeditation and engagement, Ang is careful at this
point to differentiate herself from other contributors to the soap
opera moment, specifically, John Fiske. She argues that they are
involved in a project of legitimation, a claiming of positive cultural
value for this 'convenient subject':

IA: . . . these pleasures are never innocent, are never—that's why
      I think the Fiskian project is not mine.
CB: Yes, yes, now that's—can you differentiate 'cos that's—'cos
      that's—'cos also its neither the Hobson project, in fact the
      Hobson project and the Fiske project are closer.
IA: Yes, much closer, they are in the project of making something
      legitimate. (IA: 14)

The differentiation she makes is partly in the refusal of the notion
of 'innocent pleasures', which she does not expand, but which can
perhaps be most usefully related to her description of her earlier,
motivating question, 'what does it mean to like *Dallas*?', and partly
through a radical separation of her own work from a project of legitimation. Her own project is presented quite abstractly—the investigation of cultural contradiction—and its specific embodiment, the
case of *Dallas*, as convenient. The definition of her own intellectual
project at this level of abstraction anticipates comments such as

it's more like a kind of detective work or very much—the
deconstructive mode is very important, I think, in my work and
there's always this desire to show people that things are more
complicated than they think it is. (IA: 19)

She defines her own project negatively, and to an extent formally ('a
kind of detective work'), a pursuit of clues and logics, an undoing of
assumptions, a destabilizing of secure positions: 'this desire to show
people that things are more complicated than they think it is'. In this
account though, this description of a 'negative' deconstructive project is consistently articulated with a more positive project, 'to show
people'. In each account of each new project, Ang uses a term like

'show' or 'prove', and she frequently also, as we saw with the discussion of the *Skrien* board, has a very specific audience in mind: 'my writing was in fact especially for those people'.

This construction of a persona who will prove something—surely, precisely, one of the ways in which the persona of intellectual is constituted—is particularly vivid in her discussion of the period when she is doing the *Dallas* work:

> IA: Absolutely—and I'm sure I also wanted to prove something with the book, absolutely.
>
> CB: What do you think you wanted to prove?
>
> IA: I think several things. Once of course just the very simple thing that it was, that the pleasure of a programme like this is not something simple. And also, as a more academic kind of proving yourself, that it was possible to do research in this kind of area. In a way I think I had a lot of people on my mind when I was writing it—'You'll see, I will come up with something good'. A lot of people were just, 'You're doing something on *Dallas*, how is that possible?' I mean, I'm sure a lot of the women who've written about soap opera have had that experience.
>
> CB: Oh yes. Well also people just feeling it had to be a joke really, that it can't be true.
>
> IA: Yes, and they were all like, 'Ha, ha ha', that kind of reaction, 'Oh now you're doing *Dallas* I'm sure your next project will be about *Dynasty*'. I heard that more than once. (IA: 6)

Here, Ang at several points dramatizes the scenarios she recounts, going into an imaginary address to sceptics when she says, 'You'll see, I will come up with something good', but also assuming the character of the sceptics as they make bad jokes and laugh at her research. She has two clear points she wants to make—that enjoying this type of programme is not a simple matter, and that these issues are an appropriate area of serious study. She also generalizes her own experience ('I'm sure a lot of the women who've written on soap opera'), a point with which I concur in the interview, and which all the other interviews in this research support. So on the one hand we have a confident response to ridicule—the equivalent of 'I'll show you . . .'—a ridicule that all the other interviewees suffered, and on the other hand, I want to argue that there are quite specific inflections in this response which characterize an element of Ang's intellectual persona. This can be explored further in the description of the move from the soap work to the audience work:

> But certainly about this subject I think because it's about soap opera, talking about the relationship of what I've done after that,

the new project, the *Desperately Seeking the Audience* project, was very much also motivated by a kind of—that I wanted to show people that I'm not only the person of *Dallas*, that I also have something to say about these large-scale policy issues, that was a very important kind of—I'm driven to prove that what I'm doing is important, that certainly there is something about that. (IA: 8)

Here we see again the double inflection. First, Ang is quite explicit about the need to establish her ability in a 'serious' arena ('I also have something to say about these large-scale policy issues'), and one could argue that the experience of doing research on soap opera, and the type of reaction it provoked, necessitated a move into a 'heavy' field. She in fact returns to the theme of the low prestige of academic work on soap opera right at the end of the interview, arguing that there is still a need, in certain contexts, to maintain the polemic. However, in this passage she also suggests that she is 'driven to prove that what I'm doing is important', which I have suggested is the other side of her 'deconstructive urge'.

(iii) A Gendered Audience

As with most of the interviews, the description of starting the *Dallas* research, and particularly the audience part of this research, is presented as a mixture of deliberation and chance. The deliberation comes through two premises: first, 'the one thing that nobody asked about was what the viewers themselves thought about it' (IA: 4), and second, 'I was quite sure that there was something like an ideology of mass culture, but I didn't have the evidence . . .' (IA: 4). It is in relation to the first point that Ien Ang introduces the idea of chance:

It was textual analysis generally, or maybe very, very big surveys that were done by the ratings companies, that was everything that people thought could be said about the audience, and that ad that was the starting point for the book that was a real accident. Most of the ads were 'I'm looking for an Elvis Presley record, who can help me?', that kind of ad. And then I put this ad in, with the idea well maybe something will come out, maybe not—I mean that was just a complete hunch, and then I got this wonderful material and I just knew I had to do something about it or with it. So it just grew. (IA: 4)

It is the two formulations of fortune and intuition—'that was a real accident' and 'that was just a complete hunch'—which are most interesting here. First, this way of talking about a key point of access in the research recurs in other interviews, most noticeably in Dorothy Hobson's, where I discuss the strategy at length. It clearly is the case, if we take the evidence of these accounts, that a certain kind of coincidence can have considerable effects in a research project. However, if we look closely at Ang's statement, we see that not much is in fact 'accidental'—it was perhaps unusual to put an advertisement about research in a popular magazine, and she clearly thought that it was possible that nothing would come of it ('with the idea well maybe something will come out, maybe not . . .')—but she did literally, take the chance. She modifies the 'accidental' formulation slightly when she refers to the placing of the 'ad' as 'a complete hunch', a point which she develops in response to my question about a gendered audience. Although I have already quoted part of this passage in Chapter 5, the introduction to the interviews, I want here to look at the whole sequence:

> CB: Do you think you had an idea about a female audience, a gendered audience?
>
> IA: Absolutely, absolutely, from the very beginning.
>
> CB: Can you say anything more about that? So you were expecting it to be women—obviously you placed it in women's—it's a women's magazine? so you were expecting women to write?
>
> IA: Yes.
>
> CB: It was so obvious you didn't think about it?
>
> IA: Yes, it was obvious to me. And the point is that those kind of things—I do think like in cultural analysis intuition is a very good thing. When you know a culture and you live in it yourself and you're sensitive enough you can see those kind of things. That's the problem with a lot of the hard-core Social Sciences that they would never, never use that whereas I think that's where—that brings you further. They won't accept that fact unless they have hard statistics a little bit, and that seems like calculated ignorance at times on their part. It was also quite clear just in talking about it. In fact the first person who pointed—who told me that she liked watching *Dallas* was my sister, who has always been a very avid television fan and she was—at that time it was in the very beginning of *Dallas*, the very first season, and I didn't see it and I was not very aware of it yet at that time, but she told me to watch it. (IA: 7)

The first point to make about this passage is the way in which I have to work quite hard to get Ien to say anything much about the gendered audience, which I think rather supports her point about the obviousness of this fact. However, the more significant point is the move from a hard-line defence of the role of 'intuition' in cultural analysis to the introduction of her sister. Just as earlier in the interview, Ien had

talked of being the only *Skrien* writer to comment on her personal response to *Dallas*, we have here the role of a family member in encour-
aging her to watch. Although on the one hand, Ien argues quite
convincingly that there was a certain arbitrariness in the choice of
Dallas, on the other she demonstrates a theoretical and methodological commitment to the significance of personal experience, which
was, in the feminist approach to soap opera, seen as one of the key
characteristics of the genre. The point can be developed through an
analysis of Ien's discussion of the viewers' letters she receives in response to the ad:

> I do remember reading those letters and being very, very much
> reassured by the recognition I found. Somehow, the letters, a lot
> of those letters—none of the letters was quite surprising to me.
> Of course the details were—but not—in a way I already knew
> which theory would be correct, some sort of intuition that I had
> and in a way, like for example the melodramatic aspects, this idea
> of suffering, that I found most interesting [*laughs*]. It was really
> the thing I found most interesting about *Dallas*, and I didn't see
> that at all in the press clippings etc. etc. but they were very clearly
> present in the letters so that in that sense I found sort of, hey,
> you know, I'm not the only one (IA: 5)

This comment has its own poignancy, again matched in other interviews, and clearly marked by Ang herself when she laughs after saying
that it was the idea of suffering that she found most interesting. But
there is also here a very complicated dialectic of recognition at both
an experiential/emotional and a theoretical level. Thus, in a classic
formulation which recalls very strongly feminist accounts of the discovery of 'the personal as political', she says that the letters enable her
to think, 'hey, you know, I'm not the only one', and discusses the relief
of recognition, 'I do remember . . . being very, very much reassured'.
At the same time, she is pursuing a theoretical agenda: 'in a way
I already knew which theory would be correct, some sort of
intuition . . '. These two vectors are condensed in the quiet phrase
'none of the letters was quite surprising to me', which pulls together
the emotional recognition and the theoretical arguments about 'the
ideology of mass culture'.

In this assertion of the value of intuition in cultural analysis, the
recognition of the skills and competences of everyday life, Ang is
making a theoretical argument, but she makes it, in part, as the position demands, feelingly. The refusal of what she calls 'calculated ignorance' produces passages of analysis such as this:

> Because when you speak about real viewers then you must allow
> for contradiction, the pleasure in *Dallas* is a certain pleasure but

it also—people are also always a little bit disappointed. That's always there. Maybe that's not so clear in this book, but that's how I look at it now, it's much more—it's always a combination of pleasure and displeasure and the way in which watching a soap opera is on the one hand very pleasurable but on the other hand there are always things missing that you would have liked—the story to go, whatever, those kind of—that tension, that's I think the most important thing that still needs to be developed perhaps, theorizing about the viewing experience. (IA: 13)

Here, Ien extrapolates from her own experiences in combination with what she learnt from other viewers. The passage moves from 'you' speaking about 'real viewers' to 'people' (who are also always a little bit disappointed), to the speaking 'I', to the combination of these figures in the key analytic statement 'it's always a combination of pleasure and displeasure and the way in which watching a soap opera is on the one hand very pleasurable but on the other hand there are always things missing that you would have liked'. The ambivalence of watching is very precisely delineated and quite clearly delineated from inside the experience. This 'inside-ness' is in some ways the opposite of the marginality also present at several different levels in this interview. It is an inclusion in a viewing community, but also, as this last section has suggested, in a gendered identity, while at the same time, much of the interview is concerned with not occupying stable positions, and indeed with a deconstructive urge to be 'else-where'—a key constituent of doing intellectual work. So once again we see how complex are the positions from which the soap opera work emerged.

10

'A Sense of Trying to Valorize Soap Opera as Women's TV': Ellen Seiter

ELLEN **S**EITER was working as an Associate Professor teaching Telecommunication and Film at the University of Oregon at Eugene at the time of this interview. She went to Eugene in 1981 after completing her Ph.D. at North Western University in Evanston, Illinois. Going to North Western involved a return to Chicago for Ellen since her family had lived there when her father was alive: 'When he was alive we lived in a big house in the northern suburbs of Chicago and were even the first Catholics on the block—quite a sign of coming up in the world.'[1] Ellen describes her background as 'Irish-American Catholic, middle class—but precariously so due to early death of male head of household for three generations in a row. High on cultural capital (all four grandparents college-educated) but very short on cash.'[2] The early death of her father particularly affected Ellen, the youngest of five siblings. She says:

> After he died we moved for the first time to San Diego and my mother began to move around quite a lot . . . By the 1970s the other siblings had left home and my mother and I set off on a rather unconventional life, moving frequently and living a life of a more precarious—not to say downwardly mobile—status. She never again owned any real estate, we lived in modest apartments in which she and I had to share a bedroom, we didn't have a car, we didn't have health insurance, etc. And I went through school as far as I could as fast as I could because I still had social security money from my father coming in until I was 21.[3]

---

1 Author letter, 7 Oct. 1993.

2 Author questionnaire.

3 From Ellen's 7 Oct. 1993 letter additional to the author questionnaire. She prefaces this letter observing: 'I've noticed from my classes and in my research that no one resists reduction to classic sociological demographics as much as academics, so here I go, resisting away.' There is in fact considerable symmetry in the balance between the amount of extra-interview family background information Ellen gave me and the

Ellen published two articles on soap opera in the early 1980s, both of which argue against the contemporary contempt for the genre (Seiter 1982*a* and *b*). In particular, she uses Umberto Eco's semiotic theories of active reading to validate the skills and competencies of the female soap opera viewer, and so she offered a very early feminist argument about both the activity and the skills of the woman viewer. She continued to write on daytime serial drama, popular television, German women film-makers, and family melodrama throughout the 1980s, but the emphasis on television increased as the decade progressed (Seiter 1985*a*; 1985*b*; 1986; 1987). This became most pronounced after she won a Fulbright scholarship to Germany for 1986/7. With Hans Borchers, Gabriele Kreutzner, and Eva-Maria Warth, Ellen was funded by the Volkswagen Foundation for a cross-cultural study of the reception of American soap opera which was based in Eugene and Tuebingen, West Germany between October 1986 and March 1988. This ambitious project required fieldwork which was carried out in pairs by the team (different combinations, but always one German member). Most of the fieldwork utilized long semi-structured interviews with individual viewers, but Kreutzner, Seiter, and Warth also conducted all-female group discussions (Seiter et al. 1989*a*). During this period, Volkswagen also supported a week-long international symposium on 'Re-Thinking the Audience: New Directions in Television Research' of which Ellen was the chief organizer. Some of the proceedings of this conference were then published as *Remote Control*, edited by the research group (Seiter et al. 1989*b*). This volume contains the only account in English of the research project in a composite article which has several sections explicitly authored by different individuals. Seiter and Kreutzner, in their co-authored contribution, report on their interviews with women with particular attention to their investigation of Tania Modleski's model of the 'ideal mother' viewing position for soap opera viewers (Modleski 1982). Seiter and Kreutzner argue that their research findings undermine the possibility of textually deducing the viewing positions adopted by real viewers. They suggest that their interviews invalidate the particular explanatory power Modleski attributes to a Freudian-derived repression hypothesis about female anger and argue that Modleski's 'ideal mother' position is one most accessible to middle-class white women. Working-class women are found to transgress the norms of femininity suggested in Modleski's article to be the necessary attributes of the soap opera viewer. They express anger, frequently identify jubilantly with the villainess, and tend to refuse the all-forgiving, all-understanding ideal mother position (Seiter and

significance of both her family of origin and her own family in the interview. That is, Ellen was the only person to write a letter additional to the questionnaire, and she is also the one who discusses her family most in the interview.

Kreutzner 1989: 237–42). This report on the Tuebingen project in English is disappointingly short, but even this brief account gives some sense of the complexity of the material produced in interviews with soap opera viewers.

Ellen Seiter's final reflections on the Tuebingen project took the form of an article published shortly before this interview, 'Making Distinctions: Case Study of a Troubling Interview' (Seiter 1990). This article reflects in some detail on the power relations in one of the interviews from the Tuebingen project, using the work of Pierre Bourdieu to think about the complex interplay of attitudes to television watching among the participants in the interview. Ellen uses this analysis to make a series of proposals—including, where possible, the publication of full transcripts—about the conduct of media ethnographic work. At the time of this interview Ellen was in the concluding stages of research on commercial children's culture which focused particularly on attitudes towards, and usages of, television. This has subsequently been published (1993) as *Sold Separately: Children's Television, Toys and Advertising* to considerable media response in the United States, and has been followed by *Television and New Media Audiences*, which deals mainly with different cultures of television in childcare.

This was the most informal of all the interviews, conducted when Ellen Seiter was staying at my house in Birmingham with her family in 1990. Ellen's young daughter, Anne, made her presence felt at various points in the interview, and there were several parenting breaks. This meant that the interview was very long, but also more disconnected than the other interviews. Ellen is the only one of my interviewees with young children and much of the latter part of the interview was spent in a discussion of children, feminist ideas about gender, and parental attitudes to children's television viewing. Clearly, this is to some extent a discussion of the research project that Ellen was at that point engaged in, and the last section of the interview analysis below investigates the relationships Ellen poses between the new work and the earlier work on soap opera. However, in some ways there is a decisive shift in balance from what can still be called interview, to what is more properly 'conversation', and conversation that is repeatedly sparked by Anne's appearances and 'noises off'. As with the latter part of the Terry Lovell interview, a discussion about the literary canon, I have not used this later material.

This visit was Ellen's first chance to watch British television in a domestic context in a sustained manner, and the comparison of British and US television forms a recurring topic in the interview. She is the only US interviewee, and these concerns do not emerge in any comparable manner in the other interviews. I start the analysis of the interview by discussing Ellen's observations about the differences between British and US television, and then move on to the two main themes of the interview: soaps in relation to Ellen's family of origin, and soaps in the academic context and her experience as researcher and teacher. The final part of the analysis deals with the move to the children's television project, and some retrospective comments about the soap project.

(i) British and US Contexts for Research on Soap Opera

In the period in which this interview was conducted, there was considerable debate about the future of British broadcasting which had been provoked by the publication of the Government Green Paper 'Competition, Choice and Quality', which included the proposal that the ITV franchises would be awarded to the highest bidder. That is, although there was discussion of the 'quality threshold', these proposals marked a significant shift away from a public service ethos towards a more straightforwardly commercial one. This could be seen as a move closer to the more straightforwardly commercial US TV system. As already mentioned, I was interested in this debate at the time, and particularly in the way in which I thought there was a demand that radical critics of television should re-engage with notions of 'quality' (Brunsdon 1990). At one point in the second part of this interview I explained about the Green Paper and what I thought was at stake:

> CB: ... does that make sense?
>
> ES: It does make sense, and of course the whole issue about what's happening now—there was always something very reassuring to hear people in Britain talking about American television like it's OK because of course there's this enormous weight of guilt of cultural imperialism, right—but there is the other side of that, from the US side as well which is this sort of horror and at just how far things have gone and how much they've burgeoned—(ES: 2.23)

The jump Ellen makes here, in the context of a discussion about 'quality', is to move to a retrospective comment about what it was like to be from the USA and to hear the British popular culture/cultural studies defences of US television. This defence was particularly reassuring because it came from a radical political position, one that would recognize—and be expected to bewail the effects of—American cultural imperialism. Ellen points here to a feature of the history of the study of popular culture which seems easily forgotten in the current wave of attacks on cultural populism, which is the significance of the non-US originated defences of US popular culture.[4] However, she

---

4 For example, Hebdige (1981) and Ang (1985).

moved on to interrogate the grounds on which she found the British defence of US television 'reassuring' a little later in the interview, where she pursues the differences of the two national broadcasting environments:

ES: . . . and then you look at PSB [Public Service Broadcasting] in the States, I've been thinking about that since I've been here, you look at PSB in the States and there's not anything worth defending, I mean there's really almost nothing worth defending, it's abominable TV, it's disgusting in its high culture—

CB: Just terrible, I mean just, I could never watch it, I mean when I was—

ES: —and it's so self-congratulatory and it's just terrible, but I think one thing that at least ought to come out now is that, it's like there's been this miscommunication going on over—

CB: —a sort of camaraderie—

ES: —over Europeans liking American TV and the reasons why Americans talking about American TV being both more guilt-ridden and in a certain way more important at home. Because I—since just being here this week I realize, I mean the TV is just really a lot [*pause*] better here.

CB: But what does that mean? [*laughter*] (ES: 2.28–2.30)

I completely misunderstood what Ellen is trying to say here when I interject 'a sort of camaraderie'—which is, indeed, what there has been between researchers on popular television across the Atlantic. But what she is trying to say is that it was to some extent founded on misunderstandings, that watching US imports in Britain is quite different to watching the same shows in the USA. We might have thought we were talking about the same thing, but we weren't: 'it's like there's this miscommunication going on'. In the current context, I think this point is particularly important in relation to what all the different researchers meant by 'soap opera'. She and I met, and became friends talking about what we thought about how viewers dealt with soap operas.

At that point, I had never seen any US daytime soaps, and she had never seen any British ones. In a way, the imprecision was not incorrect, because it was the connotational and metaphorical value of 'soap opera' with which we were concerned. What Ellen raises here, though, is real differences of the overall national broadcasting contexts, something which has not been much attended to in cultural studies literature. She suggests that it now seems to her that the defence of US popular culture by Europeans has in some sense been taken literally by Americans like herself, whereas in fact the context in which the Europeans are seeing the US material is equally significant.

(ii) Starting to Work on Soap Opera

There are two main vectors in Ellen Seiter's account of starting to work on soap opera, one constituted through relationships with her family, particularly her mother and sister, the other through college/academic work. Not surprisingly, these two structuring sets of relationship are in some ways quite closely imbricated, which I will discuss after outlining Ellen's presentation of each. As with all the interviews, this conversation is marked by a strong self-consciousness which is differently articulated, using different frameworks, in each interview. Thus for example, Terry Lovell constantly contextualizes each element of her account in relation to contemporary British theoretical debate and the interview itself, whereas reference points for Dorothy Hobson are drawn mainly from a discussion of interviewing techniques and developments within the British television industry. Ellen Seiter, who discusses the significance to her of Pierre Bourdieu's work on the sociology of taste within the interview, and who had recently published an article which uses this work, is I think implicitly using a workaday 'Bourdieuian' schema to reflect on the story she tells (Bourdieu 1984). An example of this, which I think governs much of her discussion of teaching and child-rearing, is her account of how she began to watch *General Hospital* in 1979:

> What happened was I met a woman who started the programme at that time—Lisa Lewis—and she and I would go to the cafeteria every day and eat our lunch at two o'clock, which was the only time graduate students hung out with the staff in the cafeteria. It was a huge room with like maybe seventy-five seats and it was the first [*inaudible: one word*] projected television video thing so we were watching that then, just about every day and the group got larger, you know, larger and larger, and some men would come and watch too, although none of the men I was involved with of course, they wouldn't be caught dead [*laughs*]. So I decided that I would write about that . . . (ES: 1.4–15)

> so then I just started writing about *General Hospital*. And that was by the way, a time, 1978–9, when like *millions* [*her emphasis*] of people in the United States started watching specifically *General Hospital* at that time, and when *General Hospital* had a producer that started trying to reach younger women, they brought in William M—so—, and there was this plot around Luke and Laura, that you know, so although I wasn't aware of that at the time, to be the age that I was then and to start watching that show, you know it was definitely a mass movement [*laughter*]. (ES: 1.10)

What Ellen does here is to embed her own, autobiographical account ('I met a woman who just started [watching] the programme') into an informed retrospective account of the demographic targets and profiles of *General Hospital* at this period. Once again, there is the vivid evocation of the ritual of soap viewing ('and she and I would go to the cafeteria every day and eat our lunch at two o'clock', 'and the group got larger, you know, larger and larger'), the very clear memory of the daily commitment, and then the slightly ironic recognition of being 'called' by a series of strategies of the production team. Thus the production detail ('when *General Hospital* had a producer that started trying to reach younger women') prepares the ground for the recognition that what she had experienced as a set of unique and individual choices was also a wider social pattern in the USA ('you know, it was definitely a mass movement'). It is this embedding of personal choice within wider social trends and patterns of taste, 'and that was by the way, a time, 1978–9, when like *millions* of people in the United States started watching specifically *General Hospital*', with its ironic juxtaposition of 'millions' and 'specifically', which I understand to be deeply informed by the work of Bourdieu, and this set of preoccupations with taste and place recurs throughout the interview as we shall see below.

The other point to note here is the inscription of gender through the discussion of male viewers. As with Christine Geraghty's account of her father's viewing, there is here a heavy reliance on shared understanding between the two of us having the conversation, indicated most strongly by the use of 'of course'. Thus Christine says, 'My father despises television of course', counting on my familiarity with attitudes to television among the British middle classes, and particularly middle-class men, to decode the strength of the investment in 'despises', to see through the 'of course' that this would be the only attitude to television her father would consider it appropriate to have. And there is also, of course, a recognition of a certain irony, given his daughter's interest. With Ellen, similar assumptions are in play, despite greater cultural differences, when it comes to talking about men and soap opera, and there is a similar reliance on what can be left unsaid. The irony is perhaps more explicit, as she is describing what is for her a formative viewing pattern while a student: 'and some men would come and watch too, although none of the men I was involved with of course, they wouldn't be caught dead [*laughs*]'. She laughs—we both laugh—at the recognition that while she is getting involved in these programmes which she will write about as women's culture, she is involved with men who couldn't possibly be seen to watch them. This is laughter about contradiction, about wanting to assert the significance of traditionally undervalued feminine concerns and pleasures, but at the same time having romantic investments in much more macho and misogynous forms of masculinity. We can laugh, perhaps slightly ruefully, at the impossibility of our own desires—implicit here is the recognition that neither of us would have considered suitable as a romantic partner a man who *did* watch soap opera in 1979.

The graduate group viewing that Ellen describes here, which in some ways is the immediate spur to her first written work on soap opera, is preceded in her account by what she describes almost as 'soap opera familiarization' conducted mainly by her sister. Thus she describes being told how to watch, rather than being brought up to watch. Here I will offer a quite long set of sequences from the interview before comment:

> ES: ... but the real part of it was that before that when I was in college my sister who was then in law school started talking to me all the time about *The Young and the Restless* and saying you should really watch this.
>
> CB: Is that because she thought it was telling her things about her life or—
>
> ES: She just loved it. And my sister is somebody who aspires— my sister was in sociology and she likes to think of herself as completely normal, she likes to read the *National Enquirer*, and she likes to have her finger on the pulse of sort of popular culture and she has been consistently sort of my informant— (ES: 1.5–16)

But what happened because it's very clear to me about just sort of the introduction to soap operas, because nobody watched, my mother always worked, and nobody, there was no daytime television, she [*sister*] started watching it during her break from classes and law school and then that year I would go up and visit her, I spent a lot of time visiting her, as a teenager, you know, sort of going wild, you know, away from home, and on this vacation she would force me to watch it, and she would ask me when she was phoning me up at college about, 'Are you watching?' you know, 'Can you find a student lounge where you can watch it?' So that was kind of the background, but I never was really around a TV enough to watch it. (ES: 1.7–18)

By this time my mother was living in Chicago and working as a legal proof-reader and she was then starting—she didn't used to have a job where you would talk about television but then there was a radio that they brought to the office where she was a legal proof-reader and her partner, a black woman lived on the south side of Chicago, was listening to the soap opera so there was that kind of interest that I, you know, then I found this time of day that I could then watch this one and then she was also talking to me about it, and both my mother and my sister, as you know, it was very important, and I was kind of horrified when my sister first

started talking about them, you know, I did think, I did kind
of wonder about her and I didn't have a particularly strong
stereotype about it, but it was just completely foreign to be doing
that. My mother then was totally open to it at her work and stuff
and clearly saw it as, you know, something that you could talk to
women who were much younger, so anyway, and then there was
this melodrama class. (ES: 1.10–1.11)

The process which Ellen describes here, her induction into soap
opera viewing, consistently elevates the family relationships in play
above the viewing. Soaps, and soap viewing, are consistently described, as with other interviewees, as a medium of exchange. Soap
viewing or listening clearly gives the viewer something to talk about:
'and her [my mother's] partner, a black woman lived on the south
side of Chicago, was listening to the soap opera, so there was that kind
of interest'. Something in common, perhaps in a context where other
differences made conversation less easy: 'My mother . . . clearly saw
it as, you know, something that you could talk to women who were
much younger.' Soap opera in this context is a useful resource which
enables the viewer to join in conversations from which she would
otherwise be excluded: 'then I found this time of day that I could then
watch this one and then she was also talking to me about it, and both
my mother and my sister, as you know, it was very important'. I think
what is noticeable here is Ellen's relief at being able to join in ('then I
found this time of day . . .'), in a context when she is away from
family members to whom she was very close ('and both my mother
and my sister, as you know, it was very important').

Like Christine Geraghty, this move into being a family that watches
soap happens relatively late—in contrast to, for example, Terry's
description of growing up with *Coronation Street*—and seems to involve the almost conscious embrace of the transactional possibilities
offered by a shared viewing. Ellen is quite clear that 'nobody watched,
my mother always worked, and nobody, there was no daytime television'. She negotiates her account of the memory of the change in family patterns quite carefully, for she has to bring together her obvious
reluctance with her later work:

> I was kind of horrified when my sister first started talking about
> them, you know, I did think, I did kind of wonder about her and
> I didn't have a particularly strong stereotype about it, but it was
> just completely foreign to be doing that. (ES: 1.10)

Because much of Ellen's subsequent work on soap opera has been
concerned to validate the skills and competencies of soap viewers, to
attack what she refers to here as the stereotype about soap viewing,
and this work in a way could be seen to delegitimate her own initial

reaction, 'I was kind of horrified . . .', this sentence has to hold together quite disparate attitudes. The strength of the initial response ('horrified') is immediately placed in relation to a sense of the social hierarchy of tastes ('I didn't have a particularly strong stereotype about it . . .'), and in what is almost a disavowal, the horror is attributed to the 'foreignness' to the family culture of discussing soaps, to a local disturbance, rather than to the wider social endorsement of the stereotype. Particularly significant in Ellen's account is the role of her sister ('she would force me to watch it and she would ask me when she was phoning me up at college about, "Are you watching?"'), both as a soap instructress and as someone who wielded authority in this field partly through her professed 'normality', the way in which she is in touch with popular culture in a way which by implication Ellen is not, or does not feel herself to be, or is not treated as if she is: 'she likes to think of herself as completely normal, she likes to read the *National Enquirer*, and she likes to have her finger on the pulse of sort of popular culture and she has been consistently sort of my informant' (ES: 1.5–1.6).

(iii) Soaps and Academic Life: 'And Then There Was This Melodrama Class'

The story Ellen Seiter tells about learning to view and talk about soap opera in her family of origin is imbricated with another story of an increasing engagement with soap opera in an academic context. This starts with taking a class on cinema melodrama at North Western University, and, like Ien Ang, reaches a particular significance in the required choice for a dissertation topic:

> So then I just started writing about it, and just kind of figuring
> out the rules of it, and applying, but at that time applying things
> about nineteenth-century stage melodrama to soap opera,
> so that by the end of that year, and Chuck Kleinhans was very
> enthusiastic about what I was writing about soap opera, so that
> by the end of that year, you know, I sort of needed a dissertation
> topic and chose that and these teen pics from the seventies . . .
> (ES: 1.11)

This is 1979, a point at which there was already a certain amount of published work on film melodrama, which concentrated particularly on the representation of the family and women therein (Elsaesser 1972; Kleinhans 1978; Mulvey 1977). Ellen Seiter is the youngest of my interviewees, and it is noticeable that she does at this stage have the option of taking a course on melodrama. Her innovation is to use material about theatrical and cinema melodrama to think about soap opera, but we also see an interest in 'figuring out the rules' of this genre which is not unlike Christine Geraghty's concern with the narrative conventions of soap opera. Significantly, in comparison with the ridicule some of the other interviewees met, Ellen was offered support by her professor, and had a good public response when she first presented her work:

ES: So I was first using all the melodrama, you know, I read Tania Modleski's thing, I read Carol Lopate, I read Renata Adler, you know, Laura Mulvey, you know, was around all that time but what I thought I was doing was, I did, you know, which I'm sometimes still interested in doing is crossing film and television stuff, and I tried to look at all the supporting materials within *Soap Opera Digest*. I'd just look at the production, the advertising packages on the films, and all of that and then I was in that Feminar group that started at the same time—

CB: Which did the *Film Reader*?

ES: Which did the *Film Reader* and did the conference. So I gave the paper at that conference and it was wildly well received, you know, a sort of very early public paper about soap opera, including that the people who put up the money for the conference, and who then had all of us to this cocktail party and stuff, I was the one—they chose my paper to go to, and they chose me to talk about because they were sort of closet soap opera viewers. (ES: 1.12–1.14)

The key element here, in terms of the way Ellen tells her story, is the way in which this paper, which was 'wildly well received', appeals particularly strongly to the non-academics present, to the conference funders: 'I was the one—they chose my paper to go to, and they chose me to talk about because they were sort of closet soap opera viewers.' Ellen's work particularly—although this is a feature of all the work I am discussing—seems absolutely poised on the making public of 'closet soap opera' viewing. There is a repeated sense of the exhilaration she feels ('wildly well received') when she uses her legitimating authority as an academic to address and sometimes celebrate the skills and pleasures of soap opera viewing. However, this legitimating exhilaration is also related to a quite complex and contradictory inhabiting of the position of the academic:

I think the thing for me was that I had, you know, I was coming out of this experimental film thing and also these sort of fantasies of being a film-maker, so when I switched over to criticism, the kind of giving up of being a film-maker was—well, already about something really popular, and that you—that's something that— all the—I mean, it still happens to me constantly that people will sort of light up and start talking about soap opera, and that it's kind of a way of being an academic with thinking that you're still kind of 'in touch' in some way. (ES: 1.14–1.15)

This passage, with all its shifts of direction in the middle, is setting up several key oppositions:

experimental film making : criticism of a popular television genre; being an academic : being 'in touch';

and I think, by implication,

being dull/bored : 'lighting up'.

I am not suggesting that Ellen is unconscious of these oppositions— indeed I understand her to be telling a story of an intellectual biography which can be most easily understood through the repeated conscious privileging of the second term in each pair. The renouncing of the fantasy of being a film-maker, the key choice here, was 'already about something really popular'. The development of the work on soap opera amplifies this dimension of the choice, and clearly offers very particular rewards:

I still like that big bang that you get in like a feminist criticism class about switching to soap opera and the way that suddenly students are talking in a way—who do not normally talk and also what happens with the women and the men in the class. So I think the initial thing to me was also getting you know—was very much a sense of trying to valorize soap opera as women's TV, and it was also a point, then in the mid-seventies, when there was all this about, the mass comm. stuff, was about the absence of women, the Gaye Tuchman stuff, the symbolic annihilation thing so a lot of the initial impulse was just to sort of say, 'Look, here's something where there are lots of women on the screen and you can—so let's talk about this because that the representation we're getting, so let's sort of take that apart.' (ES: 1.17–1.18)

The first part of this passage, recounting again the excitement and pleasure teaching this material gives Ellen ('I still like that big bang'), also offers an analysis which is constructed partly through a feminist enterprise ('trying to valorize soap opera as women's TV'). This feminist enterprise, referred to earlier in her membership of the Feminar, and discussed later in the reference to Gaye Tuchman's notion of 'the symbolic annihilation of women' (Tuchman 1978), is specifically exciting to Ellen in the context of the power relations in the classroom: 'the way that suddenly students are talking in a way—who do not normally talk and also what happens with the women and the men in the class'. The study of soap opera—the bringing of soap opera into the classroom—is clearly so enjoyable for Ellen because it has a political edge, it provokes a disruption of customary power relations.

Because, certainly in the early period of which Ellen speaks, soap opera was not a legitimate subject of academic enquiry and was also perceived as a clearly gendered genre, bringing it into the classroom, taking it seriously, disturbs and challenges both academic and social hierarchies. Later in the interview she discusses the way in which her 'heart's not in it anymore', but I think here we can see that part of the project, the project which has now made soap opera a very common part of many curricula, was the valorization of illegitimate tastes. It is in this context that her use of Umberto Eco's theories of reading was clearly strategic: 'but it was also this legitimation thing like, let's have some high theory in here to deal with it, although I still think that *The Role of the Reader* is very apt to dealing with these problems' (ES: 1.21).[5]

Just as the study of soap opera disrupts the classroom, it manages, for exactly the same reasons (popularity with women and illegitimacy as an object of study) to bridge the gap between Ellen the academic and her mother and sister:

CB: Is there a kind of political discourse in here which isn't quite coming out, which is sort of round a form that is accessible and, I don't know, do you see what I mean? And like, not wanting to be an academic academic?

ES: yes, and to me, you know, it is very explicitly wanting to still be able to talk to my mother and my sister about what I was doing. You know, like I don't really want to be spending all this time on something that nobody would ever talk to me about—yes—I mean it is that accessibility thing, and that I do believe in this thing and I sort of said the first time round that I do think that they're talked about, and they're reused, and that you could—and that old version of feminism, you know, the old idea about feminism and consciousness-raising and stuff, that you could really use them explicitly for that and that you sort of do in the classroom when you teach them. It's just that then they kind of got—things got kind of fixed on the openness of the readings, rather than just say, let's do a specifically feminist reading, and how might one actually just reproduce and encourage explicitly feminist readings of soap opera. Rather than, you know, what we kind of got at now from the interviews in Oregon is like, there is this sort of latent feminism in the readings of sort of ordinary women. But, what you sit there, and you interview them, and you don't say anything about the kind of reading you're

---

5 Eco's *The Role of the Reader* valorizes the 'open' as opposed to the 'closed' text in terms of reader activity. This was generally taken to valorize the modernist, avant-garde work, but Seiter argued that soap opera too demanded a skilled reader (Seiter 1982a).

> looking for, you know, would like to, make them very
> problematic. (ES: 1.24–1.26)

This complex passage is held together through the retention of a notion of soap opera as something that you can use, that you do things with, which is so significant in this interview. So first there is the repetition of the significance of the relationships with Ellen's mother and sister, the determination not 'to be spending all this time on something that nobody would ever talk to me about . . .'—and the 'nobody' is clearly the absence of her mother and sister—although she does go on to say that her husband watches soaps with her. So if there is a rejection of an academic career that would have as its research object something that would make her 'different', there is also a strongly politicized understanding of the classroom. This has obviously already appeared in Ellen's discussion of the disruptive qualities of soaps in the classroom. Here she speaks more explicitly about the consciousness-raising role of the feminist teacher, and then goes on to discuss the difficulties of the ethnographic fieldwork that she had recently completed as part of the Tuebingen project. The ambivalence of the feminist researcher researching 'ordinary women' is here invoked: 'there is this sort of latent feminism in the readings of sort of ordinary women. But, what you sit there, and you interview them, and you don't say anything about the kind of reading you're looking for . . .'. If I understand her correctly—and the passage is not without ambiguities—I think she is here suggesting that the traditional neutrality of the ethnographic researcher ('you don't say anything about the kind of reading you're looking for') is perhaps more problematic in terms of power than a rather more explicitly feminist engagement with the situation would be. So for Ellen, what seems partly to continue to animate her practices in relation to soap opera is a strongly politicized notion of the genre, both in its subordinate place within a clearly hierarchical culture and as a potential way in to political discussion.

It is this politicized view of soap opera—and of the potential of soap opera—and any attendant academic practices, which also partly informs Ellen Seiter's move away from work on the genre. This she discusses in relation to the racism of the US daytime soaps, and the racism of the white feminist defence of the genre:

> The other thing is that if you ever, and I think, and that was
> partly a turning point for me, if you ever want to get into looking
> at racial representation you begin to think, well, can I sort of
> endlessly defer? Do you really want to say that soap operas are so
> great when what goes on, for example, around black characters,
> is so obviously shitty, and it's obviously because you're just, you
> know, I remember giving the soap opera lecture that I get invited

to give constantly to x [African-American scholar] when she was
a student in the class and kind of feeling my cheeks burn sort of
for the first time around the very loud absences in that. Which is
one of the things that I'm getting into now is thinking is this stuff
about that the whole public/private sphere to me it seems like
from the feminist point of view the best argument that was made,
or at least the one I always wanted to make about soap operas,
was that they were dealing with the kind of unhappiness and
the public/private split and the way that that is experienced
detrimentally by women and that it was a way of airing power
relations in the family, but then you start looking at this stuff
by Aida Hurtado about where she's saying look that whole
public/private thing is really a white feminist issue, and privacy
as a privilege has not yet been experienced to the same degree,
I mean it just goes up in smoke then, the whole rationale for it.
(ES: 2.13–2.15)

This frank passage offers an account of several different stages in a
white feminist's thoughts about racism. Ellen offers an anatomy of a
range of relationships between a white self-understanding as anti-
racist and implications of this position in theory and practice. The
first is what we might call that of general intention, when an engagement with 'racial representation' is seen as necessary, is aspired to, but
is still pending. There is a political understanding that 'race' is a
significant issue, and this understanding is sophisticated in that it
incorporates a notion of the differential positioning of people in relation to this issue. The standpoint of white privilege is then articulated
and interrogated through the notion of 'deferral'. Racism is seen as
so pervasive and structuring that to engage with these issues from
the position of privilege requires a particular effort, a disruption: 'if
you ever want to get into looking at racial representation you begin
to think, well, can I sort of endlessly defer?' The notion of 'deferral' is
very precise here, in its invocation of an order of things (a world of
white privilege) which could just be left in place, despite the general
intention referred to above. To leave this world in place is recognized
as a deferral, and the available images of people of colour are also recognized as unacceptable: 'what goes on, for example, around black
characters, is so obviously shitty'. The validation of soaps as 'so great'
for women is thrown in crisis by the recognition that the world there
depicted is the privileged one of white women.

The catalyst here though, the event which Ellen recalls very vividly
as calling her on this issue, is the sensation of being witnessed by
a particular black scholar. Ellen recounts becoming conscious that
her standard lecture on soap opera does not pay what she realizes is
sufficient attention to issues of race and ethnicity: 'I remember giving

the soap opera lecture that I get invited to give constantly . . . and kind of feeling my cheeks burn sort of for the first time round the very loud absences in that.' The precision of the physical memory here ('and kind of feeling my cheeks burn') marks it as a significant experience, the embarrassment, despite other intentions, of occupying a position of white privilege ('the very loud absences'). This is clearly the 'turning point' to which she refers earlier in the passage.

This turning point leads to a third stage, that of the interrogation of existing paradigms, and their deconstruction. Here, it is the ethnic specificity of the private sphere which is revealed to be 'white'. Now Ellen moves into a theoretical interrogation of paradigms she had been using in the work on soap opera. What was seen as universal or pervasive is reseen as ethnically specific. The private/public separation, which has been analytically extremely significant for (white) feminist theory, and particularly for the analysis of soap opera, is reinterrogated, and seen as an aspect of white privilege: 'this stuff by Aida Hurtado about where she's saying look that whole public/private thing is really a white feminist issue, and privacy as a privilege has not yet been experienced to the same degree . . .' (Hurtado 1989).

For Ellen, thinking about these issues seems to radically undermine her interest in soap opera, and her sense that it is a defensible interest: 'I mean it just goes up in smoke then, the whole rationale for it.'

(iv) Leaving Soap Opera for *My Little Pony*

Ellen offers an account in which an increasing awareness of issues of racial and ethnic representation undermines her interest in soap opera[6] and, at the same time, her own life circumstances change with the birth of her first child, a daughter, in 1987. At the time of this interview, Ellen was most of the way through a long project on television and commercial children's culture. She is quite clear that one of the motives for this work was having children herself, and the way in which this transformed her television viewing and social life:

> I mean marketing is about gender differentiation because that's
> the first rule of marketing, you know, what's the first way you
> segment a market? You do it on gender. What I—it's these shows
> for girls which are the other embarrassment of what we could
> call the upper middle class, but certainly intellectuals, you know,
> you should just never let your kid, especially if you're a feminist,
> you should never let your kid do it, and one of the reasons why
> I have to is that my nieces have *My Little Pony*, you know, it's again
> this kind of refusal to change my habits, I don't want to change

---

6 It is at about this time that she writes 'Semiotics and Television' which uses the credits to *The Cosby Show* for its main example (Seiter 1987).

so much from my siblings that it actually creates conflict
(ES: 1.45–1.46)

It's saying, I'll go with my, I'll go with my family position on this
rather than—and then of course I must be worried about it to
some degree because I switched my whole field to children and
TV, but I let Anne start watching limitless amounts and playing
with whatever she wants (ES: 1.47)

Ellen explicitly invokes the same structure of 'family first' which had
informed the choice of soap opera as a research topic, and once again
shows a desire to be involved with contemporary popular culture. She
also, though, recognizes, with some irony, the special position of academics who research popular culture: 'of course, I must be worried
about it to some degree because I switched my whole field to children
and TV'. However, intellectually, the attraction also lies in the possibility of a more economically grounded analysis than was possible
with soaps. Children's television seems to offer more potential for the
realization of the 1970s Marxist-influenced paradigm of the analysis of
cultural production in which attention is paid to the economic organization of production, the commodity itself, and its consumption:

I felt that I had to respond seriously to the calls for joining
political economy and textual analysis so that's actually the major
difference and the reason why, I mean, children's television fits
sort of perfectly into that so you know it's similar in that there are
these issues of complete gender segregation but now I'm trying to
look at the way that those are mounted explicitly by a range of,
by advertising and manufacturers and market researchers—
    The thing about soap opera, you know, I did this stuff for a
project that I never wrote,—so for example I did interviews with
Esther Shapiro and these different staff writers, but—they do
think that they're sort of free agents in a way that's difficult to get
a hold on, so that if you're just dealing with the producers of the
show you can't really get at this kind of economic organization of
women as a market . . . (ES: 1.36–1.38)

But anyway, by dealing with those, you know, TV shows like
My Little Pony, it kind of solves this issue about the soap opera
producers where they think they're autonomous. (ES: 1.42–1.43)

Here Ellen offers a further insight into the ideology of soap opera producers ('they do think that they're sort of free agents in a way that's
difficult to get a hold on'), suggesting that in comparison, the producers of commodity-led children's shows have less sense of themselves as autonomous. The work on children and television involves
much that is similar to the early work on soap opera—particularly

when the programmes, such as *My Little Pony*, are members of a despised and clearly gendered genre. To discuss the new work further, though, would take us outside the bounds of this project, so I will close this final interview analysis with a brief bit of conversation between Ellen and myself:

CB: I did this talk recently—and they put to me the very very traditional critique, you know, which is, they said, 'Well but if you watch this',—and I showed them very moving bits from various bits of television, and they said, 'if you watch this, this is so degrading of your feelings'. I mean they were really offering me a high art argument, they—

ES: Like a Frankfurt School thing.

CB: Yes, almost, those kind of, well, not so much like that, but just sort of like, almost like, well it would be better to weep over a highly wrought fine art object.

ES: Yuh yuh.

CB: Weep over *The Winter's Tale*—

ES: I think it's still the existence of that that has meant that this thing has just dragged on for years and years, I think that's why I—like I get invited to talk about soap operas five times a year around the university or something and kind of go off and yeah yeah almost as a favour to the 19-year-old undergraduates who are getting sneered at by their boyfriends—

CB: That's right—

ES: But my heart's not really in it anymore [*laughs*] (ES: 2.12).

11

Commonalities: Writing Across the Interviews

BY presenting the interviews in a portrait format, I wanted to impede the transformation of the stories told there into the exemplification of another story—my story. I wanted to insist on a certain kind of intractability of the material. To suggest that the story each person told in response to my questions had a contingent and narrative particularity in which meaning and emphasis were significantly constructed internally. So, formally, I wanted to install at the core of the book the stories I was told when I asked key researchers if they could remember starting work on soap opera. By presenting these stories individually, I hope to have suggested something of the very different material grounding and circumstances of the work on soap opera, while not reducing that work to autobiography. Here, I want to address the commonalities, for all the interviewees have written significantly on soap opera, and all the research is started in the period between 1976 and 1982. All understood this work to have some connection with women, feminism, and audiences. Most have continued to be associated with this work for their professional lives. That is, all the interviewees have contributed to what is retrospectively the feminist revision of soap opera, and these contributions are commonly lumped together. So what did they say? What similarities and differences can we see, and can we draw any conclusion about these similarities and differences?

(i) Starting Work on Soap Opera: Outside the Academy	Although my interviewees are of different ages, they all started work on soap opera in the late 1970s. We can relate this directly to each of the historical maps already presented in the early part of this book. For example, *Dallas*, launched in 1978, is being broadcast internationally in the late 1970s, uniting many different audiences in the hermeneutics of Texan oil-rich patriarchy. 'Soap opera'—as *Dallas* was consistently referred to—as a term, became encrusted with newly

enriched symbolic meaning. As a set of programmes and viewing practices it became a noticeable international phenomenon which in its turn became an object of study for relatively traditional communications research (Katz and Liebes 1985). In relation to the temporal schema of feminist endeavour outlined in Chapter 1, we can see the interest of each interviewee in soap opera as an aspect of the 'return to the feminine' there sketched. That is, the interest in soap opera was, for feminists, the equivalent of interest in genres such as romance fiction and women's magazines; it was motivated, at least in part, by the same re-engagement with the feminine, but the conditions for this generically specific engagement were partly created by the expanding international market for the export of serial television drama. Feminist interest in soap opera is an effect or result of these factors, while in turn itself becoming an increasingly visible site for the reworking of meanings of both 'feminism' and 'soap opera', and thus having its own effectivity.

Given that it is through research such as the feminist work on soap opera that the academic existence of feminism has partly been constituted, what perhaps requires marking as one of the clearest findings of the interview analysis is the extra-academic origin of much of the research. Geraghty, Lovell, Ang, and Seiter all recount stories of doing critical intellectual work outside the academy. Hobson, although working within the academy, is working in one of its most politicized sites in Britain, the Centre for Contemporary Cultural Studies at Birmingham University. She is a member of the editorial group of the 'Women's Studies' journal published by CCCS/Hutchinson in 1978, one of a series of publications by CCCS designed to bring their research to a wider audience, and like many of them, marked by a profound instability of address, a hovering between an academic and a political readership (Women's Studies Group 1978). Geraghty and Lovell are members of the Women and Film Group based in London. This group brought together women in white-collar and educational posts with a loosely understood project of some juxtaposition of feminism and film. Meeting in the evenings, in people's houses, this group had a private/political agenda, rather than an academic/institutional one. I have discussed at length Christine Geraghty's description of their shared determination to find a joint project, something to focus their attention, which they understood in advance to be labelled 'women and . . .'. If this is juxtaposed with Terry Lovell's differently inflected account of the same group and project, what emerges is a strong sense of a taken-for-granted value of collective, political, intellectual work. The intellectual agenda is understood as set outside the academy, in relation to phenomena—like being a feminist and liking soap opera—that must be investigated, theoretical work that must be understood and connections (for example, between understandings of individual subjectivity and economic processes) that must be made. Ien Ang was a member of the editorial board of the Dutch journal *Skrien*, specifically recruited to write about popular television in a context where the reaffirmation of the value of classical Hollywood cinema was well under way. The project of understanding and writing seriously about popular television is conceptualized as meaningful without reference to the academy. Ellen Seiter, in a more academic context in the USA, was a member of the group of women at, or in contact with, North Western University who formed themselves as 'the Feminar' and organized a conference on Women and Film in 1981, and edited a special journal issue *Film Reader* 5 (1982). She was also associated with the editorial board of *Jump Cut*, a polemical film review magazine started in the 1970s with the specific aim of offering political criticism of Hollywood cinema.

That is, all my interviewees were, to a greater or lesser extent, engaged in a politically motivated intellectual project before they started doing the work on soap opera, and it is in this context that the work on soap opera first develops. In the period immediately after the social turbulence of the late 1960s, this project was, it seems clear, to some degree at least, an optimistic one. For people to be voluntarily engaging in often demanding and difficult intellectual work, in their own time, suggests that this work was felt as meaningful. These meanings were sought, differently, by different interviewees, in both political and personal perspectives. To say that the research starts outside the academy is to posit the historical existence of an 'outside', a leftist feminist culture which could generate and sustain reading and study groups in the 1970s. This is not the place to trace the history of this culture (these cultures), nor is it possible to generalize meaningfully across the UK, USA, and Holland. However, it is possible to trace other confirmations of the significance of this culture in Britain to certain directions of intellectual enquiry (many of which subsequently present as 'cultural studies') through accounts of the various extra-academic autodidactic reading groups mentioned, often casually, in some of the emerging histories of the left/feminist formations of the 1970s—for example Griselda Pollock's account of the formation of the Women's Art History Collective (Pollock 1993), or Denise Riley's sketch of 'some of the intellectual background to the work of people of "my generation"' (Riley 1992). What is at issue is not so much the particular intellectual formation—in Pollock's case the discipline of art history, in Riley's the engagement with Foucault—as the informing notion of an engaged, critical, intellectual practice. Denise Riley explains:

> Those of us who could somehow manage to research these
> questions saw our investigations as 'at the service of' feminist

politics and campaigns. In this we continued an aspiration of the late 1960s libertarian socialism which hoped for critical intellectual work to be done outside of the universities, to have an independent base. (1992: 124)

As Riley reminds us, her use of 'feminist' in this context is anachronistic. The preferred self-appellation of the 1970s was 'Women's Liberation', and in a way, it is precisely the passage from 'Women's Liberation' to 'Feminism' with which I am here concerned. For these groups were one of the sites of this transition. These little extra-academic groups were betwixt and between. They were engaging with feminist ideas, but their project was distinct from that of the consciousness-raising groups of Women's Liberation in the early seventies in that it was explicitly intellectual. However, this intellectual project was understood as fundamentally political. Pollock describes this extra-academic engagement with intellectual work as follows:

Across these various spaces—the stronghold of academic art history, the informal meeting of the collective in someone's front room, the visitors' balcony of the Houses of Parliament—I began to forge a practice, not *in* art history but *on* art history from the signifying spaces of the women's movement. (1993: 107)

These groups—this extra-academic space—were thus significant in both particular and more general ways to the origins of the work on soap opera here discussed. It was in groups such as the London Women and Film Group, or the not dissimilar CCCS Women's Studies Group (Brunsdon 1995), or the Chicago Feminar that much of the work on soap opera with which we have been here concerned originated, but these groups in turn were just some of the many autodidactic intellectual/political groups of the left/feminist culture of the 1970s.[1] And this culture, as the emerging accounts begin to tell us, was one place where the complexity of speaking as a woman and doing intellectual work was attempted simultaneously.[2]

(ii) The Interviewees Watch Soap Opera

All of the interviewees have watched soap opera. This may seem a rather banal observation, but one of the points that becomes very clear from the interviews is the very different investments, rituals, and

---

1 Kobena Mercer draws our attention to the continuing significance and changing constituency of this type of group in his acknowledgement of the contribution of the 'Black Gay Group in early eighties London' to his own work (Mercer 1994: p. viii).

2 Laura Stempel Mumford writes most interestingly about the absence of this intellectual space outside the academy in 1990s USA. She comments on her own absolute invisibility to most academic feminists while she is trying to work as a feminist intellectual without an institutional base (Mumford 1994a).

activities covered by the phrase 'watching soap opera'. Thus my research supports arguments about the radical contextualism of 'watching television' made by those such as Hermann Bausinger (1984) and David Morley and Roger Silverstone (1991). For some interviewees, the formative context was their family of origin, but young children, college, and work routines all feature. Most of my interviewees have watched soap opera in different ways at different points in their lives. In the discussion of Terry Lovell's interview, I posited the notion of a 'periodicity of identity'. The idea of a 'periodicity of viewing identity' has relevance for most of these stories. Theoretically, it extends diachronically and biographically some of the ways in which individual television viewing has been formulated, like Newcomb and Hirsch's 'viewing strip' (which describes the particular selections an individual makes from an evening's 'flow'), allowing us to conceptualize repeated and regular choices made by individuals in particular contexts over time (Newcomb and Hirsch 1983). Ethnographic research on television viewing has shown us the diversity of practices entailed, but has tended, for a range of reasons, to concentrate on the synchronic, the everyday, the present. These stories show us the diachronic aspects of television viewing, the way in which each individual has more and less engagement with television in general, and particular programmes, at different stages of their lives. The periodicities of identity recounted here are partly recounted through viewing practices and choices.

In the context of this particular project, in which academic attention to soap opera is investigated as a site (one of many) in which the identity of the feminist intellectual is articulated, we have particular interests in how this 'periodicity of viewing identity' is spoken of. In that all the interviewees were, by the time of the interview, *de facto* experts on soap opera, I have been particularly concerned, while drawing together the similar and contrasted ways in which they discuss their own viewing, to pay attention to the way in which this is characterized. Specifically, I have been attentive to any reference to explicit or implicit comparison between their own viewing and that of others. These others are legion—family members, peer groups, other critics, fans, women—and I have drawn attention to all statements in which they are invoked.

Two of the interviewees, Christine Geraghty and Ellen Seiter, offer vivid accounts of when they first started watching soap opera, and the complex familial interactions involved. Ien Ang was first introduced to *Dallas* by her sister. In each case, the interviewees were already at college, and for Ang and Seiter their soap viewing quickly became incorporated into college work through a choice of dissertation. So although soap opera, particularly for Seiter and Geraghty, is strongly invested with family memory, these are not memories of childhood.

Lovell, and Hobson by implication, offer a rather different account, in which soap opera, as part of available, mainstream cultures of femininity, was just *there* in the background. There is no 'starting to watch soap opera', but instead a knowledge of that viewing and related cultures that can later be drawn on. Although my project is not a sociological one, and I do not have the type of data which legitimates the sudden imposition of factors which offer sociological 'explanation', it is the case that Hobson and Lovell are nearly ten years older than the other interviewees, and that both went to college as mature students after marriage. Terry Lovell in particular, as I have already discussed, stresses the taken-for-grantedness of an involvement in commercial cultures of femininity:

> I mean, in my case, having left school at 16, and been a bank clerk for several years, I quite belonged to, very much to, a culture in which it was perfectly accept/expected that *Woman* and *Woman's Own* was something you know, you just read every week. (TL: 6)

Terry here evokes herself as a young woman in a particular culture of femininity, the contours and practices of which are completely taken for granted ('something, you know, you just read every week'). Although she is answering a question about soap opera, she does it with reference to women's magazines. This response can I think be properly understood to group together mass-circulation women's weeklies and television serials. She does not differentiate between the cultures of conventional femininity that they offer. So Terry is understanding soap opera as part of a class-specific, mainstream culture of femininity of which she was once part.

Later in the interview, speaking of a quite different phase in her life, she discusses the decision to watch *Coronation Street* in the Women and Film Group. She roars with laughter at the clearly unanticipated consequence of the decision: 'and of course we all got hooked' (TL: 3). In Terry's account, this 1970s commitment to *Coronation Street* is a return to and a revision of something already familiar. She does not— and insists that, differently, none of that group did—see herself as 'completely outside' the 'women's culture' to which she as a feminist returns.

Dorothy Hobson stresses that her knowledge of soap opera is part of an extensive familiarity with television as a whole. She describes herself as an 'avid' television viewer, and it is this, rather than any family memories, which she uses to contextualize her soap viewing, presenting herself as knowledgeable about the medium both generally and specifically.

Christine Geraghty, another member of the Women and Film Group, offers a rather more detailed account of her soap viewing. She too differentiates between periods of soap viewing, and like Seiter, whose account I discuss below, describes a late start. Geraghty offers a self-conscious periodization of viewing, which I have to a large extent discussed in the analysis of the interview, but which I want here to review in this new context. She describes a brief period of regular viewing with her father and sister:

> It was a particular thing at that particular point—and we used to watch it together, and occasionally my Mum would watch. So that it was a particular family thing at that point, I mean he doesn't watch it now. It lasted for about two years. I remember watching when Bet Lynch nearly committed suicide and we all had our hankies out. (CG: 4)

> and then once I'd left and [*sister*] got interested in other things that kind of stopped. So it was just one of those kind of 'moments' of how your viewing changes—(CG: 5)

Present within this account is a very strong insistence on the particularity of the contextual determination of the viewing. The father and two daughters ('and occasionally my mum'), all on different life trajectories, meet for thirty minutes twice a week in front of the television: 'It was a particular thing at that particular point', 'I mean he doesn't watch it now', 'and then once I'd left', 'and [*sister*] got interested in other things'. However, within this particularity, and Christine's analysis of the value of this shared viewing for this particular family discussed in Chapter 6, there is a very clear recognition of the emotional intensity of the shared viewing and vivid memories of key narrative events: 'I remember watching when Bet Lynch nearly committed suicide . . .'.

Christine is very clear about a continuing engagement with soap opera from this point—one which develops into regular *Crossroads* viewing, as well as repeated use of conversation about soap opera as a resource at work. So it is in the context of understanding herself as a committed and serious viewer that she becomes involved in intellectual work on soap opera. Like Ellen Seiter, thinking about working on soap opera initially has a formal element—how narrative works, what the rules of the genre are. This, as Geraghty says at various points in the interview, is not really a gendered interest. However, she does offer a retrospective analysis of what might be seen as gendered in the genre when she considers the complexity of the feminine identifications offered to viewers. Here, what she describes—which she says she has only just begun to work out at the end of her book— is the way in which soap opera might offer reassurance in the endless puzzle of how to be a woman:

> I think one of the reasons why I watch soap, but it only just occurred to me right at the end of all this, was that the soaps

assume that women are good at your personal life, and can handle all these things and they kind of value the way in which women do things, and I think that is true. On the other hand also they are— they assume that that is the case and I think maybe that the guilt that women feel about watching is not so much tied up with the fact that men will mock you but that actually they don't themselves always feel terribly good at—so that while on one hand soaps do value what women do, they also are I think a bit problematic for women because they make assumptions about how well you can do it, and if you actually aren't terribly good at it or feel yourself at that particular point not to have been, then the pleasure is rather more complicated than I think I've described it as. (CG: 8)

This complex passage offers several different ways of thinking the relationship between 'women', feminism, the speaker, and soap opera. It starts, in the first sentence, with a paraphrase of one of the feminist positions on soap opera: that the genre is centrally concerned with personal life, that women are seen to manage this sphere, and that validation of these feminine skills is offered herein. The relations between the 'I', women, and this lucidly summarized feminist argument are smooth, except that within this sentence, at the point which will turn out to be the substantial and difficult burden of the paragraph, there is a sudden switch from third to second person: 'women are good at *your* personal life'. This switch of personal pronoun anticipates the posing of the possibility of 'women not being good at their/your personal life'. In some ways, what is explored in the second part of this passage has elements of the early feminist critique of 'the media', in that what is being hypothesized is a gap between the personal competencies of female characters in soap opera and those of the watching women. However, this is quite different to the early feminist repudiations because it is being posed in terms of pleasure— in a train of thought that begins 'I think one of the reasons why I watch soap . . .' and concludes 'then the pleasure is rather more complicated than I've described it as'. There is here a rather more sombre note touching the difficulty of satisfactorily achieving conventional femininity, and the ambivalent pleasures of watching characters who might seem to do it better. Soap opera, presented as in some way a fiction of femininity, is here perceived as both creating and assuaging anxiety and desire. This is clearly not an hypothesis about 'other women', but a mobilization of Christine's reflections about her own—gendered—viewing to think about the complexity of the relations between femininity and soap opera. Ien Ang too reflects on the ambivalent pleasures of watching soap opera, and with similar moves in and out of the personal. Where Geraghty was negotiating the category 'women', Ien Ang negotiates that of 'real viewers'—who have earlier been discursively contrasted with the theorization of viewers in the work of a critic who will here be referred to as 'B':

> B is so ignorant a little bit, you know, about the real pleasures of 'normal' people, or 'ordinary' people. B is somehow—in love with B's theory and tries to find everything that fits into it. B is not at all speaking about real viewers I don't think. Because when you speak about real viewers then you must allow for contradiction, the pleasure in *Dallas* is a certain pleasure but it also—people are also always a little bit disappointed. That's always there. Maybe that's not so clear in this book [*Watching Dallas*], but that's how I look at it now, it's much more—it's always a combination of pleasure and displeasure and the way in which watching a soap opera is on the one hand very pleasurable but on the other hand there are always things missing that you would have liked the story to go, whatever, those kind of—that tension that's I think the most important thing that still needs to be developed perhaps, theorizing about the viewing experience. (IA: 13)

This is not the same ambivalence as Geraghty's as it is not an ambivalence focused on the performance of gender—and it should be remembered that Ang's work was concerned with *Dallas*, rather than the arguably more 'gendered' British programmes. However, it is still a profound ambivalence, and I think we can argue that it is homologous in that the theorist/critic is flitting in and out of her own experience in order to apprehend a more generalizable point. This move is in both cases signalled by the eruption of personal pronouns: 'there are always things missing that you would have liked the story to go'. However, here it is quite clear that Ang is making a bid for her experience of the contradictory pleasures of soap watching to be in some ways 'normal' or 'ordinary'—both adjectives clearly in quotes in speech—in contrast to the way in which this viewing is customarily theorized, in this case by the critic 'B'. Contextually, Ang is arguing for the necessity of empirical research with 'real viewers'. However, we should perhaps remind ourselves that one of her responses to the letters about *Dallas* that she received was the sense of being reassured:

> I do remember reading those letters and being very, very much reassured by the recognition I found . . .

> hey, you know, I'm not the only one. (IA: 5)

In this 'I'm not the only one' Ang articulates an unchallengeable identity as fan. While she is theorizing the experience of watching shows like *Dallas*, she is also clearly partaking in this experience in ways which would be recognizable to those not simultaneously theorizing.

Ellen Seiter offers the most extended meditation on the movement of the critic inside and outside 'ordinary' viewing. Ellen does this towards the end of the interview, when she is talking about reasons why she moved away from research into soap opera to research on children's television. She offers a very moving account of her own soap viewing when her mother was terminally ill in hospital:

> There's one other thing about soap operas. You see—and maybe it's an extremely pessimistic view of class relations—but I have I actually feel that soap operas are, in terms of the uses and gratifications of soap operas for women, I actually think that there's a degree of sort of pain and suffering and that the use value of soap operas as a distraction, material in terms of, really crudely putting it, sort of overcoming pain and suffering in everyday life, is at a scale that is quite unimaginable, and one of the points when I really kind of thought I'm not going to talk about this stuff any more was the time that I was most grateful in my entire life to watch soap opera was when my mother was in the hospital and sort of thought, 'Now I understand why we've been, why it's really there, and no, I don't want to talk about it any more.' (ES: 2.6–2.7)

As the interview analysis has shown, Ellen was introduced to soap viewing while a student. It was not an element of her domestic culture when she was growing up, and she clearly delineates her sister's role as 'instructress' in the watching of soap opera. She also talks about her mother's developing use of soap opera in her work context, and her own feelings of relief and inclusion when she finally finds a soap at a time she can watch. So, in the period when she is researching soap opera, it has very clear family associations, and it is also, as discussed in the interview analysis, a particular way to inhabit the position 'intellectual'.

These aspects of her life as a soap viewer and researcher Ellen discusses in some detail, but what she says here about viewing while her mother was ill also offers another way to think about her soap biography, and gives an account of a transition between one sort of viewing and another. The key passage is:

> the time that I was most grateful in my entire life to watch soap opera was when my mother was in the hospital and sort of thought, 'Now I understand why we've been, why it's really there, and no, I don't want to talk about it any more.'

Ellen, in other words, watched soap opera in a different way when her mother was dying. She was grateful for the relief and escape it offered, she found it a solace. And what she suggests about this experience was that it gave her an emotional intuition into ways which soap opera is used which she at this point realizes she had mainly apprehended intellectually: 'Now I understand why we've been, why it's really there . . .'. She describes a moment of epiphany when she experiences and uses soap opera in the way in which she has been arguing that it is experienced and used. This not only recasts our understanding of her soap biography, but it also leads her to reassert the significance of the everyday use of soap opera in this way: 'I actually think that there's a degree of sort of pain and suffering and that the use value of soap operas as a distraction, material in terms of, really crudely putting it, sort of overcoming pain and suffering in everyday life, is at a scale that is quite unimaginable.'

I would, from my own involvement with soap opera, very much endorse the way in which Ellen suggests that regular viewing of shows can offer—or be used to provide—enormous support at times of intense emotional crisis. However, here Ellen is saying something else as well: she is saying that this was a reason to stop talking about soap operas as an academic, and she is linking this to an analysis which includes class ('and maybe it's an extremely pessimistic view of class relations'). In this context, I think what Ellen is doing is making a distinction, which is governed by class, between those who talk about soaps academically (as she had done) and those in such dire straits that they can only depend on them (as she had become during her mother's illness). In line with all the decisions discussed in the interview, she chooses to make the non-academic identification: 'Now I understand why we've been, why it's really there, and no, I don't want to talk about it any more.'

So I think with Ellen Seiter the distinction between the feminist and the other woman both is and isn't valid. It is very much present in her understanding of the way she can use soap opera in the academy and, indeed, of the obligation she clearly feels to use her cultural capital to support young women in their viewing preferences. However, there is also a way, and this passage epitomizes it, that these identities are not fixed in bodies, so that in this passage, Ellen herself moves from being the feminist to being the other woman. Identities, here, are to do with modes of engagement with television, and distances from its fictions. And it is partly in this notion of distance that class enters, if we understand distance in relation to the aesthetic object in the way that Bourdieu (1984) suggests. He argues that only those that 'have enough' in every sense can occupy the position of distance from the aesthetic object that legitimate culture demands.[3] The highest aesthetic sense is, at its foundation, a sense of distance. The Ellen who watched soap opera here with such involvement is a different Ellen to

3 Although Bourdieu's work has attracted criticism, particularly for what has been called its romanticization of dominated tastes, it still seems immensely useful in this context. It is of course Ellen Seiter who introduces Bourdieu here.

the one who did her undergraduate dissertation and 'figured out the rules' of soap opera.

What is left open is the extent to which the critical work—given its particular arguments—was actually enabling in relation to the use of soap opera as an emotional resource. Did making politically motivated arguments about the value and complexity of women's viewing of soap opera—a project that is to some extent distanced from soap viewing per se—permit the erosion of this distance? This question is posed here because of the differences in the way in which Ellen describes her first reactions to her sister and mother talking about soap opera, and the much more straightforward 'use' described later. But I think it could equally be posed in relation to the accounts given by Christine Geraghty, Ien Ang, and myself—all middle class in origin, brought up with the expectation of higher education. With a certain irony, might it not be possible to argue that one of the results of our academic work about soap opera was to allow us to watch soap, not only without guilt, but, on occasion, without distance? Or to push this a little further, did the feminist endeavour which was the investigation of soap opera and its viewers tutor a class mobility in television tastes? Put slightly differently, this would be to suggest that the re-engagement and revaluation of feminine genres undertaken by (nearly academic) feminists legitimated pleasure in these games—not only for 'other women' but also for feminists.

(iii) Reactions to the Research and Becoming an Expert

When I first set up this project, I knew that there was an irony in the reception of the soap opera research that interested me. Perhaps rather in the spirit of Ien Ang's promise, 'you'll see, I shall do something good', I wanted to juxtapose the incredulous contempt with which telling people I was working on *Crossroads* was met, with the considerable influence that feminist studies of popular culture have had. Like Ien, but retrospectively, I wanted to say 'well it wasn't rubbish, was it?' Until I asked my interviewees about the reactions to their work, I hadn't realized how simultaneously they were teased and rendered experts. None of my interviewees ever revealed their research topic without immediate and vocal responses. Soap opera is a topic about which everyone has an opinion and the combination of soap opera, intellectual/academic work, and feminism proved irresistible. The project was unbelievable—it must be a joke. Hostile reactions came from both academics and television production staff. I have already discussed the response to the 'Women and Soap Opera' paper at the Edinburgh Television Festival at some length in the analysis of Terry Lovell's interview. Here, the most important element of this attack is the deeply contradictory attitudes of the programme-makers.

In Terry's account they were both vituperative in response to this feminist discussion of soap opera and deeply contemptuous of the programmes themselves:

> But what I hadn't expected, apart from the ferocity of the attack that they made—and I've never experienced anything like that before or since, I'm glad to say—but also the extent to which the professionals were really caught in a situation where they precisely inhabited some of those attitudes of contempt towards what they were doing and they were compromised in terms of their livelihood and their whole career development and they were actually only doing a professional job in the production of soap opera. But the kind of level of contempt that they themselves actually had for the punters and for the product in the end— which at the same time in professional terms they were wanting to defend and being very kind of sensitive about kind of—what we felt was they weren't really listening to what we were saying. (TL: 7–8)

This is a vivid evocation of the contradictions and compromises of television professional ideologies, one which is founded on the recognition that soap opera figures very low in the hierarchy of programmes on which career professionals would like to work. Without wanting to over-read, I think it also hints at the paradoxes of the recruitment to the British television industry, where many of those employed with a mandate to produce popular television have had exceptionally privileged backgrounds and educations: 'But the kind of level of contempt that they themselves actually had for the punters and for the product in the end . . .' (TL: 7).

The presenting group were attacked for what was taken to be their stereotypically feminist attack on a popular programme. So they were attacked for not being 'real' *Coronation Street* viewers, but, as Terry's analysis makes clear, this view of their paper to some extent involves the expression of the programme-makers' own contempt for their product, which invokes a rather different, more straightforwardly 'high culture' dismissal of soap opera. Terry evokes very clearly the career contradictions for many involved in soap opera production in this period. They can't bear what they do, they don't watch it themselves, but on the other hand they are very hostile to a critique which they perceive to come from 'not-ordinary viewers'. Given what Dyer, Lovell, and McCrindle actually argued, the hostile response is partly directed at a projection of the producers' own valuation, while also responsive to the ambivalences of the presentation towards soap opera.

Dorothy Hobson also encountered the defensiveness which is such a strong element of the contradictory professional ideology mobilized here in response to the presentation of 'Soap Opera and Women' in 1977. However, in direct contrast to the 1977 response at Edinburgh, Hobson's work presented at Edinburgh in 1985 appeared to offer succour to beleaguered production staff (Hobson 1985). Dorothy first identifies this defensiveness in her account of trying to gain access to the *Crossroads* set to observe production practices in 1981, as discussed in Chapter 8:

> but the hardest programme to get into was in fact *Crossroads*. And that was what particularly I'd been trying to get in and couldn't, but I then had an appointment with Jack Barton [the producer of *Crossroads*]—and this comes then to the nub of what soap operas were about at that time, this is back in 1981, and the reason that it was hard to get into soap operas—I mean you would think it would be hard to get into news or current affairs work, newsroom or current affairs production but it was not, it was because of the whole way that soap opera was seen at that time, and all that they were used to was press criticism. (DH: 15)

I think we can properly say that she is referring to the same defensive and beleaguered professionals as had attacked Terry Lovell and the others, but what Dorothy manages to do—through the considerable skill discussed in the interview chapter—is to finally win the trust of the programme-makers 'because I did know such a lot about the programme, so he knew it was not going to be a criticism in the conventional sense' (DH: 16).

So if, in the first instance, Dorothy met defensiveness, the trust that she was eventually granted was due in large part to the way in which she dealt with her privileged position in the Gordon affair, and the type of arguments she made about soap opera in general and *Crossroads* in particular:

> I became somebody that they saw as—I mean, not an ally, but someone who they could call upon often to speak either to about something but also on their behalf, but I was not seen as a threat in the sense that I would just slag them off, but if I was going to say something it was because of a reason, they might not agree with it, but they were always interested to enter into the dialogue about it . . .

> they were also interested in things that might be wrong, or when their storylines—I mean when I was critical of programmes or events, sometimes they would say, 'Crikey, if you think it's bad it's really got to be bad at the moment', and laugh about it, and that was a step to take, to be openly critical. Because earlier on, the criticisms that I was making about *Crossroads* were not about the production but about the amount of money spent on the

productions, so the criticism was supporting the producers, but saying to the executives, this programme needs more money. (DH: 37–8)

Dorothy comes to be perceived as the source of potentially useful criticism, as somehow—even though she disavows 'ally'—on the same side as the soap opera producers.

Ellen too got positive reactions to her first presentation of her work, at a conference organized by the Feminar:

So I gave the paper at that conference, and it was wildly well received, you know, sort of very early public paper about soap opera, including that the people who put up the money for the conference, and who then had all of us to this cocktail party and stuff, I was the one—they chose my paper to go to, and they chose me to talk about because they were sort of closet soap opera viewers. (ES: 1.13–1.14)

This is not a professional constituency, but neither is it a simply academic one. Ellen's work provides a point of contact for the conference founders, precisely because she is discussing popular culture, rather than feminist film theory (the main concern of other conference papers). Indeed Ellen's own account of her own trajectory is precisely one of consistently making choices for the popular and away from the avant-garde or the overtly theoretical.

A differently motivated choice leads Ien Ang to the study of *Dallas*, to which her colleagues' responses were occasionally vituperative. She recounts—and I remember well—the sort of joy with which people pounced on her research topic:

'I am sure your next project will be about *Dynasty*'—I've heard that more than once. (IA: 6)

In its purest form—and this nearly always involved a joke, like Dorothy Hobson's reported punchline 'What is *Crossroads*? Where is Birmingham?'—this is simple incredulity about the serious study of popular culture. In Bourdieu's terms, these jokes are part of the symbolic violence through which the distinctions in the legitimacy of the cultural field are maintained. And just as, in his 1984 study, the less legitimate art forms, such as photography or jazz, are the specialisms of those with less inherited cultural capital (upwardly mobile, first-generation educated working-class and lower middle-class men), so it is significant that it is through even less legitimate forms that highly educated women later contest the boundaries of the field. However, in this field, these reactions were articulated through a range of snobberies which have themselves become part of the intellectual agenda. Indeed, the attitudes to the study of soap opera are in some ways homologous to the attitudes to the viewing of the genre, and it is thus not incidental that much of the feminist-influenced soap opera work has as its core the defence of the genre. It should be stressed that this often involved a defence of the genre from feminist critique, as I have already documented. Hobson (1982), Brunsdon (1981), Seiter (1982*a* and *b*), Ang (1985), Dyer et al. (1981), Geraghty (1991), Allen (1985) are all centrally concerned with these attitudes to the genre, and the implied and actual attitudes to fans.

So let us return to the reaction that the interviewees recount to their early research. These responses, although articulating different views, point to the relative stability of the discursive repertoire within which soap opera was positioned in the late 1970s/early 1980s. This is a repertoire—as many of these interviewees have argued, perhaps most notably Dorothy Hobson and Ien Ang—structured significantly through the High Art/Mass Culture opposition. Soap opera can only be produced as an object of ridicule, contempt, or irony. So the reaction Terry describes at Edinburgh is a reaction from people who occupy a very contradictory position in relation to this discursive field, and hence, to some extent, misrecognize the challenge being offered. At another point they can welcome Dorothy who to some extent is making similar and certainly strongly related arguments. She, however, wishes to explicitly validate soap opera as popular culture. Ellen is welcomed by a different audience because she offers a challenge to this discursive repertoire—as do all the interviewees—which poses to her listeners the idea that their pleasure might not be wrong. Ien, however, is teased and ridiculed—which makes her all the more determined to transform the discursive repertoire within which soap opera is perceived: 'You'll see, I shall do something good!' (IA: 6).

During the 1970s, when structuralism and semiotics were first being taken seriously in the study of language and literature, a common popularizing, pedagogic device to illustrate the implications of these new theories was the inversion of mode (active/passive) in relation to the verbs 'to speak' or 'to write'. Thus instead of old humanist ideas of subjectivity and agency implied in the active 'I speak language' we got new structuralist ideas of identity constituted through pre-existing language and discursive position, as in 'I am spoken by language'. These opposed ideas about the constitution of identity—and their contradictory interrelation—form a useful background to the different accounts my interviewees give of 'becoming an expert' in relation to soap opera. For if, on the one hand, as we have just seen, their early forays into 'taking soap opera seriously'—the moment of agency—were mocked ('I suppose you're going to do *Dynasty* next!', 'Where is Birmingham? What is *Crossroads*?'), almost immediately, they were taken up and created experts.

As Christine Geraghty put it:

> And then inevitably once—then when you write something, as you know, you then instantly become an expert in it even if you aren't, and people invite you to do things and you kind of say yes and in six months time you find yourself doing it. And then inevitably you end up, if you're looking at soap operas, or being involved with anything that might be called a soap opera, then inevitably the kind of aspect about women comes in. But that certainly I guess wasn't where I started. (CG: 5)

Christine is firm about the incongruity of the designation 'expert . . . even if you aren't', in combination with the snowball effect 'and you kind of say yes and in six months time you find yourself doing it'. Dorothy Hobson describes a not dissimilar process, again, through the use of inverted commas, distancing herself from a claiming of 'expert' status, but recounting being granted it. Although she had considerable reaction to her 1981 article in *The Times* (Hobson 1981*b*), it was after her book came out in 1982 that things accelerated:

> because what, as it happened then, after the book came out, of course, I became known as the 'expert' in inverted commas 'on soaps', and so every time anything happened in any soap I was rung up to comment or I was on a programme to comment about it. (DH: 35)

These accounts in particular—but by no means only these—point to another factor in the shifting discursive field 'soap opera'. This is the narcissism and parasitism of the media themselves, the internal interest in 'a media story'. And for precisely all the reasons already discussed, particularly the metonymic and metaphoric value of soap opera, what 'expert' could be more attractive than an 'expert' on soap opera? However, once again in these accounts my interviewees take comfort from a role that can best be described as that of 'people's champion':

> One of the ways radio programmes set up the interviews was they liked to get a critic who'd slated soap operas, and me, in battle, either down the line on the phone or in a studio together. What was nice from my point of view to find that often people who could write vitriolic prose were not quite as good when it came to argument so you could [*laughs*]—but what was also good was as soon as the viewers came in on the phone line you were like the five-star golden girl because they were praising you for saying what you want, putting their own point of view very strongly, that's where you felt 'I'm not out on a limb', you know, I'm uniting an academic perspective or a new theoretical perspective which is

actually uniting with what people do think and what they didn't have much voice with at that time. (DH: 31–2)

As we have seen, Ien Ang, Christine Geraghty, and Ellen Seiter also voice sentiments similar to these here spoken by Dorothy Hobson. And in some ways this sense of being a 'five-star golden girl', of 'uniting with what people do think and what they didn't have much voice with at that time', takes us back to the beginning of the chapter and the extra academic origins of much of this work. There was a desire to speak to and of pleasures excluded not only from the academy, but also from respectable repertoires of taste. Although lambasted subsequently for populism, this type of work should also be recognized as springing from a democratic and empowering impulse. If the feminist intellectual is partly discursively constructed in opposition to 'ordinary women', who are by implication neither feminist nor intellectual, there was often also a profound connection across this division, when the privilege of intellectual work was understood as in some sense mandated politically.

(iv) 'Women' in the Interviews

Rosi Braidotti, in one of a series of meditations on the subject of feminist theory and the institutionalization of 'Women's Studies', argues that

> In feminist theory one *speaks* as a woman, although the subject 'woman', as I have argued earlier, is not an essence defined once and for all but rather the site of multiple, complex and potentially contradictory sets of experience. (1994: 199; italics in original)

My own project could be seen to offer both an interrogation and an empirical investigation of this claim. That is, if one speaks 'as a woman' in feminist theory, how should we conceptualize this speaking woman, particularly if, like Braidotti, we have an interest in constructing this figure as 'not an essence defined once and for all'. These interviews provide rich and complex illustration of some of the issues involved in speaking as a woman, revealing repeatedly the plurality and historicity of this speaking position. My own hypothesis had been that the particular kind of 'speaking as a woman' to which Braidotti refers—speaking as a feminist—was historically insufficiently attentive to the other women that this speech constructs: the other women who may also see themselves 'speaking as women', but are not thereby placed in feminist theory—and may indeed, by this very understanding, be placed outside it.[4] That is,

---

4 This is discussed in different ways by Probyn (1993) and Skeggs (1997). Skeggs asks the young working-class women with whom she has worked for several years about the meaning of feminism to them.

although it is incontestably true that second-wave feminists did claim to speak *as women*, and that this claim was both potent and necessary in that historical/political mobilization, it has seemed retrospectively a colonizing claim, a claim to inherit true womanhood—however ironical this may seem. It was this terrain that I was particularly interested in exploring in these interviews—the way in which gender was constructed and remembered as a speaking position, across work which shared, as Christine Geraghty put it, a determination to do something on 'Women and . . .'. If, as we have seen, in Chapters 2 and 3, one of the products of early mainstream and feminist research on soap opera was the construction of a figure—the 'ordinary woman', the housewife, the television viewer—who was in some ways the other of the researcher/feminist, how are these personae distributed and inhabited in these interviews?

I sought the answer to this question through direct questioning of my interviewees and through close textual analysis of the conversations. I wanted to see how we—the interviewees and I—negotiated nouns like 'women', 'housewives', 'viewers', and 'feminists' as well as pronouns like 'we' and 'they' when discussing research on soap opera. That is to say, '*speaking as* a woman', as indeed the second part of Braidotti's sentence suggests, is a very complex practice, and is negotiated very differently at different times by different women. If indeed, as Braidotti implies, the process of making feminist theory demands the construction and inhabiting of this speaking position, what can data like these interviews show us about this practice?

The analysis of the interviews conducted so far establishes how subtle and variant were the usages of pronouns such as 'we', while the shifts between personae are adroit and fleeting. Nobody speaks as *a* woman. Everybody speaks plurally, pulling together the woman or girl they were and are at different points with other much less gendered positions. People speak as daughters, as lovers, as scholars—and intermittently as classed and raced subjects. To explore some of these shifts, I want here to pay attention to the more metalinguistic features of the interviews. There are two particular areas of usage which underpin any analysis of specific observations the interviewees might make about the feminist/other women relation, and which contextually complicate any such observations. These areas of usage are only available through detailed textual analysis of transcripts and tapes, and are perhaps the most useful data in the empirical investigation of '*speaking as* woman'. It should be noted then, that these are the areas of analysis in which my own interpretations are most evidently dominant, and which were least open to negotiation with the interviewees. First, there are identifications which are governed, within the interview context, by choices about how the participants address each other—parameters of address. Secondly, there are the complex of available positions occasioned in a conversation in the present about times past. These can be grouped together as involving narrative/historical parameters.

What I am calling identifications of 'address' are constituted through the question of how the two participants address each other within the conversation. This, I would suggest, is not necessarily gendered—or certainly, does not necessarily inscribe gender, which is a slightly different matter. An example of gendered address would be the point in the interview with Ellen Seiter when she observes that none of the men she was involved with would be seen dead watching soap opera in 1979. We both laugh at this point, and this is a clear moment of the inscription of heterosexual female gendered identities. We laugh as women and feminists, reminded by her anecdote of some of the contradictions of desire that this can pose. We are gendered 'the same'. In the Seiter interview, this type of shared gendering can be contrasted with other moments when Seiter draws attention to the class differences in our backgrounds.

In a rather different way, much of the beginning of the interview with Dorothy Hobson uses gendered address in the way in which she repeatedly uses the pronoun 'we', meaning herself and me, but herself and me *as women*, now, in this conversation. However, in her use of the phrase 'what we would call popular television', Dorothy at another moment groups herself and me together as critics/academics in a way which is not gendered. So the notion of 'gendered address' allows us to specify one site of the fluctuating and differentiated constitution and presence of gendered identity within the conversations. And this gendered identity is itself very differentiated. Sometimes it is 'We women', sometimes, as with much of Terry Lovell's discussion, it combines with narrative complexity to produce a historically gendered identity, 'we women then'. Sometimes the 'we' is 'feminists' not 'women', but this too can be historically differentiated, as well as splintered between different kinds of feminism, either directly or by inference. This is further complicated by the irregular marking of class, national, and ethnic identities, as well as age difference. So, for example, Seiter and Ang both discuss the difference of the USA and Holland from the Britain where these interviews are taking place, and Seiter marks her own 'whiteness' at various points in the interview.

Thus although identities in each interview may be articulated through a relatively consistent repertoire of potential address, it is difficult to generalize across them—for example to substantiate an hypothesis about the relationship between the personae 'feminist' and 'housewife'. Instead, what can be commented on is the relatively limited range of identities that are posited, all of which could be understood to be within a feminist repertoire, and the fluency with which the speakers adopt and jettison positions. The most significant absence is precisely that of 'the housewife', who is rigorously excluded by all interviewees, often by the substitution of lengthy circumlocuations like 'young women at home with their children'. This avoidance/circumlocution strategy can only be explained by a sensitivity to the status of the nomination 'housewife' in the context of 1970s feminism, when it was seen as one of the terms through which women's labour in the home was undervalued. Certainly, there was a relatively widespread colloquial feminist deconstruction of the term, posing the absurdity—or humiliation—of being 'married to a house'.[5] The absence of this word in the interviews suggests a certain naturalization of this feminist critique in the 1990s.

All participants moved across different modes of address during the conversations. I think that the relationship of familiarity between participants contributed to a dominant mode of address between the two of us that was not necessarily gendered, while at the same time gender was a constant topic and was repeatedly reinscribed within the conversation. At the same time, I think it likely that the particular context of the interviews, the fact that the participants were already familiar with each other, may have functioned to minimize explicit articulations of difference through address, or to permit only those that were comfortable within the relationship. Thus nationality, age, and parenting were the most easily articulated sites of difference, perhaps because the imbrications of power and privilege appear more natural and are indeed less troubled sites in the culture of the interviews. At the same time, it was with the two non-British interviewees that there was most discussion of class and ethnicity, perhaps because of the way in which 'explaining your culture' is recognized as a necessary part of all international relationships. The gulfs of class within British culture are less recognized as requiring explication. This has implications for any conclusions I might draw from these interviews, while also pointing to methodological consequences for qualitative interviewing in general. It also perhaps gives us some indications of how individuals negotiate difference in the practice of everyday life.

What I have called the 'narrative/historical' parameters mark the consciousness of passed time and show us most vividly that these interviews are a type of memory work—conversations in which the participants prompt each other to remember what it was like trying to take soap opera seriously. This consciousness is inscribed in a number of ways in the interviews and comes from the temporal negotiations that partly constitute each of the interviews. Most obviously, it

---

5 Of course accompanied by long campaigns and academic work to get domestic labour recognized as labour (Malos 1980).

can be found in the descriptions of a former self which are found in each account and have already been discussed, and also in the 'whatever happened to x?' gossip which is a feature of all the interviews. But there is also the way in which a story about 'then' is being told 'now', and one of the differences between the two times is the referential value of words like 'women' and 'feminism'. The complexity lies in the way in which these different values have to be inscribed, narratively, in the conversation, exemplified most clearly in the discussion of 'women's culture'—in quotes—in the Terry Lovell interview. In this instance, she is trying to tell a story about a category 'women's culture' which meant something quite particular in the period under discussion. She doesn't want to get distracted into what this was, or her attitude to it then and now, so she uses quotation marks to signal her recognition of what is not being opened up (see Chapter 8). She is telling a story, and inscribing, formally, consciousness of shifting meanings within that telling.

Related negotiations occur around many of the key words of the project, such as 'feminism' and 'soap opera', and can only be understood through the consciousness of their shifting referential value. As Christine Geraghty observes, 'I don't think we called it soap opera then' (CG: 12). It comes from the way in which notions such as 'femininity' and 'women' were extremely contested in the period under discussion, which is generally 1976–83. Of course this contestation is not specific to this period and to this extent is always an issue in any history-making. What is specific to this period is the way in which a rather minor field, the proto-academic study of 'soap opera', and approaches to soap opera, can be seen to contain and condense many of the contemporary debates about women, feminism, and femininity. In this minor field, in this period, there is a rhetorical antagonism between two key terms, 'soap opera' and 'feminism'. 'Soap opera' connotatively means 'conventional femininity', while 'feminism' means hostility to conventional femininity. I have traced some of the contradictory impulses in play here in my discussion of the development of the study of 'women's genres', and in the study of early work in Chapter 3. This antagonism also structures Terry Lovell's account of presenting the 'Women and Soap Opera' paper to the Edinburgh Festival. In this account, Terry's analysis of the hostility that they meet is precisely that they were heard as antagonistic to soap opera because they were feminists: 'they treated us as though what we said—was the kind of thing that at that time you would have expected a group of feminists to be saying about a product like *Coronation Street*' (TL: 9). So, in the inscription of narrative and history in these interviews, we can trace the memories of the governing contours of the discursive field, and the particular frisson of the juxtaposition of feminism and soap opera.

Denise Riley, in the elegant essay on the history of the Western category 'woman' she writes to answer her question 'Does a sex have a history?', evokes the experience of going about one's everyday life, feeling like a human being, and suddenly being hailed as a woman (Riley 1988). Gendered identity, in her argument, is not only historically specific, it is experienced as fluctuating, as more or less important at different times. She is, however, in no doubt as to the necessity of organizing through this identity when it is as this group, women, that subordination is maintained. Riley's essay, along with key interventions like Donna Haraway's 1985 'Manifesto for Cyborgs' and the work of Judith Butler (1990), offer very radical reformulations of the feminist project from which much of the work under discussion here developed. That is, work like Riley's has been concerned to deconstruct any automatic belongingness to a category 'we women' for females. It is this debate which informs the second part of Braidotti's sentence about speaking as a woman with which we started this section. In this debate, the demon is often 'second-wave' feminism, which doubtless did at times construct an unthinkingly exclusive, inclusive 'we'. What these interviews suggest, however, as the interviewees think back to the late 1970s and early 1980s, is how complex the negotiations of 'feminism' and 'women' were.

The detailed analysis of these interviews endorses the developing theorization of gender identity as being a matter of considerable flux, while at the same time pointing to the way in which gender can provide a very strong 'core' identity. Evidently, the proclaimed object of enquiry in the interviews would mean that gender was an overdetermined topic and identity for both participants. However, within that overdetermination, the engagements with femininity and feminism are various and fluctuating. History, origin, and context are repeatedly cited to explain gender identifications.

That is, these interviewees recount a range of more and less prominent, more and less conscious, differently inflected gender identifications to which they have different responses. Thus I have suggested that, for example, Terry Lovell's story is best told through a notion of a periodicity of identity, in which gender is more or less prominent depending on whether she is, for example, a girl in a large farming family, a bank clerk, a married mature student, or a university lecturer specializing in 'women's studies'. Further, that the embrace of gender involved in the last occupation builds on, revises, and is quite different from, that of gendered adolescence. Ien Ang, on the other hand, tells a much less gendered story, but a story in which issues of migration and ethnic identity are central in a way that they are not for other interviewees. Hers too is a story in which the notion of a periodicity of identity is useful. As she commented on reading her chapter, she would now see the *Dallas* work as done in a period in which she was coming to terms with the contradictions of her immigrant family's desire for integration into Dutch society, characterizing the work as a 'metaphoric articulation of some of the problems and tensions of that desire for integration'. The absence of 'ethnicity' as a category inflecting gender identification for several of the white interviewees suggests, as does Ruth Frankenburg's research, that 'whiteness' as an ethnicity is not usually experienced as a 'marked' identity for those thus categorized (Frankenburg 1993). Here though, I think both my own whiteness and the indubitable whiteness of second-wave feminism in the period under discussion conspire to produce 'women' in these interviews as generally ethnically unspecified—and thus by implication white. Interesting here is Ellen Seiter's detailed account of coming to see her work on soap opera as white, thus giving a periodicity to her own interests and enthusiasms. Identity shaped through class is fluctuatingly present, particularly, if not always explicitly, in the stories of television watching and the attitudes to television in the parental home, but it is always bound up with gendered positionings.

As sociological and historical investigation, rather than political invective, will eventually confirm, the women of women's liberation in the 1970s did tend generally to be white women of middle-class and lower middle-class origin.[6] The unselfconscious inhabiting of these origins has been the subtext of much guilty breast-beating and castigation. What my research suggests is that there is something improperly voluntaristic about this approach. That is to argue that there was a certain inevitability about the blindnesses and exclusions in the feminist category 'woman' in this period. If we take the formation of this identity as something to be explained rather than simply politically abhorred, then some of my research might be useful, suspended, as it is, between ethnographical and autobiographical accounts of the second wave in one small arena.

For if we explore the implications of the periodicity and contextuality of gender identity that we find herein, we could hypothesize that only some women, at particular periods, in particular contexts, are available to identify themselves as primarily gendered. What in turn this identification involves is also subject to historical and contextual change and inflection, and the 1970s was a decade in which there was considerable explicit and public negotiation about what it meant to be a woman. This is an issue of both macro- and micro-social and historical contexts. Put simply, non-working-class white women would

---

6 Sara Evans (1979) offers an interesting account of the origins of the US women's movement in the Civil Rights movement of the 1960s, while Douglas (1995) stresses the significance of the mass media. Both point to the significant presence of white middle-class 'baby boomers' in the US women's movement. There are no equivalent accounts of the British movement, although Wandor (1990) is illuminating.

be available to have a primarily gendered identification precisely because they were not *already* identified as, for example, black and/or working class.

At the macro-level, we have to understand the rise of the women's movement as subtended by changing patterns in employment, education, family size, contraception, etc.[7] But the point is that those least encumbered by other identities subject to structural discrimination are most available to explore what they experience as a primary self-definition and site for discrimination, their gender. This is not to say that other women could not/did not conceptualize themselves as women, but it is to hypothesize the likelihood and probability of a focus on this as a defining and primary identity for a particular stratum in the absence of other strongly articulated competing definitions. This would be particularly significant for women who had not yet, or who had just, had children—for whom the profoundly gendering identity of mother was either absent or a recent shock. This macro-context in turn—a period in which there is a publicly identifiable gender agenda—makes available positions from which there can be interrogations and identifications with feminist 'woman'. However, there are also significant micro-contexts of gender appellation for each individual. These, of course, are subject to enormous variation, if not the absolute contingency at both macro- and micro-levels postulated by Ang and Hermes (1991), and will include the particularity of each family habitus, and the psychic arrangements therein, as well as, for example, watching soap opera.

Only with a theoretical model of this type of flexibility—which allows for the inscription of specificity at each level and context—can we make sense of the stories told here. These are very different tales, recounting quite different micro-histories, within a recognizably shared set of parameters (the women's movement, higher education, the investigation of popular forms, families, autodidactic political intellectual groups).

They are different stories, about different people working in different conditions, but they are also recognizably about the same thing, which we could perhaps characterize as the development, from a historically specific 'pro-woman' discourse of an equally specific 'pro-soap' discourse which has its own national inflections, but is clearly historically identifiable and has its own effectivity in the wider fields of media research, television studies, and cultural studies in the late 1970s and early 1980s. The stories told in this book do not recount the sudden discovery of the pre-existent significance of the study of soap opera for and by feminists. Instead, they reconstruct—remember—the

---

7 Wilson (1980) offers one history of the changes in the position of British women since 1945.

halting negotiation and constitution of new speaking postions, positions from which feminists could speak about soap opera. The stories told are all, at moments, quite intimate stories, for this new speaking position, that of the feminist intellectual (in its variousness), demanded considerable interrogation of already existing modes of femininity—of what it is to understand oneself as gendered female. The work of soap opera is one site on which these interrogations were conducted.

Coda: 'It's like Gum on Your Shoe'

I want to finish with an observation by Ellen Seiter about the heritage of her early work on soap opera:

> So then I went off to Oregon, and then because of being early Miss Soap Opera was kind of the thing that stuck, I mean I still have this ingrained feeling that I can't get out of that, you know, I kind of completely—like the Tuebingen thing came up at a point when I really thought that I was completely done with soap opera, that I just didn't you know that I didn't have a lot more to say about—or a lot of different—and I think in a way this audience stuff is just saying the same stuff that you did actually manage to say in the criticism, it just sort of proves it then. And I was kind of interested in disproving some aspects of the criticism so it was satisfying in that respect but I already knew from talking to my mother about what the women at work said about soap opera that that was true. So it's been this kind of thing that I just can't, you know, it's very it's like gum on your shoe or something you can't get rid of, you know, I can't believe that I'm going to this conference and again talking about soap operas when everything that I'm now doing is about, you know, this other children's TV stuff. (ES: 1.31–1.32)

Ellen's perception of her research on soap opera being like 'gum on [her] shoe' provides a tactile metaphor for the identities that are constructed for academics through bibliographies, reviews, and references. Long after she perceives herself to have moved on to other work, the invitations and citations she receives nominate her as a soap scholar. As we began to trace in the reactions to the reseach, once academic research enters the public domain it acquires a certain autonomy. Generally, this autonomous circulation is limited to academic spheres through scholarly journals and across the hyperspace of computer generated bibliographies. However, as we have already noted, the research on soap opera transgresses certain definitions of the academic to begin with, as well as offering the promise of a 'sexy' topic to media features editors. Rather as Carl André's 'pile of bricks' functioned to condense a repertoire of populist attitudes to modern art in the tabloid press, so the idea of a 'Doctor of Soap' produces an irresistible image of the idiocy of academic life.[8] My interviewees have had more and less public profiles in relation to their soap opera work, but I think we can safely say that all have attracted more media attention than is normally the case for academic research, and all have contributed to radio and television on the topic.

Dorothy Hobson has become the preferred British source for quotation on soap opera in newspapers and television, and, for example, was referred to in *The Observer*, 28 August 1994 as 'soap expert, Dorothy Hobson', when she was quoted extensively on her opinion of the likely impact of a satellite soap channel. Perhaps most interestingly in relation to the stories told here, she was invited in 1985 to address the Edinburgh Television Festival on the subject of soap opera. The response to her talk was enthusiastic (McGuigan 1992: 144–5). Her appointment to be official historian of the first five years of Channel Four was clearly partly a response to the way in which the *Crossroads* book paid attention to both producers and audience— and indeed, it should be said, was, in this way, very unusual for academic-in-origin studies of television. As she makes clear in the interview, she used the ethnographic skills developed at the Centre for Contemporary Cultural Studies to pursue this work.

Ien Ang, who has recently returned to soap opera and co-written some articles on 'post-realist soap opera', moved definitively into 'serious', critical mass communications/sociology of the television audience after the *Dallas* work (Ang and Stratton 1995). As she says in the interview, 'I wanted to show people that I'm not only the person of *Dallas*—that I also have something to say about these large scale policy issues.' The other area she has worked in, as discussed in Chapter 9, has been that of cultural identity, which has involved both personal autobiography and postmodern theory. She is currently working on issues of diasporic Chinese identities.

Terry Lovell, the interviewee least concerned with soap opera in any long-term work way, subsequently published on aesthetic hierarchy and women as audiences in a study of the novel, and has edited two collections, one on *British Feminist Thought*, the other on *Feminist Cultural Studies*. If the soap work is viewed in its chronological place in Terry Lovell's work as a whole, I think we could argue that it marks a theoretical and conceptual turning point, in that issues of gender begin there to contest the previous supremacy of Marxist paradigms in her thought. Terry Lovell has established, and become director of, the Centre for the Study of Women and Gender at Warwick University since the interview, and has recently completed

---

8 Ann Gray recounts a similar story about being labelled 'Britain's first doctor of soap' by the *Daily Express* in 1986 when her research on the domestic use of the video recorder was 'discovered' (Gray 1995).

a study of the relevance of Pierre Bourdieu's work for feminism (Lovell, forthcoming).

Christine Geraghty has now become a full-time academic teaching Communication Studies at Goldsmiths' College. She has maintained a relatively high media profile on soap opera, but has also continued to speak about soap opera/television/women at public meetings within the labour movement. The publication of her book on soap opera, which happened before she considered a move to the academy and is thus in some senses outside the academy, would be generally recognized as a prerequisite for this career move (1991). She is now working on British cinema.

Ellen Seiter, despite the gum on her shoe, has changed her primary research field to that of children's television and marketing to children. The methodological and personal reasons for this move have been discussed extensively in Chapter 10. As is also discussed to some extent in the interview analysis, although the object of study is different, there are in fact many similarities between studying *My Little Pony* in an academic context, and doing the same with soap opera. In both cases, Ellen has chosen fields in which the object of study has very low cultural prestige and much concern is expressed about consumers. She published *Sold Separately* in 1993 and had extensive media coverage in the USA, particularly on the radio where she did innumerable phone-ins. Her role was one of 'expert' who could advise parents about their children's television and toy usage. Her latest work, which involves longitudinal ethnographic studies of child-carers in relation to television, *Television and New Media Audiences* (1999) is likely to be her last work on television—she is proposing to move into Women's Studies.

I too find I have gum on my shoe, and this book is an attempt to make sense of what has turned out to be a longer term connection than I had anticipated. It is with reflection on this project that I conclude in the final chapter.

12

The Feminist, the Housewife, and the Soap Opera

THE central concern of this project turns out to be two, rather than one, kinds of cultural production. I understood myself to be investigating production of one genre of mass culture, the soap opera, as an object of study within the (mainly) British (anglophone) academy in the late 1970s and early 1980s, and the role of feminist scholarship therein. However, this investigation led me increasingly to the study of the contemporary production of a speaking position—or identity: that of the feminist intellectual as it was articulated in relation to a particular area of study. This position and identity was clearly not produced in relation to soap opera alone, and has to be understood in relation to other feminist work,[1] in relation to more general shifts in the legitimacy of the academic study of popular culture in the period of study, and also in relation to the history and theory of the intellectual.

For example, Helen Taylor makes the following observation in the introduction to her study of the female fans of *Gone with the Wind*, a classic of the feminist reinvestigation of women's genres discussed in Chapter 1:

> Over the last few years, when I have told people at work, on trains or at parties that I was writing a book about *Gone with the Wind*, almost always, they offered me an anecdote. . . . No one has ever asked me, 'Gone With the . . . What?' (1989: 1)

This provides a particularly vivid example of the way in which those studying popular culture must negotiate their place in relation to the detailed familiarity, expertise, and fandom of objects and practices already widely known outside academia. The popularity and availability of the object of study, be it rock music, romance fiction, television, or fashion, raise a series of issues in the academic study of the object,

---

1 Key self-reflexive, feminist texts which trace related histories include Pollock (1993), Miller (1991), Probyn (1993), Skeggs (1995), and Wallace (1990).

for it is evident from the initiation of the project that the researcher is not alone in her expertise—or search for expertise. That is to say, when the object of study is already in the domain of the popular, when it is already familiar and known about outside the academy, doubts are often expressed about the necessity and value of an academic engagement. These doubts come from a range of positions, including, for example, both high cultural dismissals of popular culture and fans' dismissals of academics' interpretations of their enthusiasms and activities.[2] These resistances to any recognition of the value of the study of popular culture are enhanced when the object of study, such as soap opera, is connotatively gendered as feminine.

However, as histories told in Chapters 1 and 3 suggest, many of the scholars interviewed in this dissertation were also defending their chosen object of study against feminist criticism. For not only does 'soap opera' have general metaphorical and metonymic significance, the genre also had very particular resonances for the emergent feminism of the 1970s. Initial feminist response to the genre was one of repudiation. Soap opera represented to feminists what they didn't want. That is, as we learn from the range of discursive material here analysed, in the period of our study, it can be argued that 'soap opera' and 'feminism' signify connotationally opposed understandings/practices of femininity—to feminists themselves, to television producers, and more generally. And this connotational opposition lingers. In the popular imaginary, feminists are still women who don't wear make-up, don't shave their legs and disapprove of watching soap opera, getting married, and having doors held open for them.

I have investigated how 'the feminist intellectual' was partly produced in the complicated and contradictory struggles to define a soap opera as a legitimate area of engagement for intellectual work, and the way in which these processes frequently involved more explicitly personal engagement with the study material than is conventional in intellectual work. This more explicit personal engagement, however, in combination with the originally derided object of study, in turn repeatedly threatens to undermine the cultural legitimacy of the scholarship. Each of the interviewees addresses this problem in some ways—perhaps most vivid is Ien Ang's justification of her subsequent project on the institutional construction of the audience: 'You will see, I am not just the person of *Dallas*' (IA: 8).

---

2 Simon Frith, in a review of Andrew Ross's *No Respect* and Morag Shiach's *Discourse on Popular Culture*, offers a germane comment on the relationship between intellectuals and popular culture: 'After reading Ross's celebration of pornography . . . and Morag Shiach's account of the historical exclusion of women from definitions of "the popular", my conclusion is that "popular culture" just isn't a political site. It is, indeed, a fantasy land, but the fantasies are those projected onto it by (male) intellectuals themselves: intellectuals longing, daring, fearing to transgress; intellectuals wondering what it would be *not to be an intellectual*' (1990: 235).

However, as the interviews show, there is no single figure 'the feminist intellectual', and the women who are retrospectively identified as, for example, responsible for 'the soaping of feminism' (McGuigan 1992: 140) in fact had very diverse attitudes to both feminism and soap opera. At the same time, the very fact that a scholar who understands himself to have a 'progressive' agenda can call a chapter section in 1992 'the soaping of feminism' reveals how very strongly the pejorative attitudes to the feminist scholarship on soap opera persist. The opposition soap opera/feminism is reinvoked, and the implication is clearly that a 'soaped' feminism is just a load of frothy bubbles.

Against this, I have traced the complexity of the engagement between second-wave feminism and soap opera, showing how this new object of study emerges from two different fields, feminist television criticism and 'women's genres', each of which has its origins in explicit political activity. Three salient features emerged from this genealogy. First, that soap opera emerges as a privileged area of attention for feminists in both fields. That is, in the feminist attention to television, the privileged texts have been soap opera and what I called 'heroine television', while in 'women's genres', if we restrict ourselves to the audio-visual, the privileged genres are soap opera and melodrama. This produces soap opera as an overdetermined area of study for feminist scholars. Secondly, for a range of reasons, each field has generated innovatory research into audiences/viewers/readers, repeatedly inspired or organized through an investigation of 'the ordinary woman'. Indeed, it is significantly through ethnographic research that feminist scholarship is recognized in the wider disciplines of media, cultural, and communication studies. Thirdly, in the constitution of soap opera as an object of study we see simultaneously a series of emotionally and politically charged encounters between feminism and femininity.

Put most baldly, the argument was that the constitution of a new object of study—in this instance, 'soap opera and the women who watch it'—necessitated the production of a position from which to speak about this 'object'. This produces at least two positions: 'the woman who watches soap opera' and 'the person who watches the woman who watches soap opera'. It was demonstrated that the very different materials analysed in Chapters 2 and 3—1940s US audience research and 1970s feminist writing—shared more than might have been anticipated, specifically through the figuring and refiguring of these positions. Of particular concern to all commentators was the relation between soap opera viewing and involvement in civic life. However, it is only the later feminist commentators who have to negotiate the tricky issue of their own relation both to 'the women who watch' and to viewing themselves, attracted to the genre as they were by feminism's proposal of the potential unity of all women. The juxtaposition of material from different discursive repertoires (1940s social science, 1970s feminist polemic, and 1970s soap opera publicity) suggested that not only were feminist commentators more akin to earlier researchers than they might imagine, but that they also shared the characteristic of 'worrying responsibly' with the soap opera matriarch. That is, the 1970s feminist repudiation of the housewife figure was founded partly on intolerable identities. Together, this analysis established the profound ambivalences in the second-wave feminist attitude to soap opera, as well as the relatively unrecognized role of fantasies of 'ordinariness' in both feminine and feminist repertoires.

While the early part of the book traces converging histories through the juxtaposition of stories told in different discursive registers, the latter part extends the range of material used in history-making through the analysis of autobiographical interviews. These 'interview autobiographies', analysed with particular attention to the telling of stories, as well as the stories told, can be best seen as a contribution to what Carlo Ginzburg describes as 'micro-history', one characteristic of which is that 'the obstacles interfering with research in the form of lacunae or misrepresentations must become part of the account' (1993: 28). The method of juxtaposition used foregrounds the different lacunae produced in different accounts, different history-makings, revealing the enormous complexity of determination in even such a small and unitary field as feminist scholarship on soap opera.

On the one hand, this interview analysis was addressed, at a methodological level, to debates about power relations within field-work interviews. Here, the interviews revealed how inescapable is the responsibility of the researcher, but they also yielded fascinating and often moving accounts of individual intellectual formation in relation to a specific object of study. The housewife, the shadowy figure I thought I discerned somewhere between the feminist and the soap opera in the early stages of the research, has remained in the shadows, caught sight of in glimpses. I hypothesized that much feminist intellectual work on popular feminine genres was motivated and legitimated in relation to a female non-feminist figure, variously described and thought of as 'the housewife', 'the ordinary woman', 'the average soap fan'. It was this person who read romances and told Janice Radway, wrote letters to Ien Ang, talked about her life to Dorothy Hobson. She was the person about whom Herta Herzog, Rudolf Arnheim, Carol Lopate, Tania Modleski, and Michèle Mattelart, in their different ways 'worried responsibly'. She was the person that many of these authors thought could become more 'civic-minded'. She might even become a feminist if she came to understand the role of her fiction habit—if it could be explained to her after it had been analysed.

She is clearly present in the proto-feminist work of Friedan (1963), Gavron (1966), Dunn (1965); specifically investigated in early feminist writing (Hall 1974); Oakley (1974) and the domestic labour debate (Malos 1980); central to serial drama as distinct as Helen Trent (Arnheim 1944) and *Crossroads* and a figure of concern to those writing on soap opera in both the 1940s and the 1970s. However, this other to feminism is present only in the most dispersed forms in the interviews, and usually in guises other than that of 'the housewife'. My interviewees were uniformly scrupulous in their avoidance of this appellation, although they all did, differently and at different points in their narratives, articulate some sense of the historical complexity of the relationships between feminism and women. Soap opera was usually the site or figure on or through which that was articulated, but the complexity of these relationships was increased by the interviewees' own dipping in and out of identifications.[3] However, it remains significant that all the interviewees watched and enjoyed soap opera. The pleasures and involvements explored in the articles and books which they wrote were their own pleasures—as well as those of other women. And indeed, one result of the research, as is evident from the interviews, is the extraordinarily sophisticated manner in which they appraise their own viewing involvement.

Less predicted were the plural 'others' to feminism who peopled the stories—and indeed, in at least two cases were the original source of the interest in soap opera. I, perhaps rather reductively, had expected mothers. This was because I would, to some extent, hold to the relative commonplace that one way of thinking the generation of women who composed the second-wave women's movement was as a generation of daughters—daughters who were determined that they would not grow up like their mothers. Daughters who would not be housewives like their mothers—for even mothers who did paid work outside the home in the 1940s and 1950s had still retained that primary definition. Daughters who would not watch soap opera. And indeed there were mothers for all the younger women. But perhaps more significantly, there were families of origin, fathers—and particularly sisters. These stories did, repeatedly, include female others who had grown up differently—often more conventionally in terms of a feminine career than my interviewees. Sometimes these were sisters,

3 Nancy Miller addresses the issue of identification between feminist scholar and their subjects slightly differently, in the answer to a question put to 'senior feminists by junior feminists': 'It is true that the litany label ["white, middle class, heterosexual and [above all!] East Coast American"] (saved, I was hoping comedically, by the ECA) describes a good number of feminist critics, but do you think feminist critics necessarily take themselves for the women they work on? That is a potentially more devastating question for feminist epistemology than the implications of racism. When I think about a (white heterosexual) seventeenth century aristocratic French woman writer, do I imagine she really lives in Manhattan? Is me? Maybe, but is that the bad news or the good news?' (1990: 77)

sometimes fellow students, sometimes work colleagues. There were also, perhaps not surprisingly, the students whom some of the interviewees taught. Young women whom the speakers variously felt answerable to, responsible for, impatient with, protective of. Those same young women who prompted me to think about their puzzlement when studying feminist writing on soap opera and melodrama. Young women about whom, I must conclude, we (the interviewees and I) could be found to be 'worrying responsibly'.

Can we make sense of this in the terms proposed here? My own suggestion would be that one of the changes that has occurred in the period between the doing (the research and writing in the period of our study, approximately 1976–83) and the telling (these interviews) of the first feminist research on soap opera has been a loosening of an understanding of feminism as primarily an 'identity' in favour of a rather more flexible understanding of it as a 'position' (or indeed, more than one position). That is, in the early politicized period of second-wave feminism, the movement was one with the aspiration of forging a new way of being a woman—a different kind of femininity. This new identity was forged in opposition to conventional femininity. In relation to this work, and other early research on soap opera discussed, it is useful to point to the textual construction of the non- or pre-feminist female as a significant presence—the figure I have called 'the housewife'. However, I would want to stress that this figure, whom I have called one of the personae of feminist television criticism, is not proposed as a real person—she is precisely constructed by feminism as what the feminist is not. She is the site of the 'othering' of conventional femininity, an 'othering' which is necessary for the constitution of the emergent identity, the feminist.

Listening to the interviews, going through the transcripts, I was struck by the absence of the housewife, but impressed by the nuanced sensitivity to the fleeting identifications of gender. That is, the dualism of early second-wave feminism (feminist/not feminist) has been transformed, at least for the interviewees, into a much more complex apprehension of the lures and burdens of feminine identity, as well as a continuing endeavour to apprehend gender as just one determinant of identity. If I return to the students that I taught, and their response to the certainties of early feminist writing, the interviews would lead me to conclude that it is clearly not just students in feminist classrooms who experience 'gaps' when they encounter words like 'women' and 'feminist'. All of the interviewees—and I don't mean to make them sound as if they were complaining, for they weren't—meditated at various points on the different modalities of 'being' a woman and a feminist. Thus the project as a whole would suggest that the opposition feminist/housewife was polemically and historically formative for second-wave feminism and that the exploration of this

opposition in the attention to soap opera was significant and generative. However, the evidence of the interviews further suggests that it
would be mistaken to suppose that continued attention to soap opera
should be a preferred direction for feminist research—or indeed that
research on soap opera is in some ways, essentially, feminist. It is precisely the historical specificity of the encounter between feminism
and soap opera in the late 1970s and early 1980s which the project
reveals as significant. Thus more recent work, such as that of Louise
Spence (1995), Martha Nochimson (1992), and Mary Ellen Brown
(1994), which continues to work within what we might call the 'soap-
defencist' paradigm, reproducing a defence of soap opera as 'women's
culture', tells us little new, not because there is not more information
about soap opera therein, but because the speaking positions are
taken for granted. That is to say, this project, in its exploration of the
constitution of the 'new' speaking position of the feminist intellectual—and the nervy pressing at limits this entailed—suggests that it
is this, the production of positions, rather than the object of study as
such, which was significant in the feminist encounter with soap opera.

Indeed, in relation to soap opera, this analysis would suggest that
new directions of research should follow directions suggested in the
interviews by, in particular, Ien Ang and Ellen Seiter, where the
emphasis would be on a more global perspective and a detachment
from the concerns of white femininity which have been so formative
to the study area. Here there is some precedent in the recent work of
Gripsrud (1995), Gillespie (1995), and Ang and Stratton (1995), and
the substantial body of non-English language study of, particularly,
South American soap opera.[4] Ang and Stratton (1995) in particular
have been keen to interrogate ideas such as 'cultural imperialism' in
a complex negotiation with theories of the postmodern in their
approach.

At the same time, the repeated stories of the difficulty met in the
endeavour to study a popular low cultural form which are told in the
interviews point to the significance of the feminist approach to soap
opera in legitimating the academic study of popular culture. This is
not the place to enter into further debate about the problems entailed,
but it is perhaps the moment to remember that the study of soap
opera (or, for example, romance) is the study of a subaltern field.[5]
The study of soap opera was innovatory because it addressed this hierarchy in a gendered way. It is the challenge, rather than the object of
study, as these interviews suggest, that is most significant. New challenges may require the constitution of new objects of study—or a

4 See e.g. the work of Ondina Fachel Leal and Martín-Barbero and, in English, but dealing
with Brazil, Tufte (1995).

5 Terry Lovell (forthcoming) raises more generally the issue of the success of feminist
work in subaltern fields.

return to those more established. Indeed, this may be the moment to argue for the importance of a feminist move outside expertise in 'subaltern' fields. These options in turn require the difficult production of new speaking positions. It is in this sense that this essay is historical—it maps, in a small way, the generative interaction of 'the feminist' and 'the housewife' in the 1970s. In the 1990s, although she may not be staying at home all day and watching daytime television, the feminist herself has more than a passing resemblance to a middle-aged, middle-class, heterosexual first-world white woman. She is now a generative other to the new queer politics and the post-colonial movements, just as British soap opera now features more than one 'out' lesbian, something impossible to imagine at the time of these interviews.

Appendix: Example of Interview Transcription

This appendix reproduces the first nineteen pages of the transcription of the interview with Ellen Seiter. Parts of this sequence have been subject to detailed analysis in Chapter 10, and all passages quoted there are printed in bold. Also included is my own introduction to the interview when I offer a series of formulations about the nature of the project.

No attempt has been made to render phonetic detail in the transcriptions—thus for example, laughter is rendered as '[*laughs*]', and 'ums' and 'ers' are excluded. However, in this version, some attempt has been made to render the enormously high frequency of the range of confirmatory noises made by both participants, generally through the conventional use of 'uh-huh' or 'yeah'. The appearance of 'uh-huh' or 'yeah' in square brackets during speech signifies this noisy confirmatory listening which was such a feature of all the interviews, but which is not represented in the extracts used in the analysis chapters. In the same way '[*laughs*]' signifies that the speaker laughs, whereas '[*laughter*]' signifies that both do. Punctuation has been used to some extent in transcription—for example, the use of question marks. The more difficult issues of pausing and pacing, conventionally rendered through commas, full stops, and paragraphs in written English, have in general been represented through the use of commas and dashes, where the dash designates a longer pause.

The inclusion of this lengthy extract from the very beginning of an interview is designed to function as an exemplary control for the reader. The extract provides context for the shorter passages discussed in Chapter 10, while also, in its general narrative development, showing how Ellen Seiter told her story. Against this, the emphases I have given can be measured. What immediately appears as one of my main interpretative practices is the *rearrangement* of Ellen's story. I use a very high proportion of the interview and discuss lengthy quotation in context, but I group material together in different topic groups and themes than her narrative offers sequentially.

As is characteristic of the beginnings of the interviews, most of this sequence is what I would describe a 'referential' narrative. However, in the sequence where Ellen is describing beginning to watch *General Hospital*, she moves into what I would designate 'reflection' as she meditates, with some irony, on the particular audience shifts for this show at this time. This I join in. Slightly later we find the beginnings of theoretical narrative, 'I was first using all the melodrama, you know . . .' although this is not much developed here. As a whole, the extract indicates how complex is the interweaving of identities, narrations, and histories in these accounts.

Note on Pagination The interview with Ellen Seiter, like the one with Dorothy Hobson, was transcribed with very wide margins and quadruple spacing. The extract below is the first nineteen pages of the interview. Different spacing and indeed paper size were used for other interviews, so pagination is not comparable across the interviews as an indicator of length. However, page references have been retained in the text to enable the reader to gauge the sequence in which comments were originally made.

Interview with Ellen Seiter, 21 June 1990 (opening)

CB: I mean really, as I said, my interest—there isn't an idea of ethnography [yeah]—my interest is interviews between really scholars who know each other [*laughs*], and in a way it's a kind of it's to try and think about what we went into the work doing and of course you can only give retrospective accounts [yeah], obviously the way one glosses what one did is probably quite different but that seems to me—I'm kind of interested in if you can think about how you got into it and what you thought you were doing really when you started doing it [uh-huh] and then I suppose at a later point I kind of want to if you can hold the separation—sort of see if that's what you think what you think you did so [yeah]. Do you see what I mean? [yeah] If you did what you thought you were doing. [yeah] So I don't know how . . . because you were at North Western weren't you, is that the Jump Cut crew—?

ES: So basically what happened was, I'd done a film-making degree and I just did, you know, theory and practice kind of stuff, I was making little short experimental films then I taught for a year. I got hired to replace somebody and then I decided to go back to school [uh-huh] because my mother told me why don't you get a Ph.D. because that will be a more pleasant life for you because you're obviously not going to work in the industry and you know, take the train at night to downtown Chicago and work sixty hours a week, so that's one part of it so then I was back in school and I took a melodrama class from Chuck Kleinhans, OK, [yeah] which was all movies, we read *Mommie Dearest* and saw Joan Crawford movies and that and I was in the film—it was 'Radio-TV-film', but I was in the film division so it was all film and this was 1979 when I went back to school and we could write about anything that we, we had to keep like a diary a journal and we could write about anything we wanted to and I was writing about *General Hospital* which I was watching for the first time [uh-huh]. **What happened was I met a woman started the programme at that time Lisa Lewis [uh-huh] and she and I would go to the cafeteria every day and eat our lunch at two o'clock which was the only time postgraduate students hung out with the staff in the cafeteria. It was a huge room with like maybe seventy-five seats and it was the first [*inaudible: one word*] projected television video thing so we were watching that then just about every day and the group got larger, you know larger and larger and some men would come and watch too, although none of the men I was involved with of course they wouldn't be caught dead, [*laughter*] so I decided I would write about that, but the real part of it was that before that when I was in college my sister who was then in law school started talking to me all the time about The Young and the Restless and saying you should really watch this.**

CB: Is that because she thought it was telling her things about her life or . . .

ES: She just loved it. **And my sister is somebody who aspires, my sister was in sociology and she likes to think of herself as completely normal, she likes to read the *National Enquirer* and she likes to have her finger on the pulse of sort of popular culture and she has been consistently sort of my informant,** she says look, I mean this kids' TV stuff you know she's getting into that too, she's taken me, she takes me through my clothing and she takes me through my television viewing—.

CB: So she's like Janice Radway's Dot—[*laughter*].

ES: And she, she then she became a lawyer and she doesn't get to do this stuff, basically cultural studies is what she wants . . . you know . . . and she has really wanted to do a graduate degree in sociology, but my mother told her [*laughs*] that that was too impractical and she should go to law school [*laughs*]. **But what happened because it's very clear to me about just sort of the introduction to soap operas, because nobody watched them, my mother always worked and nobody, there was no daytime television, she started watching it during her break from classes and law school and then that year I would go up and visit her, I spent a lot of time visiting her, as a teenager you know sort of going wild you know away from home and on this vacation she would force me to watch it and she would ask me when she was phoning me up at college about are you watching you know can you find a student lounge where you can watch it. So that was kind of the background, but I never was really around a TV enough to watch it, but then by the time, so that was like '73, so then back up to '79 by this time my mother was living in Chicago and working as a legal proof-reader and she was then starting—she didn't used to have a job where you would talk about television but then there was a radio that they brought to the office where she was a legal proof-reader and her partner a black woman lived on the south side of Chicago was listening to the soap opera so there was that kind of interest that I you know then I found this time of day that I could then watch this one and then she was also talking to me about it and both my mother and my sister as you know, it was very important and I was kind of horrified when my sister first started talking about them, you know I did think, I did kind of wonder about her and I didn't have a particularly strong stereotype about it but it was just completely foreign to be doing that my mother then was totally open to it at her work and stuff and clearly saw it as you know something that you could talk to women who were much younger about, so anyway and then there was this melodrama class and that was kind of so then I started writing about *General Hospital*. And that was by the way, a time 1978–9 when like *millions* of people in the United States started watching specifically *General Hospital* at that time and when *General Hospital* had a producer that started trying to reach younger women they brought in William M—so, and there was this plot around Luke and Laura that you know so although I wasn't aware of that at the time to be the age that I was then and to start watching that show you know it was definitely a mass movement. [*laughter*]**

CB: Demographically [*laughter*] you were personally choosing something that was laid out for you.

ES: Yes, that's right [*laughs*]. **So then I just started writing about it and just kind of figuring out the rules of it and applying but at that time applying things about nineteenth-century stage melodrama to soap opera, so by the end of that year, and Chuck Kleinhans was very enthusiastic about what I was writing about soap opera, so by the end of that year you know I sort of needed a dissertation topic and chose that and these teen pics from the '70s** *Highest Castles, You Light Up My Life* **and** *The Promise,* movies whose music themes are played in stores to this day constantly like the major musak numbers of [*laughter*] so—.

CB: . . . which you must recognize the minute you go into stores (laughs).

ES: **Oh yes [*laughs*] so, and but I kind of, so I was first using all the melodrama, you know I read Tania Modleski's thing I read, Carol Lopate, I read Renata Adler—you know Laura Mulvey you know [yeah] was around all that time but what I thought I was doing was I did you know which I sometimes still interested in doing is crossing film and television stuff and I tried to look at all the supporting materials within soap opera, [uh-huh] I'd just look at the production the advertising packages on the films and all of that and then I was in that Feminar group that started at the same time.**

CB: **Which did the Film Reader?**

ES: **Yeah. Which did the Film Reader and did the conference. So I gave the paper at that conference and it was wildly well received, you know, [uh-huh] a sort of very early public paper about soap opera including that the people who put up the money for the conference and who then had all of us to this cocktail party and stuff. I was the one, they chose my paper to go to and they chose me to talk about because they were sort of closet soap opera viewers.**

CB: And did they . . . I mean like, when I've talked to other people like Dorothy there's been like this moment of recognition like somebody serious is doing something or somebody is doing something [yes] serious about this thing which nobody else has done anything serious about or some—.

ES: **Yes, yeah and that you know I think the thing for me was that I had you know I was coming out of this experimental film thing and also these sort of fantasies of being a film-maker so when I switched over to criticism the kind of giving up of being a film-maker was—well already about something really popular and that you know that's something that—all the—I mean, it still happens to me constantly that people will sort of light up and start talking about soap opera and that it's a way of being an academic with thinking that you're still kind of 'in touch' in some way.**

CB: It's sort of like being not an academic academic or—.

ES: Yes, yes, which I think I have a lot invested in anyway you know, you know, that I've sort of tried to and then of course you think about teaching you know, would you rather teach *Riddles of the Sphinx* or *General Hospital* in terms of the different kinds of student reactions that you get? Like I always, I basically always had a problem in teaching film that I was lacking some conviction to convince the students that this extremely difficult stuff like Michael Snow and you know, was worth it you know I you know I knew how to do it but I couldn't really get up you know when they would sort of say 'Bleah, well you know, this is horrible' and you know and then as I went on teaching I was teaching larger and larger classes you know 250 students in a film history class you know that's been kind of a recurring issue for me that I somehow, that has made me feel that I'm kind of in the wrong business and that I should be in TV criticism, although I never get to teach TV criticism hardly ever, I teach film history and production classes, so, which always seems also easier to me to teach despite this problem of lack of conviction about taking difficult and dealing with avant-garde stuff, **I still like the big bang that you get in like a feminist criticism class about switching to soap opera and the way that suddenly students are talking in a way—who do not normally talk and also what happens with the women and the men in the class. So I think the initial thing to me was also getting you know was very much a sense of trying to valorize soap opera as women's TV and it was also at a point then in the '70s when there was all this about, the mass comm. stuff, was about the absence of women the Gaye Tuchman, the symbolic annihilation thing [uh-huh] so a lot of the initial impulse was just to sort of say, Look here's something where there are lots of women on the screen and you can, so let's talk about this because that's the representation we're getting, so let's sort of take that apart.** And then, so that was one part of the interest and then the other part was just kind of the melodramatic mode, but I was more influenced by stuff by Peter Brooks and Thomas Elsaesser [yeah]. You know I still sort of— Thomas Elsaesser's article is still kind of the the you know and that had a huge impact on me you know actually more than you know, some other things—.

CB: But also I mean I think Peter Brooks I think it's a great book you know. [uh-huh]

Bibliography

ADAMS, MARY LOUISE (1989), 'There's No Place Like Home: On the Place of Identity in Feminist Politics', *Feminist Review*, 31: 22–33.

ADAMS, PARVEEN, and COWIE, ELIZABETH (1990), *The Woman in Question: m/f* (London: Verso).

ALASUUTARI, PERTTI (1992), 'I'm Ashamed to Admit It But I Have Watched *Dallas*: The Moral Hierarchy of Television Programmes', *Media Culture and Society* 14/4: 561–82.

ALEXANDER, SALLY (1994), *Becoming a Woman* (London: Virago).

ALLEN, ROBERT C. (1983), 'On Reading Soaps: A Semiotic Primer', in Kaplan (1983*a*), 97–108.

—— (1985), *Speaking of Soap Operas* (Chapel Hill, NC: University of North Carolina Press).

—— (1987) (ed.), *Channels of Discourse* (Chapel Hill, NC: University of North Carolina Press).

—— (1989), 'Bursting Bubbles: "Soap Opera", Audiences, and the Limits of Genre', in Seiter et al. (1989*b*), 44–55.

—— (1995), *To Be Continued . . . Soap Operas around the World* (London: Routledge).

ALLEN, ROD (1977), 'Edinburgh Report', *Broadcast* 929 (12/9/1977), 10–17.

ALTHUSSER, LOUIS (1971), 'Ideology and Ideological State Apparatuses', in *Lenin and Philosophy and Other Essays* (London: New Left Books), 121–73.

ANG, IEN (1982), *Het Geval* Dallas (Amsterdam: Uitgervarij SUA).

—— (1985), *Watching* Dallas: *Soap Opera and the Melodramatic Imagination* (London: Methuen).

—— (1987), 'The Vicissitudes of "Progressive Television" ', *New Formations*, 2: 91–106.

—— (1988), 'Feminist Desire and Female Pleasure', *Camera Obscura*, 16: 179–91.

—— (1989*a*), 'Beyond Self-Reflexivity', *Journal of Communication Inquiry*, 13/2: 27–9.

—— (1989*b*), 'Wanted: Audiences. On the Politics of Empirical Audience Research', in Seiter et al. (1989*b*), 96–115.

—— (1990*a*), 'Culture and Communication: Towards an Ethnographic Critique of Media Consumption in the Transnational Media System', *European Journal of Communication*, 5/2: 239–60.

—— (1990*b*), 'Melodramatic Identifications: Television and Women's Fantasy', in Brown (ed.) (1990*b*), 75–88.

—— (1991), *Desperately Seeking the Audience* (London: Routledge).

—— (1992), 'Hegemony in Trouble: Nostalgia and the Ideology of the Impossible in European Cinema', in Duncan Petrie (ed.), *Screening Europe* (London: BFI), 21–31.

Ang, Ien (1994), 'On Not Speaking Chinese', *New Formations*, 24: 1–18.

—— (1995*a*), 'I'm a Feminist But . . . "Other" Women and Postnational Feminism', in Barbara Caine and Rosemary Pringle (eds.), *Transitions: New Australian Feminisms* (St Leonards: Allen and Unwin), 57–73.

—— (1995*b*), *Living Room Wars* (London: Routledge).

—— and Hermes, Joke (1991), 'Gender and/in Media Consumption', in Curran and Gurevitch (1991), 307–29.

—— and Stratton, Jon (1995), 'The End of Civilisation as We Knew It: *Chances* and the Post-Realist Soap Opera', in Allen (1995), 122–44.

—— and Tee, Ernie (1983), 'De televisier als kroegmaat' in *De Groene Amsterdammer* (5 Jan. 1983) (n.p.).

Angelou, Maya (1984), *I Know Why the Caged Bird Sings* (London: Virago) (1st pub. 1969).

Arnheim, Rudolf (1944), 'The World of the Daytime Serial', in Lazarsfeld and Stanton (1944), 38–45.

Ascher, Carol (1981), *Simone de Beauvoir: A Life of Freedom* (Boston: Beacon Press).

—— (1993), 'On "Clearing the Air": My Letter to Simone de Beauvoir' in Carol Ascher, Louise DeSalvo, and Sara Ruddick (eds.), *Between Women* (New York: Routledge), 85–103.

Association of Cinematograph and Television Technicians (ACTT) (1975), *Patterns of Discrimination against Women in the Film and Television Industries* (London: ACTT).

Atkinson, Paul (1990), *The Ethnographic Imagination: Textual Constructions of Reality* (London: Routledge).

Baehr, Helen (1981), 'Women's Employment in British Television', *Media, Culture and Society*, 3/2: 125–34.

Barrett, Michelle, and Phillips, Anne (1992) (eds.), *Destabilizing Theory: Contemporary Feminist Debates* (Cambridge: Polity Press).

Basinger, Jeanine (1993), *How Hollywood Spoke to Women 1930–1960* (New York: Random House).

Bathrick, Serafina (1984), 'The *Mary Tyler Moore Show*: Women at Home and at Work', in Jane Feuer et al. (eds.) *MTM: Quality Television* (London: BFI), 99–131.

Bausinger, Hermann (1984), 'Media, Technology and Daily Life', *Media, Culture and Society*, 6/4: 343–51.

Beauvoir, Simone de (1959), *Memoirs of a Dutiful Daughter* (London: Andre Deutsch and Weidenfeld and Nicolson).

—— (1963), *The Prime of Life* (London: Andre Deutsch and Weidenfeld and Nicolson).

—— (1965), *Force of Circumstance* (London: Andre Deutsch and Weidenfeld and Nicolson).

—— (1977), *All Said and Done* (London: Andre Deutsch and Weidenfeld and Nicolson).

Belsey, Catherine (1980), *Critical Practice* (London: Methuen).

Benney, Mark, and Hughes, Everett C. (1977), 'Of Sociology and the Interview', in Martin Bulmer (ed.), *Social Research Methods* (London: Macmillan), 233–42.

BENSTOCK, SHARI (1988), *The Private Self: Theory and Practice of Women's Autobiographical Writings* (London: Routledge).

BERNSTEIN, SUSAN DAVID (1992), 'Confessing Feminist Theory: What's "I" Got To Do with It?', *Hypatia* 7/2: 120–47.

BETTERTON, ROSEMARY (1985), 'How Do women Look? The Female Nude in the Work of Suzanne Valadon', *Feminist Review*, 19: 3–24.

BIRMINGHAM POPULAR MEMORY GROUP, CENTRE FOR CONTEMPORARY CULTURAL STUDIES (1982), 'Popular Memory: Theory, Politics, Method', in Richard Johnson et al. (eds.), *Making Histories: Studies in History-Writing and Politics* (London: Hutchinson), 205–52.

BLAND, LUCY, et al. (1978), 'Women "Inside and Outside" the Relations of Production', in Women's Studies Group (1978), 35–78.

BOBO, JACQUELINE (1988), '*The Color Purple*: Black Women as Cultural Readers', in Pribram (1988), 90–109.

—— and SEITER, ELLEN (1991), 'Black Feminism and Media Criticism: *The Women of Brewster Place*', *Screen* 32/3: 286–302.

BORDO, SUSAN (1990), 'Feminism, Postmodernism and Gender Scepticism', in Nicholson (1990), 133–56.

BOURDIEU, PIERRE (1984), *Distinction: A Social Critique of the Judgement of Taste*, trans. R. Nice (London: Routledge & Kegan Paul) (1st pub. 1979).

—— (1988), *Homo Academicus*, trans. Peter Collier (Cambridge: Polity Press) (1st pub. 1984).

—— (1990), *In Other Words: Essays Towards a Reflexive Sociology* (Cambridge: Polity Press).

BRAIDOTTI, ROSI (1994), *Nomadic Subjects* (New York: Columbia University Press).

BROOKS, PETER (1976), *The Melodramatic Imagination: Balzac, Henry James, Melodrama and the Mode of Excess* (New Haven: Yale University Press).

BROWN, MARY ELLEN (1990*a*), 'Motley Moments: Soap Opera, Carnival, Gossip and the Power of Utterance', in Brown (1990*b*), 183–200.

—— (1990*b*) (ed.), *Television and Women's Culture: The Politics of the Popular* (London: Sage).

—— (1994), *Soap Opera and Women's Talk* (Thousand Oaks, Calif.: Sage).

BROWNMILLER, SUSAN (1984), *Femininity* (London: Collins Publishing Group).

BRULEY, SUE (1976), *Women Awake: The Experience of the Consciousness Raising* (London: Sue Bruley).

BRUNSDON, CHARLOTTE (1981), '*Crossroads*: Notes on Soap Opera', *Screen*, 22/4 (1981), 32–7.

—— (1989), 'Text and Audience', in Seiter et al. (1989*b*), 116–29.

—— (1990), 'Problems with Quality', *Screen* 31/1: 67–90.

—— (1991), 'Pedagogies of the Feminine: Feminist Teaching and Women's Genres', *Screen* 32/4: 364–81.

—— (1993), 'Identity in Feminist Television Criticism', *Media, Culture and Society*, 15: 309–20.

—— (1995), 'A Thief in the Night', in David Morley and Huan Ksing Chen (eds.), *Stuart Hall: Critical Dialogues* (London: Routledge), 276–85.

—— D'ACCI, JULIE, and SPIGEL, LYNN (1997) (eds.), *Feminist Television Criticism* (Oxford: Oxford University Press).

BRUNSDON, CHARLOTTE, and MORLEY, DAVID (1978), *Everyday Television: Nationwide* (London: British Film Institute).

BRUNT, ROSALIND (1983), 'Street Credibility', *Marxism Today* (Dec.), 38–9.

BUCKINGHAM, DAVID (1987), *Public Secrets:* EastEnders *and its Audience* (London: British Film Institute).

BUCKMAN, PETER (1984), *All for Love: A Study in Soap Opera* (London: Secker and Warburg).

BURGELIN, OLIVIER (1972), 'Structural Analysis and Mass Communication', in Denis McQuail (ed.), *Sociology of Mass Communications* (Harmondsworth: Penguin), 313–28.

BURGIN, VICTOR, DONALD, JAMES, and KAPLAN, CORA (1986) (eds.), *Formations of Fantasy* (London: Methuen).

BUTCHER, HELEN, COWARD, ROS, EVARISTI, MARCELLA, GARBER, JENNY, HARRISON, RACHEL, and WINSHIP, JANICE (1974), *Images of Women in the Media*, Stencilled Occasional paper, Centre for Contemporary Cultural Studies, University of Birmingham.

BUTLER, JEREMY (1986), 'Notes on the Soap Opera Apparatus: Televisual Style and *As the World Turns*', *Cinema Journal*, 25/3: 53–70.

—— (1991), 'I'm Not a Doctor But I Play One on TV: Characters, Actors and Acting in Television Soap Opera', *Cinema Journal*, 30/4: 75–91.

—— (1993), 'Redesigning Discourse: Feminism, the Sitcom and *Designing Women*', *Journal of Film and Video*, 45/1: 13–26.

BUTLER, JUDITH (1990), *Gender Trouble* (New York: Routledge).

—— (1992), 'Contingent Foundations: Feminism and the Question of "Postmodernism"', in Butler and Scott (1992), 3–21.

—— and SCOTT, JOAN (1992) (eds.), *Feminists Theorize the Political* (New York: Routledge).

BYARS, JACKIE (1991), *All that Hollywood Allows* (Chapel Hill, NC: University of North Carolina Press).

CAMERA OBSCURA COLLECTIVE (1989), *The Spectatrix*, *Camera Obscura* 20–1.

CAMPBELL, BEATRIX (1987), *The Iron Ladies: Why Do Women Vote Tory?* (London: Virago).

CANTOR, MURIEL (1978), 'Where Are the Women in Public Broadcasting?', in Gaye Tuchman et al. (1978), 78–90.

—— (1979), 'Our Days and Our Nights on TV', *Journal of Communication*, 29/4: 66–88.

CANTOR, MURIEL, and PINGREE, SUZANNE (1983), *The Soap Opera* (London: Sage, 1983).

CASSATA, MARY, and SKILL, THOMAS (1983), *Life on Daytime Television: Tuning in American Serial Drama* (Norwood, NJ: Ablex).

CAUGHIE, JOHN (1980), 'Progressive Television and Documentary Drama', *Screen*, 21/3: 9–35.

CLIFFORD, JAMES, and MARCUS, GREGORY (1986) (eds.), *Writing Culture: The Poetics and Politics of Ethnography* (Berkeley and Los Angeles: University of California Press).

CLARKE, JOHN (1991), *New Times and Old Enemies* (London: Harper Collins Academic).

—— HALL, STUART, JEFFERSON, TONY, and ROBERTS, BRIAN (1975) (eds.), *Resistance through Rituals* (Working Papers in Cultural Studies 7/8).

COOK, PAM (1983), 'Melodrama and the Women's Picture', in Sue Aspinall and Robert Murphy (eds.), *Gainsborough Melodrama* (London: British Film Institute), 14–28.

—— (1999), *'It's Only a Movie'* (London: Routledge).

—— and JOHNSTON, CLAIRE (1975), *Dorothy Arzner* (London: BFI).

COOK, SAMANTHA (1990), 'A Particularly Valuable Service', in Janet Willis and Tana Wollen (eds.), *The Neglected Audience* (London: British Film Institute), 45–56.

CORNER, JOHN (1991), 'Meaning, Genre and Context: The Problematics of "Public Knowledge" in the New Audience Studies', in Curran and Gurevitch (1991), 267–306.

—— (1999), *Critical Ideas in Television Studies* (Oxford: Oxford University Press).

COWARD, ROSALIND (1984), *Female Desire* (London: Paladin).

COWIE, ELIZABETH (1984), 'Fantasia', *m/f* 9: 71–104.

CREEDON, PAMELA (1989) (ed.), *Women in Mass Communication: Challenging Gender Values* (Beverley Hills, Calif.: Sage).

CRUZ, JON, and LEWIS, JUSTIN (1994), *Viewing, Reading, Listening: Audiences and Cultural Reception* (Boulder, Colo.: Westview).

CULLER, JONATHAN (1983), *On Deconstruction* (London: Routledge and Kegan Paul).

CURRAN, JAMES (1991), 'The New Revisionism in Mass Communication Research: A Reappraisal', *European Journal of Communication*, 5/2–3: 135–64.

—— and GUREVITCH, MICHAEL (1991) (eds.), *Mass Media and Society* (Sevenoaks: Edward Arnold).

D'ACCI, JULIE (1987), 'The Case of *Cagney and Lacey*', in Helen Baehr and Gillian Dyer (eds.), *Boxed In: Women and Television* (London: Pandora), 203–25.

—— (1994), *Television and the Case of* Cagney and Lacey (Chapel Hill, NC: University of North Carolina Press).

DAVIES, KATH, DICKEY, JULIENNE, and STRATFORD, THERESA (1987) (eds.), *Out of Focus: Writing on Women and the Media* (London: Women's Press).

DOANE, MARY ANN (1987), *The Desire to Desire: The Woman's Film of the 1940s* (Bloomington, Ind.: Indiana University Press).

DOUGLAS, SUSAN J. (1995), *Where the Girls Are* (Harmondsworth: Penguin).

DOWNING, MILDRED (1974), 'The Heroine of the Daytime Serial', *Journal of Communication*, 24: 130–9.

DUNKLEY, CHRISTOPHER (1985), *Television Today and Tomorrow: Wall-to-Wall Dallas?* (Harmondsworth: Penguin).

DUNN, NELL (1965), *Talking to Women* (London: MacGibbon and Kee).

DYER, RICHARD (1977), 'Entertainment and Utopia', *Movie*, 24: 2–13.

—— (1970), *Stars* (London: British Film Institute).

DYER, RICHARD (1979), *Stars* (London: British Film Institute).

—— LOVELL, TERRY, and MCCRINDLE, JEAN (1977), 'Soap Opera and Women', in *Edinburgh International Festival Official Programme*, free suppl. to *Broadcast* 926 (22 Aug. 1977), 24–8.

—— GERAGHTY, CHRISTINE, JORDAN, MARION, LOVELL, TERRY, PATERSON, RICHARD, and STEWART, JOHN (1981), *Coronation Street* (London: British Film Institute).

ELSAESSER, THOMAS (1972), 'Tales of Sound and Fury: Observations on the Family Melodrama', *Monogram*, 4: 2–15.

EVANS, CAROLINE, and THORNTON, MINNA (1989), *Women and Fashion: A New Look* (London: Quartet).

EVANS, SARA (1979), *Personal Politics: The Roots of Women's Liberation in the Civil Rights Movement and the New Left* (New York: Alfred A. Knopf Inc.).

FEMINIST REVIEW COLLECTIVE (1986), *Waged Work: A Reader* (London: Virago).

—— (1987), *Sexuality: A Reader* (London: Virago).

FEUER, JANE (1984), 'Melodrama, Serial Form and Television Today', *Screen* 25/1: 4–17.

—— (1992), 'Reading *Dynasty*: Television and Reception Theory', in Jane Gaines (ed.), *Classical Hollywood Narrative: The Paradigm Wars* (Durham, NC: Duke University Press), 276–93 (paper presented at International Television Studies Conference, London, 1986).

FILM READER (1982), 5.

FINCH, JANET (1984), ' "It's Great to Have Someone to Talk To": The Ethics and Politics of Interviewing Women', in Colin Bell and Helen Roberts (eds.), *Social Researching: Politics, Problems, Practice* (London: Routledge and Kegan Paul), 70–87.

FISKE, JOHN (1987a), *Television Culture* (London: Routledge).

—— (1987b), 'British Cultural Studies and Television', in Allen (1987), 254–90.

—— and HARTLEY, JOHN (1978), *Reading Television* (London: Methuen).

FLITTERMAN, SANDY (1983), 'The Real Soap Operas: TV Commercials', in Kaplan (1983a), 84–96.

FLITTERMAN-LEWIS, SANDY (1987), 'Psychoanalysis, Film and Television', in Allen (1987), 172–210.

—— (1988), 'All's Well that doesn't End: Soap Operas and the Marriage Motif', *Camera Obscura*, 16: 119–28.

—— (1990), *To Desire Differently: Feminism and the French Cinema* (Urbana, Ill.: University of Illinois Press).

FOUCAULT, MICHEL (1970), *The Order of Things: An Archaeology of the Human Sciences* (London: Tavistock).

FRANKENBERG, RUTH (1993), *White Women, Race Matters* (London: Routledge).

FRANKLIN, SARAH, LURY, CELIA, and STACEY, JACKIE (1991a) (eds.), *Off-Centre: Feminism and Cultural Studies* (London: Harper Collins Academic).

—— (1991b) 'Feminism and Cultural Studies', *Media, Culture and Society*, 13/2: 171–92.

FRENTZ, SUZANNE (1992), *Staying Tuned: Contemporary Soap Opera Criticism* (Bowling Green, Ohio: Bowling Green State University Press).

FREUD, SIGMUND (1973), *New Introductory Lectures on Psychoanalysis* (Harmondsworth: Penguin Books).

—— (1975), *The Psychopathology of Everyday Life* (Harmondsworth: Penguin Books).

FRIEDAN, BETTY (1963), *The Feminine Mystique* (London: Penguin).

FRITH, GILLIAN (1989), 'The Intimacy which is Knowledge: Female Friendship in the Novels of Women Writers', Ph.D. thesis, Department of English and Comparative Literature, University of Warwick.

FRITH, SIMON (1990), 'Review Article: Ross, Shiach, Collins', *Screen* 31/2: 231–5.

GAINES, JANE, and HERZOG, CHARLOTTE (1990) (eds.), *Fabrications: Costume and the Female Body* (London: Routledge).

GALLAGHER, MARGARET (1981), *Unequal Opportunities: The Case of Women and the Media* (Paris: UNESCO Press).

—— (1984), *Employment and Positive Action for Women in the Television Organisations of the EEC Member States* (Brussels: Commission of the European Communities (V/2025/84)).

—— (1985), *Unequal Opportunities: Update* (Paris: UNESCO Press).

—— (1987), 'Redefining the Communications Revolution', in Helen Baehr and Gillian Dyer (eds.), *Boxed-In* (London: Pandora), 19–37.

—— (1992), 'Women and Men in the Media', *Communications Research Trends*, special issue 12/1: 1–36.

GAMMAN, LORRAINE, and MARSHMENT, MARGARET (1988) (eds.), *The Female Gaze: Women as Viewers of Popular Culture* (London: The Women's Press).

GARNHAM, NICHOLAS (1973), *Structures of Television* (London: British Film Institute).

GAVRON, HANNAH (1966), *The Captive Wife* (Harmondsworth: Penguin).

GEERTZ, CLIFFORD (1973), *The Interpretation of Culture* (New York: Basic Books).

—— (1988), *Works and Lives: The Anthropologist as Author* (Cambridge: Polity Press).

GERAGHTY, CHRISTINE (1981), 'The continuous serial: a definition', in Dyer et al. (1981), 9–26.

—— (1983), '*Brookside*: No Common Ground', *Screen* 24/4–5: 137–41.

—— (1989), '*EastEnders*', in Therese Daniels and Jane Gerson (eds.), *The Color Black* (London: British Film Institute), 149–51.

—— (1991), *Women and Soap Opera* (Cambridge: Polity Press).

—— (1992), 'British Soaps in the 1980s', in Dominic Strinati and Stephen Wagg, *Come on Down: Popular Culture in Post-War Britain* (London: Routledge), 133–49.

—— (1995), 'Social Issues and Realist Soaps: A Study of British Soaps in the 1980s/1990s', in Allen (1995), 66–80.

GILBERT, SANDRA, and GUBAR, SUSAN (1979), *The Madwoman in the Attic: The Woman Writer and the Nineteenth Century Literary Imagination* (New Haven: Yale University Press).

GILLESPIE, MARIE (1995), *Television, Ethnicity and Cultural Change* (London: Routledge).

GINZBURG, CARLO (1993), 'Microhistory: Two or Three Things that I Know about It', *Critical Inquiry*, 20/1: 10–35.

GLASGOW UNIVERSITY MEDIA GROUP (1976), *Bad News* (London: Routledge and Kegan Paul).

GLEDHILL, CHRISTINE (1987) (ed.), *Home is Where the Heart Is: Studies in Melodrama and the Woman's Film* (London: British Film Institute).

—— (1988), 'Pleasurable Negotiations', in Pribram (1988), 64–89.

—— (1992), 'Speculations on the Relationship between Soap Opera and Melodrama', *Quarterly Review of Film and Video*, 14: 103–24.

GRAHAM, HILARY (1984), 'Surveying through Stories', in Colin Bell and Helen Roberts (eds.), *Social Researching* (London: Routledge and Kegan Paul), 104–24.

GRANITE (1990), *For Business Only: Gender and New Information Technologies* (Amsterdam: SISWO).

—— (1992), *NICTS and the Changing Nature of the Domestic* (Amsterdam: SISWO).

GRAY, ANN (1987), 'Behind Closed Doors: Video Recorders in the Home', in Helen Baehr and Gillian Dyer (eds.), *Boxed In: Women and Television* (London: Pandora), 38–54.

—— (1992*a*), *Video Playtime: The Gendering of a Leisure Technology* (London: Routledge).

—— (1992*b*), 'Turn Your Living Room into a Frontier of Technology: Gender Relations and New Technologies in the Home', in GRANITE (1992), 99–110.

—— (1995), 'I Want to Tell You a Story: The Narratives of *Video Playtime*', in Beverley Skeggs (ed.), *The Production of Feminist Theory* (Manchester: Manchester University Press), 153–68.

—— (forthcoming), 'Audience Reception Research in Retrospect: The Trouble with Audiences', in Pertti Alasuutaari (ed.), *The Inscribed Audience* (London: Sage).

—— and McGUIGAN, JIM (1993) (eds.), *Studying Culture* (Sevenoaks: Edward Arnold).

GREENBERG, BRADLEY S. (1980), *Life on Television: Content Analyses of US TV Drama* (Norwood, NJ: Ablex).

—— ALTMAN, ROBERT, and NEUENDORF, KIMBERLEY (1987), 'Sex on the Soap Operas: Afternoon Delight', *Journal of Communication*, 31/3: 83–9.

GREENE, GAYLE, and KAHN, COPPELIA (1993), *Changing Subjects: The Making of Feminist Literary Criticism* (New York: Routledge).

GREER, GERMAINE (1971), *The Female Eunuch* (London: Paladin).

GRIPSRUD, JOSTEIN (1991), '*Dynasty* Is History—*Dynasty* As History', Paper to the Fourth International Television Studies Conference, London.

—— (1995), *The Dynasty Years* (London: Routledge).

GROSSBERG, LAWRENCE (1997), *Bringing It All Back Home* (Durham, NC: Duke University Press).

HALL, CATHERINE (1974), 'History of the Housewife', *Spare Rib*, 29: 15–17.

—— (1990), untitled interview in Micheline Wandor (ed.), *Once a Feminist* (London: Virago), 171–82.

—— (1992), *White, Male and Middle Class: Explorations in Feminism and History* (Cambridge, Polity Press).

HALL, STUART (1973), 'Encoding and Decoding in Television Discourse' (Birmingham: Centre for Contemporary Cultural Studies: Stencilled Occasional Paper no. 9).

—— (1980), 'Introduction to Media Studies at the Centre' in Hall et al. (1980), 117–22.

—— (1986), 'New Ethnicities', in Kobena Mercer (ed.), *Black Film, British Cinema*, ICA Document no. 7 (London: ICA), 27–31.

—— (1990), 'The Emergence of Cultural Studies and the Crisis in the Humanities', *October*, 53: 11–23.

—— (1992), 'Cultural Studies and its Theoretical Legacies', in Lawrence Grossberg et al. (eds.), *Cultural Studies* (New York: Routledge), 277–86.

—— CONNELL, IAN, and CURTI, LIDIA (1976), 'The "Unity" of Current Affairs Television', *Working Papers in Cultural Studies*, 9: 51–94.

—— HOBSON, DOROTHY, LOWE, ANDREW, and WILLIS, PAUL (1980) (eds.), *Culture, Media, Language* (London: Hutchinson).

—— and WHANNEL, PADDY (1964), *The Popular Arts* (London: Hutchinson).

HALLORAN, JAMES (1970), *The Effects of Television* (London: Panther).

HAMMERSLEY, MARTIN (1990), *Reading Ethnographic Research* (Harlow: Longman).

HANSEN, MIRIAM (1986), 'Pleasure, Ambivalence, Identification: Valentino and Female Spectatorship', *Cinema Journal*, 25/4: 6–32.

HARAWAY, D. (1985), 'A Manifesto for Cyborgs: Science, Technology and Socialist Feminism in the 1980s', *Socialist Review 15/80: 65–107* repr. in Nicholson (1990).

HARPER, SUE (1983), 'Art Direction and Costume Design', in Sue Aspinall and Robert Murphy (eds.), *Gainsborough Melodrama* (London: British Film Institute), 40–52.

HEATH, STEPHEN, MacCABE, COLIN, and PRENDERGAST, CHRISTOPHER (eds.), (n.d. [c.1974]), *Signs of the Times* (Cambridge: n.pub.).

HEBDIGE, DICK (1981), 'Towards a Cartography of Taste', *Block* 4: 39–56.

HERMES, J. (1993), 'Easily Put Down: Women's Magazines, Readers, Repertoires and Everyday Life' Ph.D. thesis, University of Amsterdam.

—— (1995), *Reading Women's Magazines* (Cambridge: Polity).

HERON, LIZ (1985) (ed.), *Truth, Dare or Promise: Girls Growing Up in the Fifties* (London: Virago).

HERZOG, HERTA (1944), 'What Do We Really Know about Daytime Serial Listeners?', in Lazarsfeld and Stanton (1944), 3–33.

HMSO (1988), *Broadcasting in the '90s: Competition, Choice and Quality* (Cmnd 517), London.

HOARE, QUENTIN, and NOWELL-SMITH, GEOFFREY (1971) (eds.), *Antonio Gramsci: Selections from the Prison Notebooks* (London: Lawrence and Wishart).

HOBSON, DOROTHY (1978*a*), 'A Study of Working Class Women at Home: Femininity, Domesticity and Maternity', MA Diss. University of Birmingham.

HOBSON, DOROTHY (1978*b*), 'Housewives: Isolation as Oppression', in Women's Studies Group (ed.), *Women Take Issue* (London: Hutchinson), 79–95.

—— (1980), 'Housewives and the Mass Media', in Hall et al. (1980), 105–14.

—— (1981*a*), 'Now that I'm Married . . .', in McRobbie and McCabe (1981), 101–13.

—— (1981*b*), 'Meg's Fate: TV Tycoons Write Off the Viewers', *The Times* (7 Nov. 1981) (no page ref.).

—— (1982), *Crossroads: The Drama of a Soap Opera* (London: Methuen).

—— (1985), 'Slippery Soaps', *Edinburgh Television Festival Programme* (London: *Broadcast* (16 Aug. 1985), 43–45).

—— (1989), 'Soap Operas at Work', in Seiter et al. (1989*b*), 150–67.

—— (1990), 'Women Audiences and the Workplace', in Brown (1990*b*), 61–71.

HOGGART, RICHARD (1958), *The Uses of Literacy* (Harmondsworth: Penguin).

HOLLAND, PAT (1987), 'When a Woman Reads the News', in Helen Baehr and Gillian Dyer (eds.), *Boxed in: Women and Television* (London: Pandora), 133–50.

HOLLWAY, WENDY (1982), 'Identity and Gender Difference in Adult Social Relations', Unpublished Ph.D. thesis, University of London.

—— (1989), *Subjectivity and Method in Psychology* (London: Sage).

HONEYFORD, SUE (1980), 'Women and Television', *Screen* 21/2: 49–52.

HOOKS, BELL (1989), *Feminist Theory: From Margin to Centre* (Boston: South End Press).

—— (1991), *Yearning: Race, Gender and Cultural Politics* (London: Turnaround Press).

HOUSTON, BEVERLE (1984), 'Viewing Television: The Metapsychology of Endless Consumption', *Quarterly Review of Film Studies*, 9/3: 183–95.

HURTADO, AIDA (1989), 'Relating to Privilege: Seduction and Rejection in the Subordination of White Women and Women of Color', *Signs*, 14/4: 833–55.

HUYSSEN, ANDREAS (1986), 'Mass Culture as Woman: Modernism's Other', in his *After the Great Divide* (Bloomington, Ind.: Indiana University Press), 44–62.

INDEPENDENT BROADCASTING AUTHORITY (1977*a*), *Annual Report and Accounts 1976–1977* (London: IBA).

—— (1977*b*), *TV and Radio* (London: IBA).

—— (1978*a*), *Annual Report and Accounts 1977–1978* (London: IBA).

—— (1978*b*), *TV and Radio* (London: IBA).

INTINTOLI, MICHAEL (1984), *Taking Soaps Seriously* (New York: Praeger).

JELINEK, ESTELLE (1980) (ed.), *Women's Autobiography: Essays in Criticism* (Bloomington, Ind.: Indiana University Press).

JENNINGS, ROSALYN (1998), 'Watching from the Margins: Female Television Audiences', University of Warwick, unpublished Ph.D. thesis.

JOHNSON, RICHARD (1991), 'Frameworks of Culture and Power: Complexity and Politics in Cultural Studies', *Critical Studies*, 3/1: 17–61.

—— (n.d. [*c*.1993]) 'Two Ways of Remembering: Exploring Memory as Identity', unpublished paper.

JONES, ANN ROSALIND (1993), 'Imaginary Gardens with Real Frogs in Them', in Greene and Kahn (1993), 64–82.

JORDAN, MARION (1981), 'Character Types and the Individual', in Dyer et al. (1981), 67–80.

JOURNAL OF COMMUNICATION INQUIRY (1987), 'The Feminist Issue', 11/1.

JOYRICH, LYNNE (1988), 'All That Television Allows: TV Melodrama Postmodernism and Consumer Culture', *Camera Obscura*, 16: 129–53.

KAPLAN, ALICE (1993), *French Lessons* (Chicago, Chicago University Press).

KAPLAN, E. ANN (1983*a*) (ed.), *Regarding Television* (Los Angeles: American Film Institute).

—— (1983*b*), 'The Case of the Missing Mother: Patriarchy and the Maternal in Vidor's *Stella Dallas*', *Heresies*, 4/4: 81–5.

—— (1987), 'Feminist Criticism and Television', in Allen (1987), 211–53.

—— (1992), *Motherhood and Representation* (New York: Routledge).

KAPLAN, CORA (1986), *Sea Changes: Culture and Feminism* (London: Verso).

KATZ, ELIHU, and LIEBES, TAMAR (1985), 'Mutual Aid in the Decoding of *Dallas*', in Philip Drummond and Richard Paterson (ed.), *Television in Transition* (London: British Film Institute), 187–98.

KATZMAN, NATAN (1972), 'Television Soap Operas: What's Been Going On Anyway?', *Public Opinion Quarterly*, 36/2: 200–12.

KAUFMAN, HELEN (1944), 'The Appeal of Specific Daytime Serials', in Lazarsfeld and Stanton (1944), 86–107.

KAUFMAN, BETTE J. (1992), 'Feminist Facts: Interview Strategies and Political Subjects in Ethnography', *Communication Theory*, 2/3: 187–206.

KAUFFMAN, SUE (1968), *Diary of a Mad Housewife* (London: Michael Joseph).

KILBORN, RICHARD (1992), *Television Soaps* (London: Batsford).

KINGSLEY, HILARY (1988), *Soapbox: The PaperMac Guide to Soap Opera* (London: Macmillan).

KLEINHANS, CHUCK (1978), 'Notes on Melodrama and the Family under Capitalism', *Film Reader*, 3: 40–7.

KRISTEVA, JULIA (1979), 'Le Temps des femmes', *Cahiers de recherche de sciences des textes et documents*, 5: 5–19 (trans. into English as 'Women's Time' by Alice Jardine and Harry Blake, and repr. in *The Kristeva Reader*, ed. Toril Moi (1986), 188–213).

—— (1987), 'My Memory's Hyperbole', in Domna C. Stanton (ed.), *The Female Autograph* (Chicago: University of Chicago Press), 219–35 (1st pub. 1984).

KUHN, ANNETTE (1984), 'Women's Genres', *Screen*, 25/1: 18–28.

—— (1995*a*), *Family Secrets* (London: Virago).

—— (1995*b*) (ed.), *Queen of the 'B's: Ida Lupino behind the Camera* (Trowbridge: Flicks Books).

LAGUARDIA, ROBERT (1977), *From Ma Perkins to Mary Hartman: The Illustrated History of Soap Operas* (New York: Ballantine Books).

LAING, STUART (1986), *Representations of Working-Class Life 1957–1964* (Basingstoke: Macmillan).

LANDY, MARCIA (1991) (ed.), *Imitations of Life* (Detroit: Wayne State University Press).

LAURETIS, TERESA DE (1984), *Alice Doesn't: Feminism, Semiotics, Cinema* (London: Macmillan, 1984).

—— (1987), *Technologies of Gender: Essays on Theory, Film and Fiction* (Bloomington, Ind.: Indiana University Press).

—— (1990), 'Upping the Anti [*sic*] in Feminist Theory', in Marianne Hirsch and Evelyn Fox Keller (eds.), *Conflicts in Feminism* (New York: Routledge), 255–70.

LAZARSFELD, PAUL (1969), 'An Episode in the History of Social Research: A Memoir', in Donald Fleming and Bernard Bailyn (eds.), *The Intellectual Migration: Europe and America, 1930–1960* (Cambridge, Mass.: Harvard University Press), 270–337.

—— and STANTON, FRANK (1944) (eds.), *Radio Research 1942–1943* (New York: Duell, Sloan and Pearce).

LE DOEUFF, MICHÈLE (1991), *Hipparchia's Choice: An Essay Concerning Women, Philosophy etc.* (Oxford: Blackwell); trans. of *L'Étude et le rouet* (1989: Paris: Seuil).

LEAL, ONDINA FACHEL (1990), 'Popular Taste and Erudite Repertoire: The Place and Space of Television in Brazil', *Cultural Studies*, 4/1: 19–29.

LEWIS, LISA (1992), *The Adoring Audience: Fan Culture and Popular Media* (London: Routledge).

LIEBES, TAMAR, and KATZ, ELIHU (1990), *The Export of Meaning: Cross-Cultural Readings of* Dallas (New York: Oxford University Press).

LIGHT, ALISON (1984), ' "Returning to Manderley": Romance Fiction, Female Sexuality and Class', *Feminist Review*, 16: 7–25.

LIVINGSTONE, SONIA (1990), *Making Sense of Television: The Psychology of Audience Interpretation* (Oxford: Pergamon).

—— (1991), 'Audience Reception: The Role of the Viewer in Retelling Romantic Drama', in Curran and Gurevitch (1991), 285–306.

LOPATE, CAROL (1977), 'Daytime Television: You'll Never Want to Leave Home', *Radical America*, 11/1: 33–51 (1st pub. 1976 in *Feminist Studies*, 3 (Spring–Summer), 69–82).

LOPEZ, ANA (1995), 'Our Welcomed Guests: Telenovelas in Latin America', in Allen (1995), 256–75.

LOVELL, TERRY (1980), *Pictures of Reality: Aesthetics, Politics and Pleasures* (London: British Film Institute).

—— (1981), 'Ideology and *Coronation Street*', in Dyer et al. (1981), 40–53.

—— (1987), *Consuming Fiction* (London: Verso).

—— (1990) (ed.), *British Feminist Thought* (Oxford: Blackwell).

—— (1995) (ed.), *Feminist Cultural Studies* (Aldershot: Edward Elgar).

—— (forthcoming), 'If I was a Lad, Do You Think I would say I'm a Lass?: Bourdieu and the Feminist Project', *Feminist Theory* no. 1.

LULL (1991), *Inside Family Viewing* (London: Routledge).

LURY, CELIA (1991), 'Reading the Self: Autobiography, Gender and the Institution of the Literary', in Franklin et al. (1991*a*), 97–108.

McCORMACK, THELMA (1983), 'Male Conceptions of Female Audiences: The Case of Soap Opera', in Ellen Wartella et al. (eds.), *Mass Communication Review Yearbook* (Beverly Hills, Calif.: Sage), 273–83.

McGUIGAN, JIM (1992), *Cultural Populism* (London: Routledge).

McRobbie, Angela (1982*a*), '*Jackie*: An Ideology of Adolescent Femininity', in Bernard Waites et al. (eds.), *Popular Culture: Past and Present* (London: Croom Helm), 263–83.

—— (1982*b*), 'The Politics of Feminist Research: Between Talk, Text and Action', *Feminist Review*, 12: 46–57.

—— (1991), *Feminism and Youth Culture: From* Jackie *to* Just Seventeen (Basingstoke: Macmillan).

—— (1994), *Postmodernism and Popular Culture* (London: Routledge).

—— (1996), '*More!* New Sexualities in Girls' and Women's Magazines', in James Curran et al. (eds.), *Cultural Studies and Communications* (London: Edward Arnold), 172–94.

—— (1998), 'The Es and the Anti-Es: New Questions for Feminism and Cultural Studies', in Marjorie Ferguson and Peter Golding (eds.), *Cultural Studies In Question* (London: Sage), 170–86.

—— and Garber, Jenny (1975), 'Girls and Subcultures: An Exploration', *Working Papers in Cultural Studies*, 7–8: 209–22.

—— and McCabe, Trisha (1981) (eds.), *Feminism for Girls* (London: Routledge and Kegan Paul).

Malos, Ellen (1980), *The Politics of Housework* (London: Allison and Busby).

Mann, Denise, and Spigel, Lynn (1988), *Camera Obscura*, 16: special issue on the female consumer.

Marcus, Laura (1994), *Auto/Biographical Discourse: Criticism, Theory, Practice* (Manchester: Manchester University Press).

Martín-Barbero, Jesus (1995), 'Memory and Form in the Latin-American Soap Opera', in Allen (1995), 276–84.

Martín-Barbero, Jesus, and Muñez, Sonia (1992) (eds.), *Television y melodrama* (Bogota: Tercer Mundo Editores).

Masterman, Len (1980), *Teaching about Television* (London: Macmillan).

—— (1984), *Television Mythologies* (London: Comedia).

Matelski, Marilyn J. (1988), *The Soap Opera Evolution* (Jefferson, NC: McFarland).

Mattelart, Michèle (1975), 'Chile: The Feminine Side of the Coup—When Bourgeois Women Take to the Streets', *Casa de las Americas* (repr. in Mattelart (1986)).

—— (1982), 'Women and the Cultural Industries', *Media, Culture and Society*, 4/11: 133–51.

—— (1986), *Women, Media and Crisis: Femininity and Disorder* (London: Comedia).

Maynard, Mary, and Purvis, June (1994) (eds.), *Researching Women's Lives from a Feminist Perspective* (London: Taylor & Francis).

Mayne, Judith (1988), '*LA Law* and Prime-Time Feminism', *Discourse*, 10/2: 30–47.

—— (1993), *Cinema and Spectatorship* (London: Routledge).

Mellencamp, Patricia (1986), 'Situation Comedy, Feminism and Freud: Discourses of Gracie and Lucy', in Modleski (1986), 80–95.

—— (1990) (ed.), *Logics of Television* (London and Bloomington, Ind.: British Film Institute and Indiana University Press).

Mercer, Kobena (1994), *Welcome to the Jungle* (London: Routledge).

MILLER, NANCY K. (1988), *Subject to Change* (New York: Columbia University Press).

—— (1990) (participant: non-authored compilation), 'Conference Call: Questions put to Senior Feminists by Junior Feminists', *differences*, 2/3: 63–85.

—— (1991), *Getting Personal* (New York: Routledge).

—— (1993), 'Decades', in Greene and Kahn (1993), 31–47.

MILLET, KATE (1971), *Sexual Politics* (London: Hart-Davies).

MITCHELL, JULIET (1971), *Women's Estate* (Harmondsworth: Penguin).

—— (1974), *Psychoanalysis and Feminism* (Harmondsworth: Penguin).

—— and OAKLEY, ANN (1976), *The Rights and Wrongs of Women* (Harmondsworth: Penguin).

MODLESKI, TANIA (1979), 'The Search for Tomorrow in Today's Soap Opera', *Film Quarterly*, 33/1: 12–21.

—— (1982), *Loving with a Vengeance: Mass-Produced Fantasies for Women* (Hamden, Conn.: The Shoestring Press).

—— (1983), 'The Rhythms of Reception: Daytime Television and Women's Work', in Kaplan (1983*a*), 67–75.

—— (1986), *Studies in Entertainment* (Indiana: Indiana University Press).

—— (1991), *Feminism without Women* (New York: Routledge).

MOI, TORIL (1985), *Sexual/Textual Politics* (London: Methuen).

MOORES, SHAUN (1993), *Interpreting Audiences* (London: Sage).

MONTGOMERY, MARTIN (1991), '*Our Tune*: A Study of a Discourse Genre', in P. Scannell (ed.), *Broadcast Talk* (London: Sage), 138–77.

MORLEY, DAVID (1980), *The Nationwide Audience* (London: British Film Institute).

—— (1986), *Family Television* (London: Comedia).

—— (1989), 'Changing Paradigms in Audience Studies', in Seiter et al. (1989*b*), 1–15.

—— (1992), *Television, Audiences and Cultural Studies* (London: Routledge).

—— and SILVERSTONE, ROGER (1991), 'Communication and Context: Ethnographic Perspectives on the Media Audience', in Klaus Bruhn Jensen and Nicholas Jankowski (eds.), *A Handbook of Qualitative Methodologies for Mass Communication Research* (London: Routledge), 149–62.

MORRIS, MEAGHAN (1988), *The Pirate's Fiancée* (London: Verso).

—— (1990), 'Banality in Cultural Studies', in Mellecamp (1990), 14–43.

—— (1994), ' "Too Soon Too Late": Reading Claire Johnston, 1970–1981', in Catriona Moore (ed.), *Dissonance: Feminism and the Arts 1970–1990* (St Leonards, and Woolloomooloo NSW: Allen and Unwin in association with Artspace), 126–38.

MORRISON, TONI (1993) (ed.), *Race-ing Justice, En-gendering Power* (London: Chatto and Windus).

MULVEY, LAURA (1975), 'Visual Pleasure and Narrative Cinema', *Screen*, 163: 6–18.

—— (1977), 'Notes on Sirk and Melodrama', *Movie*, 25: 53–6.

—— (1986), 'Melodrama In and Out of the Home', in Colin MacCabe (ed.), *High Theory/Low Culture* (Manchester: Manchester University Press), 80–100.

—— (1989), *Visual and Other Pleasures* (Basingstoke: Macmillan).

MUMFORD, LINDA STEMPEL (1994*a*), 'Telling My Story: The Narrative Problems of being an Independent Scholar', *Narrative*, 2 (Jan.), 53–64.

—— (1994*b*), 'Confessing TV: Critical Practice and the Autobiographical Gesture in Feminist Television Studies', Paper delivered to the fourth *Console-ing Passions* Conference, Tucson, Arizona.

—— (1995), *Love and Ideology in the Afternoon* (Bloomington, Ind.: Indiana University Press).

NARIMAN, HEIDI (1993), *Soap Operas for Social Change* (Westport, Conn.: Praeger).

NEWCOMB, HORACE (1976), *Television: The Critical View* (New York: Oxford University Press) (5th edn. 1994).

—— and HIRSCH, PAUL (1983), 'Television as a Cultural Forum: Implications for Research', *Quarterly Review of Film Studies*, 8/3: 45–55.

NICHOLSON, LINDA (1990) (ed.), *Feminism/Postmodernism* (New York: Routledge).

NOCHIMSON, MARTHA (1992), *No End to Her: Soap Opera and the Female Subject* (Berkeley and Los Angeles: University of California Press).

NOWELL-SMITH, GEOFFREY (1977), 'Minelli and Melodrama', *Screen*, 18/2: 113–18.

O'CONNOR, ALAN (1989) (ed.), *Raymond Williams on Television* (London: Routledge).

OAKLEY, ANN (1974), *Housewife* (Harmondsworth: Allen Lane).

—— (1981*a*), *From Here to Maternity* (Harmondsworth: Penguin).

—— (1981*b*), 'Interviewing Women: A Contradiction in Terms', in Roberts (1981), 30–61.

—— (1984), *Taking it like a Woman* (London: Jonathan Cape).

OLNEY, JAMES (1988), *Studies in Autobiography* (New York: Oxford University Press).

O'NEALE, SONDA (1985), 'Reconstruction of the Composite Self: New Images of Black Women in Maya Angelou's Continuing Autobiography', in Mari Evans (ed.), *Black Women Writers* (London: Pluto), 25–36.

OPIE, ANNE (1992), 'Qualitative Research, Appropriation of the "Other" and Empowerment', *Feminist Review*, 40: 52–69.

PARKER, IAN (1992), *Discourse Dynamics: Critical Analysis for Social and Individual Psychology* (London: Routledge).

PARKER, ROZSIKA (1984), *The Subversive Stitch: Embroidery and the Making of the Feminine* (London: The Women's Press).

—— and POLLOCK, GRISELDA (1981), *Old Mistresses* (London: Routledge and Kegan Paul).

—— —— (1987), *Framing Feminism: Art and the Women's Movement 1970–1985* (London: Pandora).

PASSERINI, LUISA (1990), 'Mythbiography in Oral History', in Raphael Samuel and Paul Thompson (eds.), *The Myths We Live By* (London: Routledge), 49–60.

PATERSON, RICHARD (1981), 'The Production Context of *Coronation Street*', in Dyer et al. (1981), 53–66.

PEARCE, LYNNE, and STACEY, JACKIE (1995), *Romance Revisited* (London: Lawrence and Wishart).

PENLEY, CONSTANCE (1992), 'Feminism, Psychoanalysis and the Study of Popular Culture', in Lawrence Grossberg et al. (eds.), *Cultural Studies* (New York: Routledge), 479–94.

PERSONAL NARRATIVES GROUP (1989), *Interpreting Women's Lives* (Bloomington, Ind.: Indiana University Press).

PETRO, PATRICE (1986), 'Mass Culture and the Feminine: The "Place" of Television in Film Studies', *Cinema Journal*, 25/3: 5–21.

PHOENIX, ANN (1991), *Young Mothers?* (Cambridge: Polity Press).

—— (1994), 'Practising Feminist Research: The Intersection of Gender and "Race" in the Research Process', in Maynard and Purvis (1994), 49–71.

POLLOCK, GRISELDA (1977), 'Report on the Weekend School', *Screen*, 18/2: 105–13.

—— (1988), *Vision and Difference: Femininity, Feminism and the History of Art* (London: Routledge).

—— (1993), 'The Politics of Theory: Generations and Geographies', *Genders*, 17: 97–120.

PRESS, ANDREA (1987), 'Deconstructing the Audience: Class Differences in Women's Interpretations of Television Narratives and Characters', Ph.D. Diss. University of California at Berkeley.

—— (1990), 'Class, Gender and the Female Viewer', in Brown (1990*b*), 158–80.

—— (1991*a*), *Women Watching Television: Gender, Class and Generation in the American Television Experience* (Philadelphia: University of Pennsylvania Press).

—— (1991*b*), 'Working-Class Women in a Middle-Class World: The Impact of Television on Modes of Reasoning about Abortion', *Critical Studies in Mass Communication*, 8/4: 421–41.

PRIBRAM, E. DEIDRE (1988) (ed.), *Female Spectators: Looking at Film and Television* (London: Verso).

PROBYN, ELSPETH (1989), 'Take My Word for It: Ethnography and Autobiography', *Journal of Communication Inquiry*, 13/2: 18–22.

—— (1993), *Sexing the Self* (London: Routledge).

RABINOVITZ, LAUREN (1991), *Points of Resistance* (Urbana, Ill.: University of Illinois Press).

—— (1992), 'Soap Opera Bridal Fantasies', *Screen*, 33/3: 274–83.

RADFORD, JEAN (1986) (ed.), *The Progress of Romance: The Politics of Popular Fiction* (London: Routledge and Kegan Paul).

RADNER, HILARY (1995), *Shopping Around* (New York: Routledge).

RADWAY, JANICE (1984), *Reading the Romance: Women, Patriarchy and Popular Literature* (Chapel Hill, NC: University of North Carolina Press).

—— (1988), 'The Book-of-the-Month Club and the General Reader: On the Uses of "Serious" Fiction', *Critical Inquiry*, 14/1: 516–38.

—— (1989), 'Ethnography among Elites: Comparing Discourses of Power', *Journal of Communication Inquiry*, 13/2: 3–11.

—— (1994), 'Romance and the Work of Fantasy: Struggles over Feminine Sexuality and Subjectivity at Century's End', in Cruz and Lewis (1994), 213–32.

Rakow, Lana (1986), 'Rethinking Gender Research in Communication', *Journal of Communication*, 36/4: 11–26.

—— (1992) (ed.), *Women Making Meaning* (New York: Routledge).

Rée, Janet (1990), untitled interview in Wandor (1990), 93–106.

Reid, Evelyn Cauleta (1989), 'Viewdata: Television Viewing Habits of Young Black Women in London', *Screen*, 30/1–2: 114–21.

Riley, Denise (1988), *'Am I That Name?' Feminism and the Category of 'Women' in History* (Houndmills, Basingstoke: Macmillan).

—— (1992), 'A Short History of Some Preoccupations', in Butler and Scott (1992), 121–9.

Roberts, Helen (1981) (ed.), *Doing Feminist Research* (London: Routledge and Kegan Paul).

Roberts, Robin (1991), 'Music Videos, Performance and Resistance: Feminist Rappers', *Journal of Popular Culture*, 25/2: 141–52.

Rose, Gillian (1995), *Love's Work* (London: Chatto and Windus).

Rose, Jacqueline (1983), 'Femininity and its Discontents', *Feminist Review*, 14: 5–21.

—— (1986), *Sexuality in the Field of Vision* (London: Verso).

—— (1988), 'Margaret Thatcher and Ruth Ellis', *New Formations*, 6: 3–28.

Rose, Tricia (1990), 'Never Trust a Big Butt and a Smile', *Camera Obscura*, 23: 109–31.

Ross, Andrew (1989), *No Respect: Intellectuals and Popular Culture* (New York: Routledge).

Rowbotham, Sheila (1973a), *Woman's Consciousness, Man's World* (Harmondsworth: Penguin).

—— (1973b), *Hidden from History* (London: Pluto).

—— Segal, Lynne, and Wainwright, Hilary (1979), *Beyond the Fragments: Feminism and the Making of Socialism* (Newcastle and Islington: Newcastle Socialist Centre and Islington Community Press).

Rutherford, Jonathan (1990), *Identity: Community, Culture, Difference* (London: Lawrence and Wishart).

Schlesinger, Philip, et al. (1992), *Women Viewing Violence* (London: British Film Institute).

Schröder, Kim Christian (1987), 'Convergence of Antagonistic Traditions? The Case of Audience Research', *European Journal of Communication*, 2: 7–31.

Schwichtenberg, Cathy (1994), 'Reconceptualizing Gender: New Sites for Feminist Audience Research', in Cruz and Lewis (1994), 169–80.

Scott, Joan W. (1988), 'Gender: A Useful Category of Historical Analysis', in her *Gender and the Politics of History* (New York: Columbia University Press), 28–52.

Screen Editorial Group (1992), *The Sexual Subject: A Screen Reader in Sexuality* (London: Routledge).

Seiter, Ellen (1981a), 'The Promise of Melodrama: Recent Women's Films and Soap Operas', unpublished Ph.D., Northwestern University.

—— (1981b), 'The Role of the Woman Reader: Eco's Narrative Theory and Soap Operas', Paper to the Society for Cinema Studies Conference, New York.

Seiter, Ellen (1982*a*), 'Promise and Contradiction: The Daytime Television Serial', *Film Reader*, 5: 150–63.

—— (1982*b*), 'Eco's TV Guide: The soaps', *Tabloid: A Review of Mass Culture and Everyday Life*, 5: 35–43.

—— (1985*a*), 'The Political is Personal: Margarethe von Trotta's *Marianne and Juliane*', *Journal of Film and Video*, 37/2: 41–6.

—— (1985*b*), 'The Hegemony of Leisure: Aaron Spelling Presents *Loveboat*', in Philip Drummond and Richard Paterson (eds.), *Television in Transition* (London: British Film Institute).

—— (1986), 'Feminism and Ideology: The *Terms* of Women's Stereotypes', *Feminist Review*, 22: 58–81.

—— (1987), 'Semiotics, Structuralism and Television', in Robert C. Allen (ed.), *Channels of Discourse* (London: Routledge), 29–65.

—— (1989), 'To Teach and to Sell: Irna Phillips and her Sponsors 1930–1955', *Journal of Film and Video*, 40/1: 223–47.

—— (1990), 'Making Distinctions: Case Study of a Troubling Interview', *Cultural Studies*, 4/1: 61–84.

—— (1993), *Sold Separately: Children's Television, Toys and Advertising* (New Brunswick, NJ: Rutgers University Press).

—— (1995), 'Mothers Watching Children Watching Television', in Skeggs (1995), 137–52.

—— (1999), *Television and New Media Audiences* (Oxford: Oxford University Press).

—— Borchers, Hans, Kreutzner, Gabriele, and Warth, Eva-Maria (1989*a*), 'Don't Treat Us Like We're So Stupid and Naive', in Seiter et al. (1989*b*), 323–47.

—— (1989*b*) (eds.), *Remote Control: Television, Audiences and Cultural Power* (London: Routledge).

—— and Kreutzner, Gabriele (1989), 'Resisting the Place of the "Ideal Mother"', in Seiter et al. (1989*b*), 237–42.

Shiach, Morag (1989), *Discourse on Popular Culture* (Cambridge: Polity).

Shostak, Marjorie (1989), ' "What the Wind Won't Take Away": The Genesis of *Nisa—The Life and Words of a !Kung Woman*', in Personal Narratives Group (1989), 228–40.

Shotter, John, and Gergen, Kenneth (1989) (eds.), *Texts of Identity* (London: Sage).

Showalter, Elaine (1977), *A Literature of Their Own* (Princeton: Princeton University Press).

Silj, Alessandro (1988), *East of Dallas* (London: British Film Institute).

Silverstone, Roger, and Morley, David (1990), 'Families and their Technologies: Turo Ethnographic Portraits', in Tim Puttnam and Charles Newton (eds.), *Household Choices* (London: Futures Publications), 74–83.

Skeggs, Beverly (1997), *Formations of Class and Gender: Becoming Respectable* (London: Sage).

—— (1995) (ed.), *The Production of Feminist Cultural Theory* (Manchester: Manchester University Press).

Skirrow, Gillian (1986), 'Hellivision: An Analysis of Video Games', in Colin MacCabe (ed.), *High Theory/Low Culture* (Manchester: Manchester University Press), 115–42.

SMITH, VALERIE (1990), 'Black Feminist Theory and the Representation of the "Other"', in Cheryl A. Wall (ed.), *Changing Our Words* (London: Routledge), 38–57.

SNITOW, ANN (1992), 'Feminism and Motherhood', *Feminist Review*, 40: 32–51.

SPARKE, PENNY (1995), *As Long as It's Pink: The Sexual Politics of Taste* (London: Pandora).

SPENCE, JO (1986), *Putting Myself in the Picture* (London: Camden Press).

—— and HOLLAND, PATRICIA (1991) (eds.), *Family Snaps: The Meaning of Domestic Photography* (London: Virago).

SPENCE, LOUISE (1995), ' "They Killed Off Marlena but She's on Another Show Now": Fantasy, Reality, and Pleasure in Watching the Daytime Soap Operas', in Allen (1995), 182–98.

SPIGEL, LYNN (1992), *Make Room for TV: Television and the Family Ideal in Post-War America* (Chicago: University of Chicago Press).

—— (1995), 'From the Dark Ages to the Golden Age: Women's Memories and the Television Reruns', *Screen*, 36/1: 16–33.

SPIVAK, GAYATRI C. (1986), 'Imperialism and Sexual Difference', *Oxford Literary Review*, 8/1–2: 225–40.

—— (1987), *In Other Worlds: Essays in Cultural Politics* (New York: Methuen).

—— (1993), *Outside in the Teaching Machine* (New York: Routledge).

STACEY, JACKIE (1992), *Star-Gazing: Hollywood Cinema and Female Spectatorship in 1940s and 1950s Britain*, Ph.D. Birmingham University.

—— (1994), *Star Gazing: Hollywood Cinema and Female Spectatorship* (London: Routledge).

STANTON, DOMNA (1987), *The Female Autograph* (Chicago: University of Chicago Press).

STANLEY, LIZ (1990*a*) (ed.), *Feminist Praxis* (London: Routledge).

—— (1990*b*), 'Feminist Auto/biography and Feminist Epistemology', in Jane Aaron and Sylvia Walby (eds.), *Out of the Margins: Women's Studies in the Nineties* (Lewes: Falmer Press).

—— and MORGAN, DAVID (1993) (eds.), 'Auto/Biography in Sociology', special issue, *Journal of the British Sociological Association*, 27/1.

—— and WISE, S. (1983), *Breaking Out: Feminist Consciousness and Feminist Research* (London: Routledge and Kegan Paul).

STEDMAN, RALPH (1971), *The Serials* (Norman, Okla.: University of Oklahoma Press).

STEEDMAN, CAROLYN (1982), *The Tidy House* (London: Virago).

—— (1986), *Landscape for a Good Woman* (London: Virago).

—— (1989), 'Women's Biography and Autobiography', in Helen Carr (ed.), *From My Guy to Sci-Fi* (London: Pandora), 98–111.

STEIN, GERTRUDE (1973), *Everybody's Autobiography* (New York: Vintage) (1st pub. 1937).

STERN, LESLEY (1978), 'Oedipal opera: "The Restless Years"', *Australian Journal of Screen Theory*, 4: 39–48.

STUART, ANDREA (1990), 'Feminism, Dead or Alive?', in J. Rutherford (ed.), *Identity* (London: Lawrence and Wishart), 28–42.

SWANSON, GILLIAN (1981), '*Dallas*', *Framework*, 14: 32–5.

TAYLOR, ELLA (1989), *Prime-Time Families: Television Culture in Postwar America* (Berkeley and Los Angeles: University of California Press).

TAYLOR, HELEN (1989), *Scarlett's Women:* Gone with the Wind *and its Female Fans* (London: Virago).

THURBER, JAMES (1948), 'The Listening Women', in his *The Beast in Me and Other Animals* (New York: Harcourt Brace), 251–60.

TORGOVNICK, MARIANNA DE MARCO (1994), *Crossing Ocean Parkway* (Chicago: Chicago University Press).

TRINH, T. MINH-HA (1989), *Woman, Native, Other: Writing, Postcoloniality and Feminism* (Bloomington, Ind.: Indiana University Press).

TUCHMAN, GAYE (1978), 'The Symbolic Annihilation of Women by the Mass Media', in Tuchman, Daniels, and Benét (1978), 3–38.

—— DANIELS, ARLENE K., and BENÉT, JAMES (1978) (eds.), *Hearth and the Home: Images of Women in the Mass Media* (New York: Oxford University Press).

TUFTE, THOMAS (1995), 'How Do Telenovelas Serve to Articulate Hybrid Cultures in Contemporary Brazil?', *Nordicom Review*, 2: 29–36.

TULLOCH, JOHN (1989), 'Approaching the Audience: the Elderly', in Seiter et al. (1989*b*), 180–203.

—— and MORAN, ALBERT (1986), *A Country Practice: 'Quality Soap'* (Sydney: Currency).

TURNER, LYNETTE (1991), 'Feminism, Femininity and Ethnographic Authority', *Women: A Cultural Review*, 2/3: 238–54.

US COMMISSION ON CIVIL RIGHTS (1977), *Window Dressing on the Set: Women and Minorities in Television* (Washington: Commission on Civil Rights).

VALASKAKIS, GAIL (1989), 'Partners in Heritage: Living the Tradition of Spring Spearing', *Journal of Communication Inquiry*, 13/3: 12–17.

WALKERDINE, VALERIE (1986), 'Video Replay: Families, Film and Fantasy', in Burgin et al. (1986), 167–99.

—— (1990), *Schoolgirl Fictions* (London: Verso).

—— (1991), 'Behind the Painted Smile', in Spence and Holland (1991), 33–45.

—— (1997), *Daddy's Girl* (Basingstoke: Macmillan).

—— and LUCEY, HELEN (1989), *Democracy in the Kitchen* (London: Virago).

WALLACE, MICHELE (1990), *Invisibility Blues: From Pop to Theory* (London: Verso).

WANDOR, MICHELINE (1990) (ed.), *Once a Feminist* (London: Virago).

WELDON, FAY (1971), *Down among the Women* (London: William Heinemann).

WICKE, JENNIFER (1994), 'Celebrity Material: Materialist Feminism and the Culture of Celebrity', *South Atlantic Quarterly*, 93/4: 751–78.

WILLEMEN, PAUL (1971), 'Distanciation and Douglas Sirk', *Screen*, 12/2: 63–7.

WILLIAMS, RAYMOND (1961), *The Long Revolution* (London: Chatto and Windus).

—— (1972), *Drama in Performance* (Harmondsworth: Penguin) (1st edn. 1954; 2nd edn. 1968).

—— (1974), *Television, Technology and Cultural Form* (London: Fontana).

WILLIAMSON, JUDITH (1986), 'The Problems of Being Popular', *New Socialist* (Sept.), 14–15.

WILSON, ELIZABETH (1980), *Only Halfway to Paradise* (London: Tavistock).

—— (1985), *Adorned in Dreams: Fashion and Modernity* (London: Virago).

WINSHIP, JANICE (1985), ' "A Girl Needs to Get Streetwise": Magazines for the 1980s', *Feminist Review*, 21 (Winter), 25–46.

—— (1987), *Inside Women's Magazines* (London: Pandora).

—— (1991), 'The Impossibility of *Best*: Enterprise Culture Meets Domesticity in the Practical Women's Magazines for the 1980s', *Cultural Studies*, 5/2: 131–56.

WOMEN and FILM GROUP (1976), '*Coronation Street*', Paper to *Images of Women in the Media* conference, Polytechnic of Central London, London.

WOMEN'S STUDIES GROUP (1978) (ed.), *Women Take Issue* (London: Hutchinson).

ZOONEN, LIESBET VAN (1994), *Feminist Media Studies* (London: Sage).

Index